THE DOG LIVED
(AND SO WILL I)

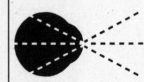
This Large Print Book carries the
Seal of Approval of N.A.V.H.

THE DOG LIVED (AND SO WILL I)

A MEMOIR

TERESA J. RHYNE

THORNDIKE PRESS
A part of Gale, Cengage Learning

Detroit • New York • San Francisco • New Haven, Conn • Waterville, Maine • London

GALE
CENGAGE Learning·

Thorndike Press® Large Print Inspirational
The text of this Large Print edition is unabridged.
Other aspects of the book may vary from the original edition.
Set in 16 pt. Plantin.

LIBRARY OF CONGRESS CATALOGING-IN-PUBLICATION DATA

Rhyne, Teresa J.
    The dog lived (and so will I) : a memoir / By Teresa J. Rhyne. — Large print edition.
    pages cm. — (Thorndike Press large print inspirational)
    ISBN-13: 978-1-4104-5690-8 (hardcover)
    ISBN-10: 1-4104-5690-0 (hardcover)
    1. Rhyne, Teresa J. 2. Breast—Cancer—Patients—United States—Biography.
3. Dog owners—United States—Biography. 4. Dogs—United States—Health.
5. Human-animal relationships—United States. I. Title.
RC280.B8R523 2013
616.99'4490092—dc23   2012050188

Published in 2013 by arrangement with Sourcebooks, Inc.

Printed in Mexico
1 2 3 4 5 6 7 17 16 15 14 13

AUTHOR'S NOTE

Because I'm a lawyer, I worry about protecting the innocent (and sometimes that means me and my publisher). Therefore, some names, identifying characteristics, and places in this memoir have been changed. Some characters in this book are actually composites of a few people, and some scenes are composites of different events, combined for the sake of story and my sanity. Conversations and events are rendered accurately to the best of my memory, but please remember my brain has been through chemo.

For Chris, who keeps my glass not only half-full, but topped off — and helps me see it that way as well.

"Two coyotes we, up high as November comes upon us. The holidays soon after, then April, summer just around the corner, then the leaves change, and here we are once again. Trouble lurks, my dear, our future uncertain, just as always, but right now, we two share the sky, just high, so high."

— *Markus Pierson*

CONTENTS

PART I

CHAPTER 1
BAGGAGE

I should not have asked him to pick me up at the airport. Was I that lonely and desperate already? I grabbed my carry-on from overhead luggage. Too late now. He'd be there waiting, appropriately enough for me, in baggage claim. *Or not.*

Now a new fear charged through me. It was embarrassing enough that I'd emailed him from an Internet café in Ireland admitting that I missed him and asking him to pick me up, but what if he didn't do it? What if no one was there to greet me? Cab fare home would not be nearly as expensive as all the therapy it would take to get over that psychic wound. I walked down the narrow aisle of the plane, moved along by the impatience of my fellow passengers, who, I imagined, all had someone there in the airport happily awaiting their arrivals, holding signs and flowers and ready to sweep them off their feet in enthusiastic embraces.

No wonder they were rushing.

"I love your scarf, by the way," the flight attendant said, smiling and fresh-looking even after a twelve-hour flight.

I looked down at my long, flowing, brightly colored, hand-knitted scarf. "Oh, thanks. I actually bought this at my cousin's shop in Athboy outside Dublin." Maybe if I engaged in a long conversation with the flight attendant, I'd never have to get off the plane. Maybe she'd be able to give me a ride home when the inevitable happened.

"Was it McElhinney's?" she asked in the same Irish brogue as my cousins.

"Yes. How funny that you knew that," I said as the crowd surged forward, moving me past her.

"Lovely shop. Such beautiful things. And you look smashing." Her grin seemed sincere. "Bye-bye."

But the compliment did not comfort me. Me looking smashing was not a good sign. Long ago my friend Stacey had told me that she always could tell when my life was falling apart because I'd look so pulled together. If I was perfectly dressed and groomed and presenting well to the world, she knew I had on my armor and was suited up to, as it were, tilt at my own windmills. If I looked smashing, it was because some aspect of my life was being smashed to pieces.

I was on this flight home after I'd gone to Ireland with my brother and a cousin, ostensibly to celebrate their fortieth birthdays but mostly to escape my lonely household following my second divorce and the death of my two old dogs, all in the past six months. So, by Stacey's analysis, yeah, I should look impeccable.

My trip had been wonderful, though, and it had mostly served its purpose of getting me out of my own head and on toward a new life. And I'd have been in a much better mood if I hadn't so foolishly asked a man I'd only been dating a few months to pick me up at the airport. For god's sake, I wasn't even supposed to be dating. I'd sworn off dating. I'd sworn off men. I had my life all carefully planned out now, and relationships were a thing of the past. No future involvements. None.

As I approached the escalator, I immediately saw Chris standing at the bottom. Even from that distance his bright blue eyes were noticeable — heck, his eyelashes were even long enough to be noticed. He was tall, with a head of massively thick salt-and-pepper hair that also made him stand out. And he was wearing his light blue plaid

17

button-down shirt. My favorite shirt. He looked handsome.

I couldn't help but smile. I had missed him. And I had so many great stories to tell him that I knew we'd laugh over . . . right after a hot bath together, a bottle of wine, and . . . well, the stories might have to wait. As would my carefully laid-out life plan, apparently. I stepped off the escalator and into his arms.

"After all those cold days traipsing around Ireland, this feels really, really good," I said, sinking farther down into the bathtub, both for the soothing wash of hot water and to keep my middle-aged body covered by bubbles. My townhome had the largest bathtub I had ever seen. The depth of the tub allowed me the modesty I still felt — the bubbles came up to my collarbone — but it was more than that. The grand tub stretched out over six feet in length and nearly four feet in width, taking up two-thirds of the bathroom. Thus, despite how tall we both were, Chris and I easily fit in the bath together facing each other. There was also plenty of space on both sides for a champagne bucket and candles.

"Feels good to me too, and I haven't been traveling. Are you tired?" Chris asked, refilling my glass with champagne.

"A little. But I slept pretty well on the plane. And it would be better for combating jet lag if I stayed awake a few more hours."

"I can help you with that," Chris said, leaning in for a kiss.

I returned the kiss. "I'm sure you can."

Chris raised his eyebrows in a playful leer. He leaned back. "Tell me about your trip."

I loved that he loved my stories. And I had certainly brought a wealth of them home from Ireland, where I'd been visiting my grandfather's family. I told Chris about one family member in particular who'd kept me laughing — my second cousin, Seamus. I knew he'd make Chris laugh, too.

On our second night in Ireland several family members gathered at a pub for dinner. Cousin Colleen, the one I'd traveled over with, had said her Irish boyfriend would be joining us as well. My brother had a few conversations with Colleen about this mysterious Irish boyfriend and was beginning to doubt he was real. He never showed up when he was supposed to. Several more relatives and friends joined us that evening, but Mysterious Irish Boyfriend was not among them. We passed two hours in the pub waiting for a table large enough to seat all fourteen of us. Or perhaps it would only be thirteen. Many phone calls and drinks later, MIB was still MIA.

When we were finally seated for dinner at 11:00 p.m., Colleen excused herself to make yet another phone call.

My brother Jay asked another cousin, Claire, "So you guys have never actually met this dude, right?"

"Never. She's wasting 'er time."

"Do you think he actually exists?"

"If he does, he's a fookin' bastard." This came from Seamus, Claire's brother, and an early-on favorite of mine if only for his pronunciation of the F word, which he, like a lot of my Irish relatives, used liberally. Seamus to me was prototypically Irish — lanky, pale, redheaded, with a fondness for drink and hysterical commentary.

When Colleen returned to the table, Seamus accosted her.

"Coosin, what're you doin'? Leave it alone. The bastard ain't coming."

"I'm worried he had an emergency at work. Or he can't find the place."

"He's a fookin' plumber. What kind of emergency can he be 'avin' that he can't bloody call? T'is the only pub in the village called Inn Moderation. He'd find it if he was tryin'."

I saw this as extremely sage advice.

Colleen saw it differently. "I just think he can't find it. He didn't grow up here and it's late and he's probably tired, don't you think? I know he'd want to be here. He said so last night. I just want to give him directions if he needs them."

Seamus flung his hands in the air, "Coosin! If a man wants to fookin' find a woman, he'll fookin' find 'er!"

I told the story, mimicking my cousin's Irish brogue as best I could. My efforts were rewarded when Chris burst out laughing. "Seamus is a genius."

"My thoughts exactly," I said.

"I'm going to remember that. 'If a man wants to fookin' find a woman, he'll fookin' find 'er.' "

"And don't you think it works so much better in that accent? Jay and I can't stop saying *fookin'*. We add it to fookin' everything."

"Absolutely. It's hilarious. And what he says is true." Chris looked right at me. "I found you."

At once, I became intensely interested in the bottom of my champagne glass, looking deep inside it. I emptied the liquid to get a better view of the bottom.

This was just a fling. This was about great sex and fun times. I was not what he was

21

looking for. How could I have been? He was twenty-nine years old. I was forty-one. He lived in west Los Angeles. I was sixty miles east in a far less glamorous locale. He was young, single, and handsome. I was . . . well, I was not young and I was still licking my wounds following my second divorce. My *second* divorce. I was not what anyone was looking for.

He held my right foot and massaged the arch gently.

When he began to trace a delicate line up my leg with his finger, I relaxed. See, it's only sex. That's what he's looking for. So much better! Not like a relationship at all. Phew. Sex I can do; it's just all that other stuff I'm not so good with.

I was good at math, though. I had easily determined the common denominator in my two divorces was me. Considering that none of the marriages surrounding me in my childhood had been happy or had survived into my adulthood, this should not have come as a surprise to me, but it had. I was good at a lot of things, but marriage, it turned out, was not one of them. So six months earlier when I'd left my second husband and moved into this rented townhome, I'd vowed to begin what I, perhaps too affectionately, had dubbed my alphabet life.

Like Steve Martin's character in *The Jerk,* all I needed was B, C, and D: books, coffee, and dogs. That's all I needed.

B was for Books — I lined my living room walls and one of the spare bedrooms with mismatched, heavily loaded bookcases and stacked the rest of the books in piles all over the house where no one could tell me they were messy.

C was for Coffee — by the gallons, with no one around to tell me the grounds got in the white tile grout and were messy.

And D was for Dogs — I had my two beagles, Richelieu and Roxy, and had told my law partner from whom I rented the townhome not to bother changing out the ugly green carpet since my dogs were old and might be messy. By this I meant I was old and messy and intended to remain gloriously so. (I find one of the many great things about dogs is that they don't mind being blamed for things that aren't their fault.)

Then a friend from college reminded me I was not likely to survive without adult beverages. Which, I think, is why we have college friends, isn't it?

So I added A for Alcohol — by which I

meant wine. Okay, and martinis. And right, also I meant margaritas.

A, B, C, and D. I had packed my alphabet into a moving van and left married life behind.

That sound you hear is not just the moving van's screeching brakes — it's fate laughing in my face.

I had seven weeks with both dogs in my new place — enough time to settle into a pattern of walks and meals, to chart out who got which portion of the bed and the couch, and to establish our home of three. By the end of April, my thirteen-year-old beagle Richelieu had a series of seizures and eventually, sobbing and cursing but knowing it was best for him, I had to let him go.

In August, the congestive heart failure that the veterinarian had told me would come finally did, and I lost Roxy, too. I came home from work to find her dead in the middle of my living room, right in front of all of those bookcases. My friend Stacey drove me to the vet's office as I held Roxy's body and shook with sadness and tears. As she drove me back, I was curled into the passenger's seat, sobbing again.

When I returned home, all that greeted me was that hideous green carpet. I was five months into my alphabet life, and already I was missing a letter. I had wanted to be alone, but not that alone. I never wanted to be without my dogs. Dogs were the only consistent relationship in my life, and now they were gone, too.

The silence suffocated me for a few weeks. I considered getting another dog, but I'd learned the great cosmic curse that all dog lovers learn eventually — you may have the unconditional love, devotion, and near-perfect companionship of a dog, but only for twelve to fifteen years, if you are lucky. Then your heart breaks. I didn't think I could take that pain again.

And that's when I'd escaped to Ireland.

But now I was back and I was dog-less, sitting naked in a steamy bubble bath, sipping champagne with a young, handsome man. Did I have my shit together or what?

"Hey," Chris jostled my leg underwater, "you still awake?"

"Yeah," I set my champagne glass down and rallied a smile. "I can tell you the rest of the Ireland stories in the morning. We have better things to do now."

"I like that," Chris said, moving toward me and wrapping me in his arms.

I blew out the candles before rising from the water.

■ ■ ■ ■

By the time Chris woke, I was on my third cup of coffee and ready to talk. About Ireland. I regaled him with stories of country drives and castles and singing in pubs and my cousin that snuck us into a private club in Limerick without letting us know he wasn't a member, and the green cliffs and spectacular scenery, the tiny roads and roundabouts (which I dubbed "roustabouts"), the beautiful Irish faces, and that I stood nearly a foot taller than most all of my relatives. Chris listened and laughed and asked questions.

"We got to see our great-grandparents' graves, which was cool, even if it meant we also had to attend mass."

"Yeah, I didn't think you'd get ten days in Ireland without going to mass." Chris and I had both been raised Catholic; both had gone to Catholic schools, and both were of Irish descent, although Chris was mixed with German. But being raised Catholic is its own special bond, particularly if one survives Catholic school. "Did nuns leap out and begin swatting your knuckles with rulers? Or was it just the proverbial lightning strike?"

"Neither, surprisingly. And I avoided

confession, since we only had ten days."

"Is divorce legal there yet? Maybe in that country you're still married."

We were sitting up in bed, and while I at least had a nightie on, Chris was naked. "That would make me a sinner of a whole different kind."

"A sexy sinner. I like it." We both laughed, until he said, "Probably the one glitch in your plan to recover from your divorce was picking a staunchly Catholic country. Did your divorces come up while you were there? How did you explain that?"

"I didn't. I just avoided the whole topic." I tried to sound more cavalier than I had felt. In truth, I felt like I had worn a scarlet "D" the entire time I was in Ireland, especially given that I never met one divorced person. "They probably think I'm a spinster. If anyone asked about kids or spouses, Jay and I both answered by talking about his wife and kids."

"Clever. So no one ever asked about a husband? You never had to explain your lack of kids?"

"Well, cousin Seamus circled around it at the end. On our last morning there we were in Claire's kitchen saying good-bye to everyone. Seamus hugged me good-bye and whispered, 'I still don't understand why some fella hasn't thrown 'is leg around ya and claimed ya as 'is own.' "

"Cousin Seamus strikes again! He is hilarious."

"He did make me laugh a lot."

"So did you explain that several men had tried the leg-throwing bit and it hadn't really worked out?"

And how would I explain that? I'd only recently been able to sort through it myself. With lots and lots of therapy. I chose my first husband without any knowledge of what a healthy relationship might look like. I only understood that traditional marriage (mom home, dad working several jobs, kids running amok) had not worked for anyone I knew and looked completely unenjoyable. It was not for me. So I chose someone exotic (Croatian-born; spoke three languages), intelligent (we met in law school), handsome (Willem Dafoe on steroids . . . and wait, we'll get to that), and infinitely charming. I still managed to be surprised that he was also a narcissistic, substance-abusing, spendthrift womanizer who thought I'd stay home and have his blond-haired, blue-eyed babies while he . . . well, see above.

It then made perfect sense that the next spouse I chose was an ultra-conservative,

Midwestern momma's boy who was as safe as . . . well, as safe as the confines of his undiagnosed (and untreated) obsessive compulsive disorder required him to be. So yes, I understood I'd done my own version of Goldilocks ("this one's too hot, this one's too cold, this one's too hard, this one's too soft . . ."). But that didn't mean I expected most folks to understand.

Chris knew my Goldilocks story. I shared it with him before we were even dating. Back before we'd crossed the line from friends in a writers' group together to friends in a bathtub together. Back when I thought he was merely humoring a middle-aged woman through her divorce over cocktails while waiting for our writers' group meetings to start. Back before I realized we were meeting for hours before our writers' group meeting started.

"No," I said. "I'm not sure my Goldilocks story can translate to Irish Catholic. I just let it go. I'd like to leave them thinking well of me."

"I'm sure they did. And knowing you made mistakes and you own up to the mistakes would not have changed that."

He really was a nice guy. "You think?"

"Well, if it did, they're fookin' bastards."

And funny. Man, he's funny.

■ ■ ■ ■

Monday came and I had to get out of bed for something other than food and bathroom breaks. I had to get to work. Chris left at six in the morning for the hour drive back to his reality. He'd agreed to my "only every other weekend" rule (this makes it a nonrelationship, you understand) so we wouldn't be seeing each other for another two weeks. Time to return to lawyer mode.

"I put your mail in three piles — client stuff, urgent stuff, and boring stuff," my assistant, Michelle, said. She followed me into my office.

"Can I get my coffee first? And then I think I'll just start with the boring stuff."

She lowered her voice. "They had a partnership meeting while you were gone. I don't think it went well. Nobody seems to be talking to Gerald. Or he's not talking to them. I can never tell. And the other three are in and out of each other's offices with the doors closed, a lot."

Good-bye, vacation. Good-bye, leisurely, sexy weekend. Hello, office politics and client needs. "Thanks. I can't really deal with that yet." I set down my purse, flipped on my computer, and headed for coffee.

30

I was able to have a semi-rational discussion with two of my law partners as to what had, once again, set off Gerald, a despicably miserable man hell-bent on being as difficult as possible over as many petty details as he could dream up to soothe his pathetic ego. This time it was over the lack of clarity in the ice cubes produced by our break room refrigerator icemaker. He wanted a newer model refrigerator and he wanted it now. My more sane partners had declined to spend three thousand dollars for pretty ice cubes.

By Thursday, I was fully absorbed into my work, Ireland having faded to a blissful memory. I practiced estate planning, which means I deal with death and taxes (and thus frequently joked that I'd always have a job). I had a client recently diagnosed with bone cancer who needed his trust updated and quick. I would be meeting with him either at the hospital next week or in my office over the weekend. There was a lot to do.

"Do you want to talk to Destiny at the pet adoption center?" my secretary announced over the speakerphone.

"How can I not answer when Destiny calls?" Oh, if only I'd known this joke would be on me.

I'd been on the board of directors for the

Mary S. Roberts Pet Adoption Center off and on for more than fifteen years, and they were aware of my recent dog losses. I had adopted Roxy from there when she was eight years old and newly diagnosed with a heart murmur. The staff sent me a sympathy card when she passed away.

"Well, I know you are back from vacation, and we waited a few days, but I wanted to let you know . . . we have a beagle in. I took him from the Moreno Valley shelter just before he was scheduled to be euthanized. Are you ready for another dog?"

My irrational love of beagles was well known, as Roxy had been the fourth beagle I'd adopted and I'd found homes for many others by baying their praises as the perfect dog for anyone — small and cute enough for women; short-haired, compact, and sporty enough for men; high-energy and of a tolerant, playful temperament for children. I loved beagles, and like any woman in love, I overlooked a lot of the less-than-charming characteristics of the breed.

But was I ready for another dog?

No. I wasn't. Ireland had been a welcome respite from my heartache, but I wasn't yet healed. I'd begun to think maybe I'd shrink my alphabet life even further to just A, B, and C. And wait . . . maybe a beagle isn't a perfect dog for everyone. Maybe I had found the limit. A young beagle is not a town house dog. A beagle is not a dog for a single woman working long hours. A beagle is not an only dog. A beagle is a pack dog. A beagle is a dog for my old life, not this new life I was vaguely forming. A beagle would not be a good idea.

But oh, how I adore beagles.

My love of beagles dates back to the summer between my sophomore and junior years of college. I had wanted to be away in a Semester-at-Sea program, but my father wanted me at a family reunion. Since Dad was paying the bills, both for my tuition and any traveling I did, I found myself in rural Georgia for summer vacation. Initially, I was sullen and sulking over the injustice as only a teenager can. But one of my uncles raised beagles for hunting, and I quickly found myself spending most of my days playing with litters of beagle puppies. Soon enough I was visiting and playing with my cousins as well. There is nothing cuter than a beagle puppy, and I quickly forgot Istanbul, Athens, and Barcelona in favor of tri-colored, round-bellied, baying balls of fur in Gray, Georgia. My uncle was willing to send a puppy home with me, but I had college to finish. And then law school. I got my first beagle puppy two weeks after finishing law school, and my beagle love affair was launched.

My heart may have hardened in many places, but the spot for dogs remained soft. And they'd rescued this beagle with me in mind. I should stop by out of courtesy. For good measure, I also assured myself that this particular dog wasn't ready for adoption yet, so it was safe to just look.

Caution, meet wind.

Destiny walked me to the kennel where the beagle was held, still in isolation for the last of the required three days. I heard the beagle howl long before I was in front of his kennel. Beagle howls are distinctive in a bloodcurdling sort of way. There is a reason the French call them *be' gueules* ("gaping mouths"), but to me it's a call to home. This particular howl, though, this was no ordinary beagle baying.

The dog greeted me with frantic, insistent, raspy howls. When Destiny opened the kennel door and leashed the dog, he ran to me, jumped up on my legs, stretched his muzzle up toward me, and "Aaaaaarrrooooooo-oo'd" away into my face. I laughed and bent down to pet him, reminded again how happy and adorable beagles are. He curled himself into me, turning so I could scratch his back. Now that he had received human contact, he quieted, if only for a moment. I stroked his soft, rounded head and noticed a few unusual things about him. First, there was his coloring — he had the usual black saddle markings of the breed, but where most beagles would be brown or beige, this dog was red. And where you'd expect to find a patch of solid white, this one was dappled white, appearing gray and mottled. His nails were black and looked to be painted that way by some goth teenager. His eyes appeared to have black guy-liner any emo-rock band member would envy. And again there was the howling. He sounded as though he'd suckled whiskey from his mother's teats and had been chain-smoking since birth.

He quivered under my hand as I petted him. He stayed close by me, pushing up against my leg, my hand, any part of me he could reach. Mostly he was pushing into my heart. I noticed another unique charac-teristic. His left ear flopped backward, turn-ing inside out and staying that way. I'd flip it back down, making him a proper droopy-eared beagle, but eventually the ear would flop right back over again. He looked up at me, one long, floppy ear forward and one backward, big kohl-lined brown eyes plead-ing.

He was cute. He liked me. And in that moment, we both knew he was coming home with me. I just had to trust that "he's cute and he's coming home with me" worked out better with dogs than it had with men.

The dog had to wait out the mandatory three-day holding period and I had to go back to work, which should have given me enough time to consider whether this dog was a good idea for me. It should have.

"I can pick him up on Saturday, right?" I said to Destiny.

"Saturday morning."

"That will give me time to get some food and a crate for him." I petted the dog's domed head. "I'll be back, buddy. I'll come get you tomorrow."

"I knew he'd be perfect for you." Destiny leashed him and led him back into the ken-nel.

The baying started instantly: *Aaaaaarr-rooooooooo!! Aaaaaarrrooooooooo!!! Aaaaaarrooooooooo!!! This is not happening! Take me with you now! Now, I say! Noooooooow!!!*

I could still hear the howling as I drove away, already missing him and feeling guilty for leaving him. I didn't stop for even a moment to consider that howl coming from my townhome. Women in love can overlook many bad traits.

Each of the beagles I'd shared my life with in the past had their own color schemes. The beagle I'd adopted after law school was Raz (short for Razumov, thank you, Joseph Conrad), and she had yellow collars and leashes her whole life. Blue for Rabu (short for Rabushov — an unintentional transmutation of the otherwise literary name Rubashov, with apologies to Arthur Koestler, but really, what kind of a nickname would "Rub" have been?); red, naturally, for Richelieu (as in Cardinal) and pink for my Roxy-girl (right, I didn't name her; I adopted her when she was already eight years old). On Saturday morning, I bought the new beagle a dark green leash and collar, along with a crate and its comfy cushion with soft cotton on one side and dark-green water-slick covering on the other.

On the way to the pet adoption center, I thought about a name for this new beagle. I was thinking I'd move away from the "R" names. I'd picked the green color because this beagle was so red and I was just back from Ireland so naturally I associated red hair with "Irish." Maybe I'd give him an

Irish name to go with his green theme. An Irish name might fit. I thought of the cousin who'd made me laugh so much on my trip. Seamus might be a good name for the dog. Maybe it would even bring us some Irish luck. But a name has to fit a dog. We'll see, I thought, as I parked in front of the adoption center. We'll see.

Destiny brought the noisy, jumping, ecstatically happy beagle to the "greeting room" so I could get to know him. That didn't take long. He stopped howling as soon as I petted him and turned his attention to sniffing out my purse and me, in that order. He must have found something he liked, because he jumped up next to me on the bench and planted himself against me, leaning in and looking up at me. He was mine and I was his. The decision wasn't even mine.

I put the new green collar on him, and he howled and jumped and cracked me up about a hundred different ways on our drive home, including barking every time the car came to a stop — *Don't forget me! I'm back here! Right here! Don't leave me back here! I'm here!!!* Right then, I knew. My red, whiskey-howling, funny little beagle was so obviously a Seamus. (When a dog wants to fookin' find a woman, he'll fookin' find 'er.)

When we arrived home, beagle Seamus followed me into the house and raced around, checking out every inch of the townhome and lingering anywhere there was a faded scent of Richelieu and Roxy. He wore himself out sniffing, howling, and jumping on and off my lap. Finally, he joined me on the couch, snuggling up against me as I petted his head and rubbed his belly. He relaxed. I began to notice how soft his coat was. And especially his long ears. That's when I noticed the inside of his right ear had a two-inch surgically straight scar running down its length. I ran my finger along the scar. Wherever he started out in life, they had cared enough to microchip him, neuter him, and stitch up whatever had happened to his ear.

Destiny had told me he'd been found by Animal Control roaming the streets of a nearby town, and no one had come to claim him at the pound. No one answered the phone when they tried the number listed in the microchip information either. When his time was up at the pound, she saw him and selected him for a second chance, bringing him and three other dogs back to the center where they would stay until homes were found for them. That was two days before she'd called me to give him that second chance.

Sitting together on my couch, I petted and scratched the dog and found several favorite spots he wanted rubbed — his belly, behind his ears, the top of his round head. He was sweet, soft. And those kohl-lined eyes of melted chocolate melted my heart. He was young — only one or two years old. I'd have plenty of time with him, I assured myself. No more pain. No more heartbreak. Not for a long, long while.

I continued to pet the dog, softly and slowly. My house wouldn't be lonely anymore. My alphabet life was back on track. And this was a sweet, sweet dog. After a few minutes, Seamus moved his left front paw over my right leg and, looking up at me, leaning far into me, he claimed me as his own.

CHAPTER 2
MAN MEETS DOG

"You got a dog?" Chris sounded incredulous and mildly frightened in our nightly phone call.

"Yes. Another beagle. He's sooooooo cute. Wait till you meet him. You'll love him."

"Okay. Well, I guess I'm just surprised. You hadn't really mentioned that."

Was I supposed to? Had we crossed some threshold where I was now supposed to be getting his input on — or worse, his approval of — decisions I made? No! No, we certainly had not. "I wanted another dog. I'm sure I'd mentioned that much. Remember, my whole alphabet life? The 'D' part of it? That was for 'dogs.'"

"Oh, I'm aware of it. I just . . . well, I guess I thought you'd wait awhile."

Wait for what? "I didn't exactly go looking, but the pet adoption center called and pretty much once they told me it was a beagle, I was a goner."

He paused, weighing his words. "I'm not much of a dog person."

Not a dog person? How had I missed that? I knew he was a Republican, and I overlooked that. I knew he was inappropriately young, and I was working on overlooking that. How did I miss that he was not a dog person? I looked down at Seamus, curled up on the pillow next to me. Seamus breathed in deeply and exhaled, his breath causing his jowls to flop noisily, as if to agree it was a ridiculous thought. Not a dog person?

"Wow. I did not know that," I said.

"Is it a small dog?"

"He's a beagle."

"I heard that. But is it small?"

"He's not an it. And beagles are beagle-sized."

"That's not helping. How big is he?"

He doesn't know how big a beagle is? He really was not a dog person. Further proof this could not be a relationship. "He weighs about thirty pounds. Oh, and I named him Seamus."

"I'm sure your cousin will be flattered. The good news is I'm mostly only afraid of big dogs. So we should be fine. I hope."

Afraid of big dogs? If I had a yard, now that I lived on my own, I'd have a Doberman and probably a German shepherd and another half dozen beagles, all adopted from the pet adoption center. I'd be that middle-aged, divorced woman stereotype, only with dogs instead of cats. And I was dating someone who was afraid of big dogs? How does my life get away from me like that?

At least he was willing to meet Seamus. I hoped they'd get along, but I knew which one was staying if it came down to that. My week with Seamus had been challenging, but the little dog had kept me so entertained. My home was suddenly filled with energy. I'd almost forgotten how exuberant young dogs — and particularly beagles — can be. I walked Seamus in the mornings and again when I came home at night, but he'd still race around the house, throw his toys up in the air, and beg me to chase him around, which I did of course. I was rewarded with serious cuddling time as Seamus snuggled up against me. He was the first beagle I'd ever had that enjoyed being petted this much. Usually, a beagle lasts a couple of minutes of petting and then his nose and boundless excitement sends him bouncing off in another direction. But Seamus was as enthusiastic about cuddling as he was about his food. I knew Seamus was staying. I'd made a commitment to

Seamus. But the truth was I didn't want to have to choose Seamus over Chris.

When Friday night rolled around, I prepared for the introduction of the beagle to the boyfriend. I walked Seamus in the morning and again in the evening. I walked him for longer than normal and hoped I'd deplete a little of that beagle energy. Then I lit the fireplace, chilled the wine, and prepared some late-night snacks.

Usually, Chris waited out the Los Angeles traffic and didn't leave his place until after eight at night, which meant he'd arrive between nine and ten. I'd always liked that schedule. I could still have dinner or drinks with a friend, attend any social or community functions I needed to, or just be home relaxing and reading before his arrival. This night, though, I was anxious for his arrival. I had not thought about the possibility of Chris and Seamus not getting along. I hadn't thought about Chris at all when I decided to adopt Seamus. I hadn't thought about much when I decided to adopt Seamus; that was becoming clear.

Seamus followed me around as I got the house ready and was particularly attentive when I was in the kitchen. He sat with perfect doggie posture, head tilted to the left, mouth slightly open, and eyes wide and

44

focused, watching my every move from only a foot away. I spread crackers on a plate, did my best to artfully arrange the cheese selection, added some salami slices, and then prepared bruschetta, realizing too late that the garlic was not a good idea for a romantic evening. Still, the food was nicely displayed and about as close to domestic as I get.

I brought the two plates of seduction into the living room and set them on the coffee table. The fireplace gave a nice glow to the room, so I dimmed the light. Candles would be nice, I thought. I walked to the dining room, grabbed two of the three candles from the table, and headed back into the kitchen for matches. As I did, the phone rang. Caller ID told me it was Chris at the front gate of my complex.

I buzzed him in and turned to talk to Seamus. "You'll like him. Just be nice, okay, buddy?"

But Seamus was no longer at my feet.

"Seamus?"

No answer. No jingling tags as the dog made his way to me.

"Seamus? Come here, buddy."

No response.

I walked to the living room.

"Seamus!!"

45

Both plates of food were on the floor. Seamus was inhaling every bit of food no matter how large. With each step I took toward him, he gulped that much more quickly and in larger bites. The tomato-garlic topping had splashed onto the carpet and the couch. The cheese, or what few pieces remained, peeked out from under the now upside-down and broken Italian ceramic serving plate.

"Shit! Seamus!" I reached for his collar to pull him back from the mess, but he gulped and bolted away from me. I picked up the two pieces of ceramic, and as I rose up and turned to dispose of them, Seamus dashed in and gulped down two more pieces of cheese.

"Seamus, stop it!" I yelled, as though a beagle has ever been commanded away from food. I knew better, but I'd forgotten the rules of basic dog training. It had been a long time since I had a new dog. I decided I'd scoop up as much of the food as I could, placing it on the largest of the broken ceramic pieces while maneuvering my body between Seamus and the spilled food for as long as I could. When I stood, I could see that Chris had let himself in the front door.

"I knocked, but I don't think you heard me," he said.

Seamus, finally, stopped his vacuum cleaner imitation and turned to the noise at the door.

Before I could even say hello, Seamus growled. A low, slow growl that I had not heard in our week together.

"Seamus, no. It's okay. It's fine, buddy." I tried to sound relaxed, in control.

Chris stepped back. "Is he going to bite me?"

"I don't think . . ." I didn't get to finish. Seamus howled loudly, looking from me to Chris and back again, increasing the volume and urgency of his howl. Chris stayed frozen at the front door, five stairs up from the sunken living room where Seamus and I were. When Seamus bolted in Chris's direction, I dropped what I was holding — bruschetta and cheese remains once again crashing to the floor — and lunged for Seamus's collar. I caught him at the third step. Chris had backed all the way up against the door. Seamus strained at his collar, howling up the stairs toward Chris.

"Sorry. This maybe wasn't the best introduction," I shouted above the raspy howl.

I pulled Seamus off the stairs, and hunched over, holding him by the collar, walked him back into the den where his bed and toys were located. I put him in his bed.

"Seamus, sit." I pointed a finger in his face, which always means "I'm being serious." Any dog knows this. Except a beagle.

Seamus looked away. He looked around me, watching for another appearance by Chris, but he did not leave his bed. I spread the fingers on my right hand, palm outward, in front of his face. "Stay." He shrunk back and turned his glaring eyes away from me. "Stay," I repeated, for good measure and to verbalize my hope.

"Okay, Chris, let's try this again. Come on into the den."

"You are kidding, right?" Chris said, remaining glued in the stairwell.

"He's not going to attack you. He's a beagle."

"You keep saying that. But all I hear is 'dog.' He's a dog."

"It's okay." This was wishful thinking only. I had no idea.

Chris walked into the room, and while Seamus growled again, he did not come out of his bed and he stopped when I corrected him. When Chris and I sat on the couch, Seamus came over, quietly and a bit more calmly, sniffing Chris's pants and paying no attention to me. Chris petted the dog's head, and I noticed he looked about as comfortable as I did when people forced me to hold or coo over their babies. But, okay, there was no growling or fighting. And neither one looked like they'd be biting the other anytime soon.

"Isn't he cute?" I ventured.

Chris widened his eyes at me. "You heard him growl at me, right?"

"Well, he didn't know you, and you walked right into the house. I think it's good that he growled."

"Maybe, but it's still going to take me a while to get past that to 'cute.' "

"Well, you two get to know each other and I'll get us some wine." I stood up and went into the kitchen. Seamus followed me.

"He's not that interested in getting to know me. Kinda rude, don't you think?" Chris said.

I laughed. "Dog has no manners." I opened a bottle of wine and poured two glasses, at which point the dog lost interest and roamed out of the kitchen.

I handed a glass to Chris and sat next to him on the couch. We clinked our glasses together. "To another great weekend of decadence," I said.

"Indeed."

We sipped and smiled and kissed. Our weekend had begun.

After a few minutes, Chris put his glass

down. "I'm sufficiently emboldened now. Where's this rascally dog?"

I looked about. And where was Seamus? He was always in the same room with me, except when . . .

"Seamus!" Much too late, I remembered the mess in the living room. I jumped from the couch and raced to the living room. Seamus was down on his belly, with his snout and one paw reaching underneath the couch. He was also lying in the tomato-garlic formerly bruschetta mix.

"Oh jeez. Seamus." I clapped my hands. "Stop!" He stopped the pawing and sat upright, shifting his weight back and forth, right to left, whining and staring from me to under the couch, back to me, back to the couch.

I knelt down next to him. "Oh, right, and I'm supposed to get that for you?"

He howled his response and wagged his tail, spreading the tomatoes deeper into the rug.

I couldn't help it; I laughed. He was so oblivious to any trouble, to any wrongdoing whatsoever. He was solely focused on his goal. I ran my hand under the sofa and brought out the slice of toasted baguette, with remains of bruschetta, delicately seasoned with dog hair. I handed it to Seamus.

"I cannot believe you just did that," came Chris's voice from behind me.

"Um . . . yeah. Well . . ." I waved my arm in the direction of the broken plate and tomato stains. "I'm pretty sure we won't be eating it."

"Still. The dog probably should not be rewarded."

"Says the 'not a dog person.' " He probably had a point, but it was not one I was going to concede. Not from my prone position on my wet, stained rug with shards of Italian ceramics and tomato smears surrounding me. No sirree. I had my dignity.

"It's not like I've never been around a dog. My parents have a dog. And she does not get table scraps."

I had the urge to mimic the "she does not get table scraps" in that child's voice that usually says "neener neener" with the drawn-down, lemon-sucking face, which was probably further indication that I knew I had been caught doing something wrong. Naturally, I turned to my cohort in crime for support, which I'm sure Seamus would have given me had he not been so busy sucking the carpet.

"Okay, well, can you just hold the dog while I clean this up?" I said.

"Uh, no. You hold the dog. I'll clean up

this disaster."

Oh. Well, okay. I'd much rather hold a dog than clean a house. There was an upside to his dog aversion.

Seamus stopped howling and growling at Chris after the mess was cleaned up and there was no food in sight. We joked that perhaps he just thought Chris was a food burglar and once there was no food at risk, his work was done. He slept.

Well, let me amend that — Seamus slept until Chris got up in the middle of the night and stepped on him on the way to the bathroom.

AR! AR! AR! AR! AR! AAAAAARR-ROOOOOOOOO! This was easily translated from beagle-speak to *Asshole! You scared the shit out of me!* because Seamus leaped onto my bed, ran up next to my head, and turned to face Chris. Seamus may have been shaking, but he was still up to calling out the perpetrator in no uncertain terms.

I sat up, cradled the dog, and checked for broken limbs, despite the fact that the dog had just leaped up three feet onto the bed. "What happened?" I turned on the bedroom light.

Chris stood, naked, in the hallway, looking distraught and more frightened than the dog. "I didn't see him on my way to the bathroom. The dog has a bed upstairs, another one downstairs, two couches, and a recliner he could sleep on, and he sleeps in the middle of the hallway?"

"You stepped on him?"

"No. I nearly fell on my face trying not to step on him."

"He's scared." I wrapped both arms around Seamus, and he leaned into me, but he continued to look at Chris.

"He's a hypochondriac."

"The dog is a hypochondriac?"

"I did not hurt him."

"I don't think you did. He'll be fine," I said, rubbing Seamus's now exposed belly as he flopped onto his back and stretched out across the side of the bed Chris had been sleeping on. "Go to the bathroom and come back to bed."

When Chris returned to the bedside, Seamus did not acknowledge him and made no effort to relinquish any space.

"A little help here?" Chris said. "I can tell you're laughing at this."

"Sorry. But that is kinda funny. He doesn't normally sleep on the bed, but he seems to be communicating something here."

"Gee, I wonder what?"

They had not made good first impressions on each other. Still, it could have been worse, I tried telling myself. I wondered, though, had I given the dog the sense that Chris was temporary, whereas the dog himself intended to be a permanent part of my life? Had I created an accomplice in my charade already?

While Seamus and I established a routine for the two of us during the week — walks, cuddles, sharing our meals (well, my meals; I let him have his kibble all to himself), Chris and I continued with our Friday night tradition — wine or chilled champagne, fire going, music playing. And Seamus continued to ruin it all by howling and growling at Chris when he arrived and lunging for the food. Shrimp cocktail, cheese, crackers, strawberries, pizza, stuffed mushrooms, quesadillas, and éclairs all became a Friday night staple for Seamus.

Although I never again left a plate of food in a room without me, the beagle was a quick study. He easily figured out that there were certain moments when Chris and I, while physically present in the room with the appetizers, were decidedly not paying any attention to the food. If we leaned toward each other for a kiss, Seamus made his move too, deftly sweeping in and inhaling whatever happened to be on the plate. I so frequently lost the battle that I began to plan the menu so it didn't include any foods dangerous to a dog. Even a dog that was part garbage disposal could get poisoned by chocolate, macadamia nuts, grapes, onions, or garlic.

When Chris eventually started doing most of the weekend cooking, he'd either arrive with bags of groceries or head out on Saturday mornings, returning with bags of groceries. As my every-other-weekend rule began to slip and Chris visited more often, eventually Seamus concluded that Chris = food. He stopped growling and began to look forward to Chris's arrival as much as I did, anxiously pacing about after dark on Friday and looking at me with that "Food guy here yet?" face. If Chris was later than normal, Seamus waited at my front court-yard gate.

I knew it wasn't Chris's winning personality the dog was waiting for, but Chris seemed flattered that he'd been able to win the dog over. Until Seamus made it obvious what he was about.

One Saturday evening, as Chris began cooking dinner, he found he was missing an ingredient.

"Baby, did you put the sourdough bread anywhere?"

"No, I haven't seen it."

We opened cupboards and checked the countertops, and Chris double-checked the trunk of his car, thinking he'd left a bag of groceries there. Nothing.

He walked around the kitchen counter to the other side, in the dining room.

The bread wrapper and a few — but not many — crumbs were on the floor. Telltale paw prints were on the wall below the counter.

"You won't believe this," Chris said.

"Oh, crap. Seamus got it?"

"So much for bread with dinner."

"There's no way he can eat an entire loaf of bread," I said. I looked around but didn't see a beagle in any of his usual spots. "Seamus? Seamus?"

Seamus declined to respond. I went upstairs. He wasn't on my bed. And he wasn't in the recliner in the library — his other favorite spot, especially when Chris was with us. I went back to the corner of my room where Seamus's upstairs bed was.

He was there, on his side looking every bit like one of those snakes in nature films with their bellies extended in the exact shape of a mouse or a giant egg recently consumed whole. Seamus's belly was extended in the shape of a sourdough bread loaf.

I rubbed his belly. It felt tight — stretched

to its limit. I worried what would happen if he drank water. Should I take the water away from him? Would that make it harder to digest an entire loaf of bread? I was also sure he'd eaten the bread in three seconds flat. Should I take him to the emergency room?

Chris was calmer. "He just seems uncomfortable but not in pain. He didn't choke, so let's just wait it out." And then he laughed.

"This isn't funny!"

"Are you kidding me? Look at that dog!" Chris pointed, and Seamus lifted his head.

And yeah, it was kind of funny the way the dog's belly protruded. So I laughed. Maybe Seamus would actually learn from this experience. Something besides how tasty sourdough is.

We finished dinner, without the purloined sourdough, and made our way upstairs to our bath. Our tub time was quickly becoming a tradition for us. This was how we started our weekends and where we'd recently begun to slowly, tentatively explore that maybe this was about more than sex and a good time. Maybe, just maybe we might have something here. We both looked forward to our tub talks and time spent soaking and sipping.

Seamus hated it.

Seamus hated anything that didn't involve him. Frequently he would poke his head into the bathroom or come right up to us in the tub, howl, and run away. If we had our Friday night snack in the tub with our champagne, Seamus would put his two front paws up on the tub and stare at us intently. If the rapid tail wagging didn't immediately produce his appropriate share of the food (read: all of it), he'd howl. Loudly. And not at all romantically.

On the night of his sourdough heist though, Seamus was out of it. Sleeping off his yeasty hangover, he gave us a rare respite from his antics. We quietly soaked in the hot water and silky bubbles, surrounded by silence, steam, and candlelight.

Thirty relaxing minutes later, I heard a noise. A scraping sound from the other side of the wall. Mice?

"Do you hear that?"

Chris listened. "Yeah. It's like a digging noise. Sounds like it's in the wall."

"Do you think it's a rat?"

As we listened, the noise got louder. More aggressive. And then faster. I jumped out of the tub, grabbing a towel as I went.

In installing this giant tub in the bathroom of the townhome, the prior owners had taken out the closet from one of the bedrooms and incorporated that space into the bathroom. The rest of the spare bedroom had then been turned into a cavernous walk-in closet. Not that I was complaining.

I ran to the closet-bedroom, where the noise appeared to be coming from. I flipped on the light and was confronted with the hind end of a beagle in the air, his head down, buried in a pile of my shoes. Digging deeper and more rapidly, Seamus came up with his trophy in his mouth and turned to me. Eyes widened, he dashed past me and headed for the bedroom.

"Get him!" I yelled out to Chris, who had also gotten out of the tub but had not grabbed a towel.

Chris met me in the hallway. "What was it?"

"I don't know. I hope he didn't just catch a rat."

We moved to the bedroom door and turned on the light. Seamus was curled in his bed, wrapped around half of a sourdough loaf with the other half still protruding from inside his belly. Apparently he had a job to finish. As we walked toward him, he chomped down on the bread, attempting to swallow it whole. Chris moved toward him quickly. Seamus growled and gulped simultaneously. Back off, Food Guy, this one's mine! Chris cornered Seamus and reached for the chunk of bread. Seamus clenched his jaw tighter around the loaf and curled his lip, exposing more of the bread and his teeth. Chris stopped his forward movement and looked back to me, eyes widened.

Ooh, right. Not a dog person. He was naked; the dog was growling. I could understand the hesitation. I was impressed he'd even approached the dog.

Chris turned back to Seamus and calmly, firmly said, "Seamus, no."

As Seamus quieted, I quieted, watching with a mix of alarm and respect not unlike Seamus himself. Chris stepped toward the dog again and reached down. Miraculously, he removed the remaining quarter of a loaf from the jaws of a seriously pissed-off beagle. Seamus did not snarl, growl, or snap at Chris, and he was much too bloated to chase after anyone.

"Wow. I'm impressed. You just might be a dog person yet," I said.

"I'm not sure that's a dog. He's more like a reincarnation of some third-world dictator."

"Aww. But look how cute he is." Seamus thumped his tail and looked up at us from his prone position on top of the quilt in his bed, soulful brown eyes conveying that he'd already forgiven us our transgressions.

"That's the problem — he's diabolically cute. It might be time for a coup."

The next morning Seamus awoke hungry, as usual. Nonetheless, we scaled back his serving size, and it was Chris who doled out Seamus's kibble after making him sit politely and calmly as I watched dumbstruck. There were new rules in this household of ours, and we were all learning them. We were, against all odds, becoming a household of three.

Chapter 3
A Family Outing

I loathe Christmas.

I loathe the entire month of December. (Let me get this out of the way: I also dislike chocolate and spa treatments, which once caused a friend to comment to Chris, "It's like you're dating a unicorn.") I can recall only one Christmas that was distinctly enjoyable — I was six years old, and my parents gave me a black cockapoo puppy on Christmas Eve. I named him Tippit (quickly shortened to Tippy) after watching him run around our house knocking over the cocktail glasses my parents and their friends left on the floor next to their chairs. After that, though, Christmas was a series of arguments as my parents' marriage fell apart and then a logistical nightmare over which parent's house the kids would be at when. When my parents each remarried, we struggled with how to blend families and traditions while multiplying the logistics to now include step-relatives. My siblings and I spent most Christmases driving from one home to the next. Several times I had fast food for Christmas dinner. Once we finally grew past that stage, our luck changed — for the worse.

I was away at law school when Tippy died — in December. A few years later, my brother Jay had a motorcycle accident on December 1 and wound up in intensive care, not expected to live. He spent a week in a coma and several more weeks in intensive and critical care and then a rehab facility. The family spent Christmas at his hospital bedside in the critical care unit of the General Hospital. He survived, with a twelve-inch scar down his chest, a few nuts and bolts in his body, and no memory of December. A few years after that, my father's wife Faye died from a brain aneurysm while standing in her kitchen baking Christmas cookies on December 23. Her funeral was on her birthday, December 29. The following year, my sister-in-law Jennifer lost her mother to cancer on December 14. The funeral was December 23. The year after that my stepfather Ted lost both of his parents between Thanksgiving and Christmas.

So, yeah, I loathe not just Christmas, but

the entire month of December.

Chris, on the other hand, loved Christmas and the whole holiday season. He told me how his mother decorated their entire house, starting the process in mid-November. He enjoyed the trees she put up (I noted the plural with dismay), the decorations (she collected nutcrackers), the parties (several that were lifelong traditions), the food (I can't imagine family recipes not printed on a take-out menu), and, of course, the presents. Lots and lots of presents. He even loved watching all the holiday specials on television. He enjoyed the season, and he wanted to celebrate together. With his family.

We'd only been together for six months — and "together" was a loose term. I was not ready to meet his parents. Initially, we'd kept things between us private. Not even our writer's group knew we were dating. Mostly, we spent our weekends together in my house with only the beagle as a witness, and that worked out well. Of course, even I knew that the secretive part of our relationship made it more exciting. And "it" was how I referred to whatever "it" was that I was doing with Chris. If we met each other's families, wouldn't this then be a relationship? And if I pinned the word *relationship* on it, wouldn't it just turn sour? Wouldn't we immediately become disappointed in each other? Wouldn't the sex just stop and the fighting start? (I was in therapy; there was work to be done.) But the longer we dated, the harder the secret was to keep. We began telling people on a "need to know" basis.

Chris's parents, I was sure, were the last ones who would ever need to know. I felt strongly that they would not approve of our dating. Or, more to the point, they would not approve of me. I was pretty confident a woman twice divorced and twelve years older than their baby boy was not going to be welcome news. I was more than those labels, I knew, but I still wore the marks and did not have confidence that anyone, least of all his parents, would see past them. There was no reason to upset them. When we had something to tell them — if we had something to tell them — we'd tell them, but not before. We agreed to this in the bathtub, of course, so it was a solid pact, sworn in bubbles and sealed with champagne.

We compromised on the holidays by having a non-Christmas celebration the weekend before. Chris made a skillet of paella. We shared a bottle of Tempranillo and exchanged a few small gifts by the fire. We dubbed the occasion "Mas Chris" ("more Chris," in Spanish). It was much less complicated than Christmas, to my delight.

For the actual holiday, I once again fled the scene. I left Seamus with my mother and stepfather while I flew to Missouri to be with my brother and his family. His kids were still young enough to believe in Santa, so I thought they might be a nice diversion (assuming my plane didn't crash). Once there, I stayed up late each evening to call Chris in private and emailed him regularly.

Having avoided any Christmas disasters, I also played New Year's Eve safe, home alone with Seamus. Chris spent it with his family in Florida for the Orange Bowl. He also sneaked off to call me late at night without his parents or his sisters, Kati and Courtney, knowing. Or so we thought.

As the winter transformed into spring, my rule about "every other weekend only" eroded. We spent most weekends together, but we stuck to our pact to disclose our relationship only on a "need to know" basis. Unfortunately, his mother was not part of the pact. She had a plan of her own, and it was another holiday that caused me problems this time. Shortly after Easter, she called Chris.

"You didn't show up for Easter brunch," she said.

"You guys were gone; what's to show up for?" he deflected.

"I told you I had brunch reservations at the club for you and your sisters. You didn't show. And your Easter basket is still here."

"I can pick that up later."

"That's not good enough, mister. What's your problem lately? You haven't been around. You're not calling. We never see you. It's like you don't have time for your family anymore. And Kati says you were sneaking off to call someone every night we were in Florida. So, I'm just going to ask. Are you gay?"

Chris assured me he was able to laugh.

I was horrifically impressed with her ingenuity. She knew, of course, that he was not gay.

Ingeniously coerced, Chris outed me instead. Much to my chagrin and horror, he told her all about me — including my age, my divorces, and that I lived in Riverside. Riverside! To the Newport Beach crowd, that's like saying I lived in Hicksville, just south of Dowdytown and over the hill from Crime City. What was he thinking? Three strikes. I was certain I was out.

"You couldn't have lied to her? Or just

67

made stuff up? Agreed you were gay? Or, I don't know, not said anything beyond, 'I'm almost thirty years old, I'm dating someone, and it's none of your business'? Or, 'I'll tell you something when I'm ready to tell you'?" I said.

"I couldn't think that fast. She caught me off guard. I don't know. I'm not in the habit of lying to my parents."

Well, there's that. Although I liked to think of it as "managing" parents. "But she doesn't have the right to pry into your personal life — or mine."

"Yeah. I know. But it didn't go badly. It's not as bad as you think."

"Oh, I promise you, it's as bad as I think." We were on the phone, so I couldn't see his face to know if her reaction had been bad and he was just protecting me or if he honestly felt his mother was accepting. I wouldn't have believed the latter anyway. "And, by the way, your mom still gives you an Easter basket?"

"I wondered how long it would take for you to mention that part."

"It's a lot to process. But, like, candy? Peeps? Fake grass?"

"I love Peeps. And my mother would never use that cheap, plastic fake grass."

"This is the sole exception to the Newport

Beach love of plastic?"

Chris must have been emboldened by our laughter. "They want to meet you."

"That's hilarious. And so wrong."

"I suggested brunch."

"What?" The happy little paradise we'd been building was coming under attack. The walls — our weekends — were crumbling. I patted the blanket on the couch next to me, and Seamus hopped up, snuggling into the crook of my arm. It's you and me, dog. Hello, alphabet life.

"I honestly think they're going to like you. What's not to like? You're gorgeous, you're a successful lawyer, you've got a beautiful home. And we've been dating almost a year now. My parents know that's twice as long as I've dated anyone before. I can't hide you forever."

I stayed quiet, petting Seamus and trying to get my mind to function. I was working on a valid excuse to not meet his parents while also trying not to be flattered by his description.

"And I don't want to hide you," he said.

Shit.

For the week before the brunch, I obsessed over what to wear and what to say without ever deciding on either. On the morning of the brunch I dressed in black pants, black patent-leather high heels and a black cotton sweater. Then I tore it all off my body. *It's not a funeral. Try being less literal about your feelings.*

I changed from the black pants to a black skirt with a ruffled hem. *Ah yes, very black widow at a funeral. That should make them comfortable. Why not just throw a wide-brimmed black hat and dark sunglasses on as well?* I took off the skirt and sweater and threw them in a corner of my closet.

I put on a white eyelet sundress. And I took that off too, tossing it in the pile. *Who are you kidding? Virginal white? Hilarious!*

A fuschia wraparound dress came on and off next. *What's with the cleavage, whore?*

I spent another twenty minutes determining that every item in my closet either wheezed "middle-aged loser" or shrieked "slutty gold digger," even though I had no recollection of ever shopping with those themes in mind. I was only distracted from my internal meltdown when I looked in the mirror and saw that my hair had been flattened lifeless — except in the places it was flying haphazardly outward from the static. I would have dropped my head into my hands in despair if I hadn't been so worried about smearing the mascara that I feared I'd over-applied.

With two minutes left to spare, I decided on an off-white outfit — linen pants and an off-the-shoulder blouse, both by Ann Taylor. I brushed my blond but not-too-blond hair back to life, leaving it straight and long but pushed back behind my ears, which were adorned with unobjectionable pearl earrings.

I forced myself to stop fussing and head downstairs where Chris was waiting.

"You look great," he said.

"I'm not feeling great."

"You look great. Really. You look great."

"Thanks."

"You look really great."

"Good to know you're as nervous as I am."

"Pretty much."

We drove to the Mission Inn, a beautiful hotel in downtown Riverside with Spanish architecture including a surrounding pergola, arches, tiled fountains, and massive amounts of bougainvillea reminiscent of a California mission. Conveniently located halfway between Los Angeles and Palm Springs, at one time it was a hangout for celebrities. Their brunch is a sprawling, festive affair and usually busy. I thought it would be a suitably impressive place while still giving me the protection of a crowd.

I grabbed Chris's hand as we walked through the lobby toward my certain doom.

We were on time, but his parents were already waiting at the hostess station. Chris led me toward them and greeted his father with a handshake and his mother with a hug.

"Mom, Dad, this is Teresa," Chris said.

And there it was. I was meeting the parents. Something I swore I'd never do again.

I inhaled and extended my hand. "Really nice to meet you both," I said, trying to mean it.

"I'm Trudi. It's so nice to meet you after all this time." His mother shook my hand.

Chris looks a lot like his mother, I noticed. It's from his mother that he gets his long-lashed blue eyes; thick, wavy, dark hair; and perfectly shaped nose. Her hair, though, was not salt and pepper like Chris's, but perfectly colored and styled. She wore turquoise and white and, just as Chris had said, was accessorized to perfection, including a straw and turquoise clutch purse. I was immediately aware that her clutch was one-tenth the size of the suitcase-purse weighing down my left side. I liked her style, although I was simultaneously intimidated by it.

I turned to Chris's dad and shook his

hand as well.

He was smiling. "I'm Jim. It's nice to finally meet you, Teresa."

I was caught off guard by Chris's father's size and coloring — he was shorter than Chris and of much slighter build, and his hair was light brown. He was not what I'd expected.

"You too," I said. And I returned a smile. Dads I can handle. My mothers-in-law had both been disapproving of me, although they'd handled it differently (one passively, one aggressively). But I'd gotten along with both of my fathers-in-law. There were a lot of mothers in my lifetime of baggage — my porters would need porters to carry it — but no fathers. What moms objected to (my logical mind, my lack of sentiment, my career, my independence, my lack of interest in children, my complete lack of housekeeping skills, and, most importantly, my inability to see the world as revolving around their sons), dads could generally relate to, or they simply couldn't care less. I didn't worry about meeting dads. So, despite Jim's deep voice and stern demeanor, I wasn't worried about him. Just her. Just Trudi.

We discussed the usual pleasantries over our eggs Benedict and mimosas — the weather, how Chris and I met, how much nicer Riverside was than they had known it to be in the past. I was beginning to think I could pull it off. I would pass as normal, presentable. Acceptable even. And then —

"So, Teresa, has Chris met your family yet?" Trudi said.

I could tell by the way she leaned in toward me, glanced over at Chris, and then re-focused on me, that the answer mattered. My mind didn't so much race as come skidding to a halt. My gut took over. What was it that she wanted to know? Does she want to know if she and Jim had met me first or if somehow my parents were more important and had met Chris first? Or does she want to know what sort of family I come from? Or is she gauging how serious we were? What? What does she want?

My mind fought for control. She merely asked a polite question. *Answer her.*

My gut screamed back. *But with what? What can you possibly say?*

My family is complicated, even by Southern California standards. I am never adept at answering questions about them. Even simple questions like how many brothers and sisters I had could stop me cold while I considered how much information the questioner could handle or likely wanted.

74

I hadn't grown up in a close or intact family. My parents had each married several times, and all totaled I had nine siblings of the step, half, and whole varieties. I'd had two sets of parents for most of my life. But those sets changed with the decades, bringing new supporting characters. I often said that we did not have a family tree so much as family ground cover — we spread outward and our roots are not deep.

So, had Chris met my family? Well, yes . . . sort of. Some of them. I was sure my face now matched my outfit. Egg-white. My parents had both fallen into the "need to know" category over the past couple of months.

Chris came to my rescue. "I have met her parents. They are very nice people."

"So what did your parents think?" Trudi asked, all polish and poise. What I heard was "Your parents also think this is ridiculous, correct?"

What did my parents think? I was forty-two years old. If my parents had cared whom I dated as a teenager (since they themselves were only in their thirties then and quite busy with their own dates, there is only limited evidence of this), they were long past caring whom I dated as an adult. Also, they were sitting in glass houses when it came to throwing relationship stones. I was gaining a new appreciation of this non-judgmental aspect of my family.

The truth was, when Chris met my parents, it was very simple. Casual.

When it came to my father, my brother caused a "need to know" situation by making a surprise visit from Missouri only a few weeks earlier. Chris and I had about an hour's notice to get out of bed, get showered, and get presentable before my brother and father were both on my doorstep. Surprise, indeed. I think mine was the larger surprise, although Jay (my younger brother but still with ten years seniority over Chris) and Dad both recovered quickly enough to make jokes about curfews, my having to cut up Chris's food, and my serving alcohol to a minor. My father called later both to say "how young is he?" and "he seems like a great guy and you seem happy." This was followed quickly by "just don't get arrested" and laughter.

When it came to my mother, it was Seamus who created the need for her to know about Chris.

After several months of Chris and me sharing our weekends home with only Seamus, we got the idea that it was time to spend a weekend away, just the two of us, heresy though that seemed to a certain beagle.

Seamus, however, presented a problem for us. I hated the idea of putting him in a boarding facility. He was a dog that needed and got a lot of companionship. I didn't think he'd do well with a small pen and only two ten-minute exercise sessions a day. The solution required a confession.

I babysat my mom and stepdad's dog Barbee on occasion, both in my previous life as a married person with a large yard and three (then two) beagles, and once or twice in my new life in a rented condo with one needy beagle and a secret boyfriend. Occasionally, my mother had returned the favor by watching Seamus, like when I went to Missouri for Christmas. But my mother was not dumb. If I started leaving Seamus with her on weekends, she'd want to know where I was going. And how many times can a forty-something-year-old woman head out for "girls' weekends" before an intervention is staged?

I 'fessed up to my mother and asked her to watch Seamus for me when Chris and I went to San Diego for the infamous Easter weekend that eventually provoked Trudi's outing of our relationship. I told my mother we'd stop by Sunday evening to pick up

Seamus and have Easter dinner. And yes, she'd meet Chris. I was hoping this dog-sitting sharing arrangement would work out. Chris and I had started planning a summer trip to Barcelona.

My mother and stepfather Ted lived in a town called Yucaipa, about twenty-five miles from me in the foothills where the weather is cooler than it is in Riverside. I dropped Seamus off on a Friday afternoon before heading down to San Diego with Chris later that evening.

Seamus and their dog Barbee, an Australian Shepherd mix, got along well enough but were very different dogs. Barbee was calm and serious. She also constantly patrolled the perimeter of their yard, which Seamus thought was great fun at first. He merrily chased after her, howling his excitement for the entire neighborhood to hear. Repeatedly. Shepherds herd. Beagles howl. It's not such a good combination, my mother learned.

Eventually Seamus tired of the game and wanted only to be safe and warm in the house. In the kitchen, to be precise. I had forgotten to warn my mother that Seamus had learned to open cupboards. In my house Chris installed three different types of baby locks on the cupboard below my kitchen sink (where the trash can was) before we found one that was beagle-proof. Seamus could move a lever up, press and release, and even twist a lock if there were food in the trash can behind the cupboard door. He could not, we eventually learned, figure out how to slide a bar to the right (and most of my human houseguests can't either). His specialty seemed to be a trash assault after an accumulation of at least three mornings of coffee grinds, eggshells, and grease-soaked anything in the trash. We'd come downstairs in the morning to find yesterday's breakfast strewn across the kitchen floor with a trail of coffee grinds leading to Seamus's bed.

Barbee, on the other hand, was a dog for whom one could leave a bowl of food out all day and eventually she'd eat it when she was hungry. Unless Seamus got to it first. And he always did. He also got to my mother's trash can which, from his view-point, had a clear "Seamus Eats Here" sign hanging over it. With its gaping, lidless mouth, its tasty chicken morsels, and its position in the back pantry, unguarded, unlocked, it was obviously free for the tak-ing. My mother swears he swallowed the chicken bones whole.

Mom and Ted also learned that Seamus,

like Chris and me, prefers warmth and late nights, disdaining cold and mornings. They had a difficult time and endured no small amount of beagle grumbling attempting to wake Seamus for a walk at six in the morning. But when my mother and Barbee left without Seamus for their walk and returned to find that Seamus had risen long enough to use the dining room as a bathroom, she instituted the mandatory morning walk rule.

When Chris and I arrived to pick up Seamus after our weekend away, Seamus's antics had seemed to take all the pressure off that particular "meet the parents" moment. My mother only briefly said hello to both Chris and me before she said, pursing her lips and looking in Seamus's direction, "He's quite a dog." My stepfather rolled his eyes. Seamus was seated on their couch — their off-white formal living room couch — staring wide-eyed and wagging his tail.

Easter dinner was made easier (and quicker) by tales of Seamus — Chris, it seemed, could match my mother's anecdotes of bad beagle behavior and then raise her one. Or several. I think my mom and stepdad decided that if Chris was willing to put up with Seamus, he was probably a pretty good guy, though they also called later to say, "How young is he?"

So yes, Chris had met my parents. And yes, they liked him. Why couldn't I just say that to his mother? Why did I have to be reading so much into what might be perfectly innocent, friendly questions?

Oh, like hell they were friendly. These were loaded questions intended to sniff out the enemy. And I was the enemy. My gut was fierce in its opinion.

But my mind was desperate. *Wait. Stop. You're being paranoid. They're very nice people. Look, she's smiling at you. He's refilling the champagne. They can see their son is happy. That's all a parent can want, right? Right?*

Chris had been raised in a privileged background, and his parents were used to knowing and controlling every aspect of their three children's lives. Heavy emphasis on children. It had worked out very well so far — Chris was a very polite, very well-mannered, private-schooled, Princeton-educated, oldest son of an intact, close-knit family. Chris and I had spent plenty of time soaking in bubbles talking about our families, so I knew that in his family decisions were made on high and handed down and had always been so. But he was nearly thirty years old now. He could make his own decisions. All that should matter is that he's happy. I took a deep breath.

"Both of my parents loved him. Of course. What's not to love?" I smiled brightly, but under the table my hand was reaching for Chris's thigh, as much a sign of affection as to stabilize myself. Or maybe I was claiming him.

"Well, I hope so. We like to think we raised a good son." Trudi smiled back at me. I don't think she could extend a claim on Chris from across the table. At least not physically.

Except for my own internal monologue, I was unharmed by the end of brunch. I admitted as much to Chris. His parents were polite and civil. Although I knew I was being "checked out," I did not feel harshly judged. Or, more to the point, I felt I passed whatever test I was being given. I did not look embarrassingly older than Chris, or even embarrassing. (I suspected they were expecting someone more along the lines of a truck-stop waitress or a stripper.) I did know which utensil to use when; I didn't drool or chew with my mouth open; and, I believe, I remembered to say both "please" and "thank you." I talked about my legal career in the hope that Chris's parents would see I wasn't a gold digger. Although Chris and I laughed about that concept (he had no gold of his own and I had no discernible digging skills since he was the pursuer and I was the one who resisted the relationship for so long), we suspected it was on their minds. I thought I'd alleviated that concern.

At the end of brunch, as we walked out of the restaurant, Trudi said to me, "I don't know why he kept you a secret for so long."

I was at a loss for an answer that would be socially acceptable. "Well, because we really just thought we were having mind-blowing sex, not getting into a relationship" did not seem appropriate to say to his mother; "Moms put the fear of God into me and thus I wanted to avoid this for as long as possible" also seemed, well, not quite right. I finally muttered something like, "Well, we've met now." Because, in case I haven't mentioned it before, I'm a conversational genius under pressure.

CHAPTER 4
INVADING STRANGERS

I next saw Chris's parents in June when they hosted a thirtieth birthday dinner for Chris at a restaurant in Santa Monica. We left the party at ten in the evening to catch a red-eye flight to Puerto Vallarta for four days — my gift to Chris. Although they were aware of the trip ahead of time, I vaguely felt I was kidnapping him as we left.

"There's still food. People are still here," his mother said.

"They're not going to hold the plane for us. Besides, these clowns will stay here as long as you keep the bar tab open," Chris said, referencing his friends.

I fought the compulsion to explain that despite what they may have been thinking, it is not, in fact, illegal to cross international borders with a thirty-year-old. But I decided I was being paranoid. They probably just wanted to spend more time with their son. Still, despite an enjoyable evening, my comfort level with his parents, never high to begin with, sank with each step I took out of the restaurant, my arm linked in Chris's. I did not see them again for the rest of the summer.

In early fall, I moved into my own town-home. I'd bought a place in the same complex where I'd been renting, only this one had been remodeled and upgraded in ways I never would have thought about. There were maple floors and cupboards, brushed nickel accents, modern lighting that accented the artwork, a built-in bar and wine refrigerator, and a sound system throughout the home. There was no massive tub, but there was a hot tub on the back patio with a stunning view of the city. When he saw it, before I made the offer on it, Chris dubbed it the "sleek and elegant cougar den" (making light of the many cougar jokes I'd endured), which was thereafter how we referred to it. It was perfect for me. I bought it furnished. All I needed to add were my books, my artwork, and, of course, my dog.

Moving day was typical of the complications that existed in my life. Not only did both of my parents come to help, but my ex-husband offered to as well since I was giving him back some of "our" furniture that I no longer needed. My mother spent nearly the entire day keeping Seamus under control (no easy task) and avoiding my father (a much easier task since he was likewise avoiding her). My ex-husband spent the day avoiding Chris by cleaning my already clean new townhome down the hill from my rented townhome where Chris was loading boxes of books into my brother-in-law's truck. One stepbrother showed up long enough to pick up some of the furniture I no longer needed and my ex didn't want, move a few boxes in exchange for the furniture, and then disappear again. My stepmother arrived with lunch and some friends of my father's who were really too old to be moving boxes and thus didn't bother.

And I was blissfully content with it all.

Well, I was until I went upstairs after my father and a friend had removed my mattress and box spring, thus emptying out the last of the items in my bedroom in the rented townhome. Chris was right behind me.

I stopped as I entered the room, shocked and mortified. "Do you think they saw it?" I said.

"The shiny, purple condom wrapper in the middle of the otherwise empty floor?

No, how could they?" Chris said. He laughed. I did not.

"How humiliating."

"Well, at least they know we practice safe sex."

"I'm sure that's exactly what they were thinking."

"It could have been worse. It could have been your ex helping your dad move the mattress."

Chris is better than I am at recognizing the small mercies in life.

After everyone left, we were alone in the sleek and elegant cougar den, grinning like children. We celebrated and relaxed our weary muscles in the hot tub, of course.

Seamus was equally smitten with our new place. Since the back patio opened to a hillside frequented by coyotes, he was not allowed in the backyard. Luckily, he had unfettered access to the front courtyard, courtesy of a doggie door installed by the previous owner in just the right size. The courtyard had a gate off the street, keeping Seamus safely inside but allowing him to be the first to greet visitors. He immediately began running in and out of the house through his own door on a whim, sometimes stretching out on the chaise lounge chairs outside in the courtyard and watching us through the French doors as we watched movies on the new flat-screen TV with surround sound. The place was perfect for all three of us, and we adjusted quickly. Chris began spending even more time at my place, as his job transitioned to contract work.

I unpacked boxes during the weekday evenings, feeling unhurried and saving the weekends for Chris. My life was here and settling in. There was no need to rush anything. Sometimes it took days just to get one box of books unpacked and shelved.

Seamus was about two years old by then. He still acted like a puppy. He greeted me, howled, jumped, whirled, and twirled each night when I came home from work and did much the same when I left in the mornings. Seamus responded to Chris similarly — howling, jumping, and demanding cuddles on arrival.

There was only one small adjustment to the new house that didn't go well for Seamus.

One evening as Chris and I were reading by the fireplace, lounging on the couch in the living room, Seamus emitted a low growl. A growl I hadn't heard since he'd first met Chris. Seamus stood in the middle of the living room, his back to us, facing into the dining room.

"What is it, buddy?"

He leaned his head to the left, then stepped left and growled again.

"What do you see?" I stood, but I could see nothing in the dining room.

Seamus stepped to his right. Then backed up. His growl got louder.

"Maybe there's a mouse in there," Chris said.

"Ewwww! Can you go look?"

Chris stood, and Seamus howled. But when Chris walked into the dining room, Seamus quieted.

"I don't see anything." He turned back to face Seamus and bent down to pet him. Seamus stepped out of his reach and looked around Chris, back into the dining room.

AAAAAARRROOOOOOOOO!

"Well, something's there." I walked over to Seamus and knelt down beside him, trying to match my gaze to his.

And then I saw what Seamus saw. As Seamus moved slowly to the left, back a step and to the right, then forward again, his neck extended and eyes wide, I began to laugh.

"He sees his reflection in the mirror."

"You're kidding me?" Chris laughed too. He joined me on the floor behind Seamus, a vantage point that made it clear that

Seamus was staring into the mirrored wall in the dining room.

"Who's that handsome stranger, Seamus?" Chris said. "Who is that?"

Seamus barked at his image. And we howled in laughter.

"He has a problem with handsome strangers," I said.

Seamus spent the next half hour working up his courage to approach the handsome stranger. When he finally did, putting his nose right up to the mirror, he must have decided the lack of smell emanating from the handsome stranger indicated he meant no harm. He walked away. And he never again approached or barked at the mirror.

In early November, Seamus's groomer Nancy pulled up in her customized motor home for his regular appointment. Though he didn't care much for being lifted off his feet, Seamus loved Nancy and the attention that came with a bath — as long as his face didn't get wet and the blow drying was minimal. I handed his leash to Nancy and returned to the house.

A half hour later Nancy was at the front gate with Seamus.

"I wanted to show you something," she said.

I opened the courtyard gate. Seamus bounded in, smelling fresh and looking jaunty with an orange bow imprinted with horns of plenty attached to his collar. Nancy bent down and turned Seamus around so his rear end was facing me.

"Can you see that bump on the right side of his anus?"

Not somewhere I usually look, but I looked. I could see a bump about the size of a mosquito bite. "Yes, I think. It looks like an insect bite?"

"Yes, it does. But it was there the last time I groomed him and it hasn't gone away."

Ah. "And it's been ten weeks. So it's not a bite?"

"No. It's something else." She let go of Seamus and unhooked his leash. Seamus ran howling back toward the house, scooted through the doggie door, and disappeared.

"Like what?"

"I don't know if it's anything. But unusual bumps on a dog should be checked out just like with people," Nancy said. She stood up and put the forty dollars I'd handed her into her pocket. "I'd get it checked."

I took Seamus for an exam the next day.

Dr. Davis picked Seamus up and steadied him on the metal exam table. Seamus turned his head to me with those big, caramel beagle eyes. *Really? You're going to let him poke me there?* He moved his hind end away from the doctor. I moved him back into position. He sat. I prodded him to stand up again. He turned and looked, wide-eyed, at me again. *Seriously?*

"It's probably nothing," Dr. Davis said. "I know you're worried, with all you've been through with dogs lately, but I really don't think this is anything. I'll remove it and have it biopsied to be safe."

"Biopsy? You think it's cancer?" For some reason, the word *biopsy* said "cancer" to me. Were biopsies done to look for any other disease?

"No. Hold on. I don't think so. He's young and sturdy. This could just be a wart. But I'd like to be safe and check it out anyway."

I scheduled a surgery to remove what looked like a wart on a beagle's anus as soon as an appointment was available. As it turned out, the first available surgery date was right before Chris and I were to leave for Cabo San Lucas. We'd been invited by clients of mine to be their guests. Although I hadn't yet figured out how to refer to Chris ("boyfriend" was too young, "lover" too personal), I'd come to terms with being a couple enough to even share the relationship with clients, so I'd accepted the generous offer. With Seamus now needing surgery though, I considered canceling the trip.

"Don't be ridiculous. Go. Have a good time. He's a young, sturdy dog, and I seriously doubt this is anything. You can leave him here with me," Dr. Davis said.

"Are you sure?"

"Absolutely."

I called Chris for his opinion as well.

"If he can stay with Dr. Davis, he'll be in better care than he would be at home anyway, won't he?"

"Well, maybe. But he won't be as comfortable."

"It's only four days total. Two days more than he'd be in the hospital anyway for this."

"True. And I do know they take great care of him."

Following the surgery, Seamus would need to be confined to a small space and wearing one of those large, plastic cones of shame to prevent him from chewing out his delicately placed stitches. That would be more easily accomplished by leaving him with Dr. Davis, I knew. Dr. Davis and his staff were far more immune to those pleading beagle eyes than I could ever hope to be. They'd leave the cone on, and he'd heal more quickly. And it was only four days, I repeated to myself.

Chris and I headed to Cabo San Lucas, where we spent a leisurely four days lounging in a cabana on the beach. The chips and guacamole, cervezas and margaritas, and anything else we wanted, readily available and served cabana-side, helped dissipate my concerns. Dr. Davis emailed me that Seamus made it through surgery fine, and I relaxed into my vacation. I read two books, got a tan in November, and did a decent job of not worrying too much about Seamus.

We returned late on a Sunday evening, happy and rested. I went to pick Seamus up as soon as I finished work on Monday. I approached the front desk, smiling.

"I'm here to pick up Seamus. And obviously, he's feeling well. I could hear his howling as soon as I got out of my car."

"The doctor would like to see you for a moment before you leave." The receptionist's voice was soft and kind, and she tilted her head to the side and squinted her eyes slightly, just slightly. Just enough that I worried maybe Seamus was not healing well from the surgery. Or hadn't behaved well, since that was always a distinct possibility. That would be better — just a complaint about his howling, not a medical issue. But I knew that wouldn't be the case. I knew because I'd seen this expression before, in this office. "The doctor would like to see you" is one of those statements like "We have to talk" that doesn't bode well. And just back from a relaxing and thoroughly enjoyable four days on a Mexican beach with Chris, I wasn't prepared for either statement.

I followed the receptionist to the exam room where she left me alone, seated, staring at the exam table and trying not to look at the cute baby animal photos likely meant to cheer me but having the opposite effect. I stared at the linoleum floor, avoiding not just the pictures but the charts, the jars, the vials, and even the puffs of cotton balls on the counters. I especially avoided the metal exam table. I'd spent too much time here in the past several years with my aging and ill dogs. We'd spread a blanket and laid Richelieu on that metal exam table where I held him and petted him when the injection that ended his life was administered. I had thought my time in this room was over for at least a few more years.

They brought Seamus into the room first. Dr. Davis wasn't too far behind. Dr. Davis had been the vet to my last four beagles and even the two German Shepherds and a sweet red Doberman from my first marriage. He was with me when Richelieu had to be put down, and he treated Roxy for her heart murmur. He'd given Seamus his initial health check when I had adopted him only one year earlier. Dr. Davis and I had served together on the board of directors for our local pet adoption center for the last fifteen years. He was someone I trusted with my animals completely — someone I knew to be compassionate to humans and animals alike. His voice was even softer, kinder, and more patient than the receptionist's.

"I'm sorry." He tilted his head and leaned toward me. "The biopsy came back, and it is cancer. It's what is known as a mast cell tumor. I'm so sorry. We really didn't expect this."

No, we really didn't.

I sat on the floor. Seamus immediately crawled into my lap and sniffed my face. I held the dog close and petted his head as Dr. Davis explained yet another disease attacking yet another dog of mine. I didn't hear much of what he told me. I petted Seamus and held his face to mine while I blinked back tears. I wanted to get to the safety of my car and later my home so I could fall apart in private. Dr. Davis handed me papers — a referral to a surgeon, medication, maybe a bill. I stuffed them in my purse.

I grabbed the leash and left the exam room. Seamus followed, baying away: *We're going home! It's time for home! Take me home now, Mom! Let's go home! I'd like to go home. Home is good. Also, feed me. Oh my God, feed me!! So hungry! Come on, Mom, let's go home now! Here's our car! We're going home! I love home. Food is at home! AAAAAARR-ROOOOOOOOO!!!*

I drove home, steering with one hand and rifling through my purse for tissue with the other. Tears flowed down my face, and I wiped them away again and again before giving up. I sniffed and tried to inhale deeply at the stoplight. I turned to Seamus in his crate in my backseat and petted him through the bars until the driver behind me honked. I cursed the driver in my mind. *Fuck you for not caring about anything except where you're going! Fuck you! My dog has cancer!!* I slammed my hands down on the steering wheel.

When we got home, Seamus immediately began the hard work of pulling his stitches out with his teeth. Beginning what would become a lifetime pattern, I felt so bad for him I could not reprimand him in the slightest. I couldn't say "no" or raise my voice to him. Instead, I tried simply explaining to him that if he continued to do that, I'd have to put that awful plastic cone collar back on his head and that would be awkward and uncomfortable. If that failed, I continued explaining, blubbering through my tears, I had doggie diapers at the ready to prevent him from chewing his rear end, and neither of us wants to go there. He stopped tearing at his stitches momentarily and instead cocked his head and looked at me expectantly. I just wanted to hold him and cry into his silky, soft puppy fur and feel sorry for both of us. He just wanted to have dinner, chomp on a few squeak toys, and chew on his rear end. It was Chris who had to put up with my crying, sniffling, and general ranting over the phone. I think I said "unfair" at least a dozen times, preceded by a few *fookin*'s without the Irish brogue.

I tried to get Seamus to sleep on my bed with me that night, but he wouldn't. He preferred the comfort of his own bed and toys, where there was far less drama. He slept soundly, snoring loudly. I know this because I was awake listening to it all night.

I couldn't call the veterinarian surgical oncologist until normal business hours the next day. I called at eight in the morning.

They didn't open until nine. I called at nine exactly and got a recording. I called again from work, and again, until finally I reached someone. A someone who told me the earliest available appointment was six weeks away. Six weeks! The dog could die by then.

I explained that my dog had been diagnosed with cancer. Cancer! I cried. Not surprisingly, the veterinarian oncology office did not move my dog to the front of the line of other dogs who had . . . right, cancer. But she did offer that there might be less of a wait at their Los Angeles office. That office was sixty miles away from me, but only ten miles from Chris. I called. They had an available appointment two weeks away. I took it. I'd drive sixty miles. I'd drive a hundred miles. Three hundred miles. I just needed my dog to be treated. I needed cancer to go away.

Seamus had two more weeks to recover from the first surgery before we'd be meeting a veterinarian surgeon discussing the possibility of a second surgery. I had two more weeks to try to wrap my head around the fact that my adorable, funny little beagle had CANCER.

I left work shortly after five in the evening. I'd been useless all day anyway. All I could think about was CANCER. The word was heavy in my brain. My puppy had CAN-CER. And I'd left him home, medicated, wearing a cone collar, with stitches still in his rear end. I hurried home, pulled my car quickly into my garage, jumped out, and raced into the front courtyard on my way to my front door.

Immediately, I was accosted by a yelp from behind me. And not a beagle yelp. I spun around.

"Teresa! Your dog has been barking all day. All day. It's making me crazy! How can you leave him like this? It's ridiculous. He barks all day, every day. I can't take it. I. Absolutely. Can. Not. Take it. Not anymore. No more!"

My neighbor across the street, a cotton-candy blond woman in her seventies whom I'd only met once, was at my courtyard gate, and indeed it did appear my dog, or something, had driven her insane. I think I saw foam coming from her mouth.

Seamus was at my feet in an instant. And still howling. *Ohmygawd, Mom! Where have you been! It's been terrifying here!! I've missed you! Get in the house! Get in the house now! Also, feed me!! Ohmygawd feed me! So hungry!! Oh, and pet me, yes, yes, pet me! Noooooooowwwww!!! Must cuddle noooooooooooooooowwwwwwwwww!!!*

I tried to calm and control my howling dervish of a beagle, while addressing my enraged neighbor and choking back my own tears. "I'm sorry. He's recovering from surgery. And I just found out he has cancer. So I'm sure he's a mess right now."

While I knew the dog was unaware of his diagnosis, something did seem wrong with his emotional state, even more than normal.

"I'm sorry about that, but it's not just recently. He howls all the time. Every day. All day long. All the time. I can't take it anymore. I just can't."

I was no longer crying. I was dismayed. He howls all day long? What? Neighbor, you've lost your mind. "I'm sorry. I didn't know that. I haven't had problems with him before. And often Chris is home with him during the day, so I really don't understand how it could be every day."

"Oh, Chris is gone a lot more than you think," she said, eyebrows raised meaningfully.

Great. So my dog has cancer and my boyfriend is running around servicing every female in town. Well, maybe that's why the dog was howling. "I'll see what I can do," I said.

I turned and headed through the courtyard to my front door. One glance at the doggie door and I could see what the problem was.

The cone collar was in the courtyard, right in front of the doggie door, where it had no doubt dropped when Seamus with his cone head got stuck in the opening. The door opening was not big enough for the cone to fit through. He must have barked for quite some time before eventually working himself free of the cone. He was no longer wearing cone or collar (it was attached to the cone). I thought about heading over to my neighbor's house to explain what had happened but chose instead to focus on the dog and his stitches.

Dog diapers it will be. Although as a backup plan, doggie diapers seem flawed. Beagles are not dogs to be restrained or contained or . . . put in diapers. Beagles are smart, cunning dogs with intense motivation to get what they want (usually food). Beagles are very, very clever dogs.

And not surprisingly, diapers are no match for a beagle. Complicating matters, I'd bought the wrong size — and I still dispute that a beagle could be a "large," but I'm not sure what chain of command to follow for a beagle diaper dispute. When I put the diaper on Seamus, I could only close up one side. The other side flapped open with the protruding section of adhesive tape virtually inviting him to bite it and tear the diaper from his hind end, flinging it into the middle of the living room. Or the kitchen. Or my cereal bowl. After several failed attempts with the diaper, the cone and tightened collar were returned to service. But I couldn't risk his getting stuck in the doggie door again.

I worked from home for a few days. I alternated between drafting trusts for families concerned with the legacies they'd leave to their children and shouting, "Seamus, NO!" or "Seamus, stop!" Seamus alternated between scratching at his cone, slamming the cone (and sometimes his head) into doorjambs, and lying at my feet looking up with his wide, sad eyes begging for a reprieve or at least a doughnut. My resolve weakened by the minute. Chris came over midweek and took over Seamus-watching, although I suspect he knew I needed watching nearly as much.

Finally, the stitches dissolved and I could leave the house again. I was able to return to my office, go grocery shopping, and rejoin the human race. Seamus was able to use his doggie door unencumbered, sit comfortably, and continue his mastery of the household. We'd survived the surgery, but there was still the upcoming appointment at the Veterinarian Cancer Center. As difficult as the cone of shame had been, it was nothing compared to what lay ahead. I knew he had at least one more surgery, or, I hoped he did. I hoped they'd be able to cut the cancer out.

I found myself staring at the dog — the very healthy, hyper, happy dog — wondering how he could possibly have cancer. With the cone banished, he was fine. He was back to all his usual tricks, and he was no longer subject to any humiliations, other than his person randomly bursting into tears, cursing the gods, and hugging him embarrassingly close.

My humiliations, however, were to continue. A few days before I was to take Seamus to Los Angeles to meet with the specialist, an anonymous note was slipped into my mailbox.

Neighbors,
   Your dog has been wheezing and barking for hours this evening and this is not the first time!!!!

My question to you is:

What is wrong with you "people" that

you cannot take care of your dog? Why must your dog cry and cry all night without your paying any attention to it?

Shame on you!!!!!!

For subjecting your dog to endless suffering, and your neighbors to your dog's endless barking.

Sure, I'd been a little crazed since the diagnosis, but I didn't think my status as "people" really needed to be questioned. And the dog had not been left alone all night without any attention being paid to him. More likely the dog was outside, having freely gone there of his own volition through his doggie door, in an attempt to get away from his clingy, cloying, crying wreck of a human.

What was wrong with me? What was wrong with my dog? Well, cancer is what's wrong, people! Cancer! But how to explain this to a neighbor who may not even like dogs? Was Seamus barking all day long? Chris and I both suspected the letter came from the same neighbor who'd greeted me at the gate in a rage. So was the dog bothering the whole neighborhood, or was he merely barking at the mailman and maybe the gardeners and perhaps even a pedestrian passing by and this neighbor had no tolerance for dogs?

I knew Seamus barked when I left, but it seemed he stopped after a few minutes. And he barked when I came home, but in an excited greeting sort of way. It had not occurred to me that he barked the entire time in between. Was that even possible? Had that just started happening because of the surgery and the stress he'd been under? When I lived in the rental condo, those neighbors never said anything about a barking problem.

Still, there were signs. Seamus had an unusually high anxiety level. I knew that. He hated to be left alone. He was vocal about my coming and going, his breakfast and dinner, and everything in between. I didn't like the way the neighbor was handling her complaints, but much as I wanted to, I knew I couldn't ignore them either.

CHAPTER 5
MARGINS OF ERROR

With my cougar status out of the bag, my neighbors gathering pitchforks at my gate, and the holidays approaching, it was clear my holiday curse was continuing. I'd be taking Seamus for his oncology appointment and another surgery, and I'd be spending Thanksgiving with Chris's entire family at his grandmother's house. I hoped numbers would be on my side — surgery number two would get all of the cancer, and the sheer number of siblings, aunts, uncles, and cousins at Chris's family Thanksgiving would produce at least one ally — or maybe just someone more objectionable than me.

I put Seamus's crate in the backseat of my car and opened the door to the crate. Seamus nimbly leaped up, walked into the crate, turned around, sat, and waited for me to close it. Once I closed the back door to my car, he barked until I was in the car with him and the car was started. Then he quieted and calmly sat looking ahead at the road through the crate for the entire drive. But when the car stopped, the barking began. *I'm back here! Take me with you! Is there food around? How about a burger? I smell burgers! Or the beach? Is that the beach? Take me with you! Come get me out! Get me! Let me outta here!! Nooooooooooo-ooooooooow!!!!*

We were at the veterinarian oncology office, but Seamus didn't know that. He just knew he wanted out of the car with me.

The Veterinary Cancer Center is housed in a modern facility in a gentrified Los Angeles suburb. The building has an open loft feeling to it, industrial with splashes of vivid colors — orange, magenta, lime green — and a green-tinted cement floor. The artwork is particularly attractive, including large black and white photographs of the doctors and their own animals. It's as nice as a place that you never want to be can be.

The facility was also not far from Chris's apartment, which made it easy for him to join me for the appointment. The three of us sat in the waiting room, Seamus sniffing, me sniffling, and Chris doing an admirable job of entertaining and distracting both of us.

"It's like an art gallery in here almost,

don't you think?" he said.

"I like the photography."

"And that painting," he said, pointing to a large oil painting of three women having cocktails at a bistro table, with three dogs at their feet.

"Makes me think this is going to cost me a fortune."

"I was thinking that, too." Chris stood and got a dog biscuit from the bowl on the reception counter, which Seamus had been straining to reach. He gave the biscuit to Seamus, who swallowed it nearly whole and barked for another one. "May as well get your money's worth," Chris said as he reached for a second biscuit.

A vet tech in purple scrubs walked toward us.

"See-muss?"

"It's pronounced Shay-mus," I said as I rose to greet her.

The technician wrote at the top of Seamus's chart in large letters SHAY-MUSS. (Later, when somebody mistakenly referred to Seamus as a she and I corrected her, she dutifully wrote "BOY" on the top of his chart.)

In the exam room, there was just enough time to observe more stylish animal-themed artwork and chairs covered in William

Wegman-designed fabric before the oncologist joined us. Dr. Gilbert was probably in her thirties, with a bob haircut and wide mouth with large white teeth that I managed to see despite the fact that she didn't smile.

"I'm Dr. Gilbert," she said, apparently to the manila file folder, since that's where she was looking.

"Hi, I'm Teresa," I said, extending my hand in her general direction. She didn't take it but turned her gaze to Chris instead.

"I'm Chris," he said. "And this is Seamus."

"Fine. I've reviewed the biopsy report, and I suppose you know this isn't good." She launched into a lengthy monologue of things I couldn't understand, while my mind stayed stuck on "isn't good."

"The biopsy shows a right perineal mast cell tumor, and the margins are not clean. Blah, blah, blah . . . aggressive . . . blah, blah, more blah . . . surgery . . . blah, blah . . . difficult. Blah, blah, blah, blah . . . quality of life. Blah, blah, blah . . . chemotherapy . . . Blah, blah, blah . . . The prognosis is likely a year."

I grabbed on to one of the few words I understood. "Chemotherapy for a dog?"

"Yes, it's cancer; we treat it just like we

would in a human. Dogs tolerate chemotherapy quite well actually."

I wondered if the dogs thought so.

Chemotherapy seemed almost as frightening as cancer itself. I remembered my dad,
when he'd worked in a hospital and later as
well, often commenting that the treatment
was worse than the disease. In my office,
we'd had a client diagnosed with Stage IV
breast cancer about a year previously. She
continued working throughout chemotherapy, no matter how tired or pale or bald
she got. I remember wondering why on
earth she would keep working. I thought I'd
probably quit everything if it were me. And
probably refuse the chemo, too. It was all
too horrible. But this doctor was telling me
dogs tolerated chemo better than humans.
How much better?

"What do I need to do?" My brain was
scrambling to process information, and her
mannerisms weren't helping. She continued
making notes in her file and not making eye
contact. She had yet to look at Seamus. I
didn't think she knew if the dog was a
beagle or a Rottweiler or, for that matter, a
cat.

This was her business, I supposed. And
she probably needs emotional distance. But
this wasn't business to me. This was my

dog. He shared my life. He was a vital part of the alphabet of my life. And I think I was still hoping there'd been some terrible mistake. A two-year-old dog could not have cancer. I needed empathy.

"You can do the surgery consult today with Dr. Tracey. We'll get an estimate of the cost of the recommended treatment. If that's acceptable to you, we can schedule the surgery here or in our Tustin clinic."

"If it's acceptable to me? Okay. Well, what other options are there?"

"Well, not everyone can afford surgery, so we try to give other options. In his case, without surgery and treatment, we would be discussing how to keep him most comfortable for the remainder of his life, for however long that might be. It would be a matter of sustaining a quality of life for the time we could." She was without sympathy for me or the dog. Maybe that's why she hadn't even looked at Seamus, let alone petted him like everyone else had done. Maybe that's how she got through her day — Rule Number One: no sympathy.

My dog is going to die. He's two years old, and he's going to die. I wanted to cry, but I was fighting it back. Something told me not to cry in front of this woman. Rule Number Two was probably "no crying." I quickly replaced the urge to cry with the urge to slap her. To blame her. I couldn't slap her, of course, so I was out of options. No crying, no slapping . . . and I wasn't comprehending much either. I looked to Chris.

"Is surgery what you recommend?" Chris said.

"Yes. Absolutely. We have to do at least that," Dr. Gilbert said to Chris. To me she said, "If you can't afford it, we understand. Not everyone can afford the care that's required. You just need to let me know what you want to do."

We'd been in the room with her for all of five minutes, and she seemed to feel I was wasting her time. Was I supposed to have signed papers, given my dog anesthesia myself on the drive in, and wheel him into the surgery now? Was I allowed no time to consider options? Were there options? "I want to do whatever I need to do for him," I said. "Just tell me what the best thing to do is. The cost isn't the issue." Cost was an issue, but not the issue.

"I'll set up the surgery consult," she said. And she left, without ever looking at Seamus. I handed him another biscuit to make up for her neglect.

Chris and Seamus and I waited alone in

the exam room to meet with the surgeon for the consultation.

"I hate that doctor," I said.

"She's not very warm, that's true. But it's a hard job. Maybe she's having a bad day. Anyway, she's not doing the surgery."

"Thank God for that. She's like a bitchy sorority girl. Like we're in rush and not everybody gets a bid. As though anybody wants to rush this kind of sorority." I mimicked the "Well, if you can't afford it" speech but was cut short when another doctor walked in.

The surgeon, Dr. Tracey, was a tall, thin woman with short, curly, light brown hair and a demeanor that conveyed confidence and compassion in equal measure. As soon as she entered the exam room, she sat on the floor, calling Seamus to her and pronouncing his name correctly. He gladly went to her and put his face right up to hers, sniffing her in, wagging his tail. She scratched his ears, petted his head, and only then, having won over the dog, did she address Chris and me, continuing to pet Seamus as she talked.

"Seamus is a sweetie. He reminds me of a hound I used to have. Great, great dog." Seamus crawled into her lap and turned to face me, sitting calmly. He approved.

I exhaled, relaxing slightly. This was good. She was good — a nice contrast to Dr. Sorority Chick. If someone's going to be operating on my dog, I wanted her thinking of a dog she had loved. I wanted her doing everything she'd do for her own loved one. I wanted her to save us both.

Dr. Tracey explained the cancer, the surgery, and the need for clear margins. A mast cell tumor is like a skin cancer and is common in some breeds, like boxers, but not beagles. Mast cell tumors can have a high survival rate, but can also be aggressive and terminal, particularly when the tumor is located in a highly vascular area, such as where Seamus's was, which increases the risk it has metastasized. When the tumor was excised, the pathologist would check to see if there were cancer cells in the margins of the tumor — if there were, that meant cancer cells were still left behind in the body. If the margins were clear, that meant no signs of the cancer, at least at that point.

No cancer. That would be good, I thought. He might not be terminal.

"That doesn't necessarily mean we've got it all. Cancer cells are extremely small and difficult to detect until there's a mass of them. But if we aren't seeing any cancer on

115

the edges of the tumor, we're at least hopeful the cancer has been removed."

Okay, hopeful. I'd settle for hopeful. "And
if it isn't? If the margins aren't clear, do you
do another surgery?" I said.

Dr. Tracey, still sitting on the floor, petted
Seamus and gave him a green dog-bone
shaped cookie, which she'd pulled from the
lab coat pocket he'd been sniffing. "Not in
this case. I will cut as much as I can, but
there's a limit to how much we can excise
because of where this tumor is. If I cut too
wide, he'll lose some bodily functions and it
becomes a quality of life issue. This is a
highly vascular area. It's very delicate." She
looked directly at me. "I will do everything
I can for him."

I watched as she petted Seamus gently. I
could see she cared, and in that moment I
believed her. I believed in her, and I'd trust
my dog to her care.

"Thank you," I said. "When can we do
the surgery?"

With Dr. Tracey's patient assistance, we
made arrangements for the surgery. For me
this meant paperwork and a discussion with
Chris as to whether I could skip out on the
family Thanksgiving if Seamus's recovery
necessitated it. For Seamus this meant sedation, an ultrasound, a blood draw, bone

marrow aspiration, and a few other pre-op procedures and tests that were not clear to me. The bill for the day: $2,035.68. And this was before the surgery.

Chris and I went to lunch and waited together, quietly for the most part, while Seamus was tested. I grabbed tissues and wiped my eyes and blew my nose, while Chris rubbed my back. I called my mom to see if she would be able to watch Seamus on Thanksgiving Day as he recovered from the surgery, if need be.

Later, on the way back home, with Seamus sleeping soundly in the backseat of my car, I asked Chris what I'd been afraid to ask Dr. Sorority Chick.

"Did she say Seamus has a year to live even if I do the surgery and chemo? Or is it a year if I do nothing?"

"I think it's a year even with the surgery and chemo. But we can make it a really good year for him." He reached over and rested his hand on my leg.

I cried the rest of the sixty-mile drive home.

That night Chris and I sat out in the hot tub on my back patio overlooking the city. The hot tub was our new "tub talk" locale, befitting a sleek and elegant cougar den.

"I need to do this. I know it's crazy

expensive, but I can't just let him die," I said.

"I know. It's okay. I think you should do it."

"You don't think I'm crazy for spending that much money on a dog?"

"No. I know how much that dog means to you. And you can afford it, right?"

I wasn't sure I could. No one gets a divorce, let alone two of them, and doesn't see their finances take a hit. And all the traveling I'd been doing was not cheap. And I was missing work while taking the dog to his appointments. My law partnership worked on what we'd lovingly called an "eat what you kill" system. In other words, if I wasn't working, I wasn't earning. But I didn't discuss my finances with Chris yet. "I think I can afford it. I don't really know. I just know I have to try."

"I know. He's your baby. You know I support you both."

"Thanks."

We were quiet for a few moments, our legs entwined under the hot water, each of us leaned back relaxing into the soothing jet streams of bubbles.

"It's funny, though. You'd do anything for this dog and you take really good care of him. But . . ." He paused and sat up, moving toward me, his hand coming to rest on my knee. ". . . you never wanted to have kids?"

I sat up. We'd had this conversation before. It was probably the biggest hurdle to our "is this long term?" discussions. I was maybe technically still of childbearing age physically, but I was never of a childbearing mentality. I'd been clear about that from the beginning of my relationship with Chris, as I had with my second husband. (I'd been less clear with my first husband; he, actually, probably crystallized the "no children" decision for me with his own childish behavior.) I didn't have nor did I want children. There were a lot of reasons for this, including a long line of ancestors who did not seem to have any natural maternal instincts. I felt sure I shared that much DNA. Besides, one should not have to go searching for reasons or be talked into having kids. My biological time clock never went off. I doubt it ever even existed, let alone ticked.

"No. I never did. I've always been good with dogs and never with children. It's not the same thing. I have vastly different feelings about dogs and children. I wouldn't be good being a mother."

"Oh, I think you would be. But I understand." We fell quiet again, and both of us leaned back. I watched Chris though. I could see he was thinking deeply, and I was certain I didn't want to know more just then. I had the dog to think about.

Chris and I stayed at his Brentwood apartment the night before the surgery so we could drop Seamus off early in the morning. We snuck Seamus into the "no pets allowed" apartment and hoped he wouldn't bark at each new noise or smell. He did not. He slept calmly and contentedly on the recliner in the bedroom with us, using my clothes as his pillow. He only howled when we left the apartment without feeding him. No food or water was allowed for the twelve hours preceding surgery.

We arrived at the Veterinary Cancer Center just before nine in the morning and were taken into the exam room immediately. They were certainly efficient.

Even though I'd heard it before, and Chris had confirmed it for me, I still needed to hear the prognosis again. I still hoped I'd misunderstood. When Dr. Tracey came into the room, I asked, "Did I understand correctly that even with surgery and chemo and maybe even radiation, it's likely he only has a year to live? Is that true even if you get clean margins?"

"Unfortunately, tumors in this area are usually very aggressive. Even with clean margins, and again, that's only what we can see with today's technology — so it may not be clean — chances are still high that the cancer is still there. Chemo may get it. It may not. That's what tough about these. We'll do the best we can."

Once again a staff person brought me an estimate for services, which was a detailed list of everything possible in the surgery. The estimate included a FedEx charge of $45 so they could ship the test results to a lab in New York. I signed and handed over my credit card. I'd begun to think of this card as Seamus's card. With a lot of airline miles building up. The estimate gave a low of $2,023 and a high of $2,193. The difference was the doses of anesthesia, antibiotics, and pain relief injection. I didn't know whether to hope for the high or the low estimate. I also signed for "advanced resuscitative efforts (primarily applies to patients weighing more than 50 lbs; including surgical & machine support; potential added cost of $150 to $400)." Seamus wasn't anywhere near fifty pounds, but I wasn't taking any chances. We're giving this everything we have.

I hugged and petted and kissed Seamus

until Dr. Tracey took him from the exam room and back to the hospital area. Seamus followed willingly and happily, sniffing around for more treats as he went, his nails click-click-clicking on the tinted cement as he trotted down the hall, his tail held high and swishing back and forth. Chris led me the other way down the hall.

I drove home alone and lonely, leaving Seamus at the surgery center and Chris in his apartment. At home, I sat on the couch, staring at the wall, swirling but not sipping a glass of wine. I waited.

Dr. Tracey called me at six that evening to tell me the surgery had gone well and she was hopeful for clean margins. Seamus was resting comfortably, she assured me. This brought me little comfort. I continued to hear "aggressive . . . one year . . . chemotherapy" echoing in my thoughts.

The next day, the oncology center phoned me in my office just after noon. Seamus was doing great, he was alert and eating, and I could pick him up anytime. I looked at my watch. Even if I left right then, which I was willing to do, there was no way I could get to Los Angeles and back without encountering heavy traffic. I calculated the time it would likely take. Maybe an hour and a half to get there, with a little luck. A half hour at the clinic . . . it would be three or later when I left. The worst possible time to get on a Los Angeles freeway. I'd be lucky if I got back home by 6:00 p.m. And Seamus, with stitches in his rear end and on pain medication, would be confined to a crate all that time.

I called Chris hoping he'd know some magic driving route that would help me avoid what I also knew was inevitable. There were not a lot of people in my life who I trusted enough to ask for advice and even fewer whose advice I'd likely take. Despite my lingering concerns about Chris's youth, I had begun to count on and enjoy his intelligence.

"You know, I can go pick him up now and bring him to you tonight," he said.

I had not thought of that. He was already in LA, which would shave off a few hours of driving time. But this was my dog. "No, I need to see him. I'll go get him."

"Really? I'm not sure it makes sense for you to drive all the way out here and then turn around and drive back when I'm headed out your way anyway. They said he was fine, right?"

Yes, they said he was fine. But he was my dog. I needed to see him. And wasn't I supposed to be there to pick him up? Wasn't that my obligation? Of course, it was also my obligation to pay for the surgery, so a few more hours at work would definitely be a good thing. If Chris left now, he'd probably be able to get Seamus home several hours before I would.

"Are you sure?" I was asking myself as much as I was asking Chris.

"Yes. They can just charge it to your card. I'll get him. Besides, the Moose and I have kinda bonded. I want to see him, too."

And that was true. They had bonded, and it might not have just been the food anymore. The more time Chris spent at my house, the more Seamus seemed to prefer cuddling up next to Chris, sometimes even choosing him over me. "The Moose" (derived from the first nickname "Shay-moose") was a favorite of the many nicknames Chris had bestowed on the dog. And his theme songs included "Scala-moose, Scala-moose, can you do the fandango" (sung to Queen's "Bohemian Rhapsody") and "Do You Know the Muffin Dog, the Muffin Dog, the Muffin Dog? Do you know the Muffin Dog? He looks a lot like me" (sung to, of course, "The Muffin Man"), the latter created as Seamus stood drooling at our bedside begging for the blueberry muffins we were eating.

I called the clinic and let them know to charge my credit card and release the dog to Chris. They knew Chris, since he'd gone to the appointments with me. They probably thought of Seamus as "our" dog, even if I didn't, so naturally the receptionist had no issue releasing the dog to Chris.

"That's great he can get here so quickly. We'll be ready for him," the receptionist said with no fanfare whatsoever. She had no idea how big this was for me. I'd let Chris be responsible for my dog. I was trusting him with my dog. My sick, recovering dog.

When I arrived home that evening, Seamus was on the couch, snuggled in next to Chris just as he did nearly every night with me. Seamus had even thrown his left front paw over Chris's right thigh. Everybody seemed to be doing fine — dog and man were both relaxed and happy and seemed as unaware as the receptionist had been that I'd just allowed my relationship with Chris to deepen. I'd just had an emotional growth of monumental proportions, and no one seemed to notice.

Seamus leaped from the couch and came to greet me. I could see his rear end was shaved on the right side, and there were stitches again, but he was wide awake and didn't seem to be in pain. His front lower left leg had a green Ace bandage wrapped around it.

"They sent home some pain medication and antibiotics. I gave him the pills for tonight, and the bottles are on the counter. I was thinking we'd order pizza? Moose says he wants pizza too," Chris said.

"I'll bet he does. And that sounds good. I'll order."

"Seamus wants pepperoni. And sausage."

"Probably also chicken. And extra crust."

The three of us went upstairs to bed by ten o'clock, which was much earlier than our normal bedtime. All three of us were night owls, but this had been a long, exhausting twenty-four hours, and we were tired. Seamus climbed into his own bed, spun around, moved the blanket back and forth until it was bunched up perfectly, and then flopped down with a loud "harrumph." He sighed deeply, letting his jowls flop in the wind he created. We did not put the cone on his head.

I was happy we were all together and relieved the surgery was behind us, but still, I did not fall asleep. I lay in bed thinking alternately about the Thanksgiving dinner ahead and then getting the pathology report back. I tried to focus on the fact that Seamus made it through surgery and that

Dr. Tracey thought it had gone well, but I couldn't maintain that positivity. Instead, I spent a restless night worried about clear margins and family judgments, while Seamus snored loudly and Chris slept soundly.

CHAPTER 6
JERSEY GIRL

Seamus betrayed me by recovering from surgery quickly and with no drama, such that I had no excuse to avoid Thanksgiving dinner with Chris's family. As though meeting the aunts, uncles, and cousins wasn't going to be difficult enough, we were meeting at his recently deceased grandmother's house in Pacific Palisades — a place that makes even Newport Beach look like Haiti. And as though that weren't going to be difficult enough, one of the aunts (the one in charge of the dress code, apparently) had decided we all needed to wear the sports jerseys of our favorite team — because Grandma Dugi would have liked that. Now I had to dress in a manner acceptable to meet the family, but also somehow wear a sports jersey of my nonexistent favorite team and do it fashionably enough that I was allowed through the magnetic force field that keeps the riffraff out of Pacific

Palisades. Had the edict been "wear a shirt representing your favorite dog breed," I would have had an ample selection of beagle-adorned shirts and sweaters to choose from; I could have even risen to a "wear your favorite alcoholic beverage on a shirt" occasion, and these seemed no less ridiculous themes to me. I borrowed one of Chris's vintage San Diego Charger jerseys, not because it was my favorite team, but because it was light blue and gold and I could look good in those colors. Also, it was one of his smaller jerseys — only an XL instead of an XXL. Chris wore a Barcelona soccer jersey, which, it just so happened, was one of his favorite shirts. I looked like I was in a costume; he looked like he was going out to breakfast on any normal day.

Not even the traffic helped me out. There was none (like a bad joke: When is there no traffic in Los Angeles on a holiday? When I would like there to be traffic!). We arrived early, and Chris ignored my pleas to drive around the block for a few hours — or days.

His grandmother's home was classically beautiful — bricks and tall white columns — and sat on a corner lot, which, Chris explained to me, was one of the largest lots left in the Palisades, the rest having been subdivided and populated by the modern

McMansions of the many sports and entertainment industry multimillionaires who had descended on the area in recent years. Grandmother Dugi's house, in contrast, was once owned by Mary Astor and was on the famous San Remo Drive (oh to live on a street featured in a novel!). The front lawn was huge, with stately magnolia trees, manicured shrubbery, and white roses everywhere, even in November. The house and yard looked like they'd been picked up out of Atlanta in a bygone era and dropped down in the midst of modern west Los Angeles. The estate was regal and serene. I was in a man's old, faded football jersey and functioning on about four hours' sleep per night for a week running.

We parked in front, but Chris led me across the expanse of lawn around to the back where we passed the pool and the carriage house and entered in the kitchen (like family or servants? Or one of each?). I expected that we would be the only ones in jerseys, that somehow this was a prank and when we arrived they would all be in formal attire (in my disturbed and moderately paranoid mind, pearls and hats were involved), and they would point and laugh at us.

Well, at me.

I met his aunt Peggy first. Peggy was in a USC jersey, which offered some relief but came as no surprise — she was, in addition to being a past Wimbledon doubles tennis champion, an avid sports fan and, almost as relevant, the aunt who had decreed the dress code. But then I met Uncle John and his wife Tina, also in jerseys, so I began to relax. Aunt Barbara and Uncle Ed and their three daughters — with matching "M" names and blond bobs, clean-cut husbands, and clean, glowing, well-behaved children of their own — wore identical USC jerseys. I smiled, nodded, and tried to remember names as best I could and put faces to the stories Chris had told me. Seeing the jerseys, albeit worn over dresses or outfits that implied the jerseys were temporary, loosened my shoulders (they were no longer up in my ears). That is, until I realized they were all in cardinal and gold jerseys — all of them. And there I was in blue and gold — the colors of the cross town rival, UCLA.

"Why didn't you tell me I should have worn a USC jersey?" I whispered to Chris.

"Because you went to UC Santa Barbara. Why would you wear a USC jersey?"

"Because everyone else is! I'd forgotten your family is all USC fans!"

"Not all of them. You're fine. My grand-

131

mother went to UCLA. In fact my grandmother was the first female student body
president at UCLA."

Wow. That shut me up. I was fine. I was in
Dugi's school colors! Sure, it's a Chargers
jersey, but the colors were close. Maybe
someone would notice and I'd get extra
points (because I was certain they were
keeping score).

"So what's with all the cardinal and gold?
Why wouldn't they be in your grandmother's school colors?" His grandmother
had passed away months before, and the
property was listed for sale. This was the
last Thanksgiving the family would have
together in the home Trudi and her siblings
had grown up in. So why wouldn't they have
been honoring Grandma?

"My grandfather went to USC. And so
did Ed. And Barbara. And . . ."

I stopped listening. Chris's parents and
his sisters had arrived. When I saw his
sisters, my brain finally kicked in and thus I
registered the thought right along with
Chris's intonation: "Of course, my sister
Courtney is there now, and Kati's getting
her master's there." I should have remembered that. I should have known that. I
should have planned ahead. Could I just go
home to my dog now? Please?

But his mother and father and sisters were not in USC jerseys. They were not in jerseys at all. His sisters were in dresses and impossibly high (and fashionable) heels. His mother was in black pants and a black silk blouse with white stripes and cuffs, with a large, pearly necklace. His father was in the male all-purpose "going out" outfit — khakis and a button-down shirt with loafers. I began to spin again. We'd gotten it all wrong. I looked ridiculous! Who wears dress pants and heels with a jersey tied in a side knot over a simple cotton top? Who does that? On Thanksgiving! I'm an idiot. I wanted to let out my own Seamus howl. *Take me home! Noooow! Fookers! Take me hooooooooooooooooome!!!* But I'm not a beagle. I couldn't cry, or howl, or escape through a doggie door. I sat. I stayed.

I was rescued by his "M" cousins, who each took the time to introduce themselves, their husbands, and their children and to sit and chat with me for long stretches of time.

Thankfully, Chris's parents and sisters donned their jerseys in time for dinner (and removed them later), and although his sisters and mother wore USC jerseys, his father wore his US Naval Academy sweatshirt.

Trudi approached me with an offer to

refill my wineglass. (Should I? Would I be judged an alcoholic if I accepted? Would I affront her if I declined?)

"So what do you think of all this? Crazy, isn't it?" she said.

"It's certainly memorable. I can't say I've ever had a Thanksgiving quite like this. I didn't realize the family was such sports fans."

"Well, we are, but not like this," she motioned, wineglass in hand, to her jersey-clad siblings in the living room. "This would have my mother rolling over in her grave."

"So this isn't a tradition?"

"Oh heavens, no. I don't know what Peggy was thinking. We've never done this."

Chris joined us, keeping his promise that he'd not leave me alone with either parent for longer than two minutes. "Never done what?"

"Dressed like this for Thanksgiving. Chris, please make sure Teresa understands we're not usually in costume. You don't want her thinking your family is crazy."

"Oh, I don't know, Mom, remember when Grandma Dugi had us all wear hats for Christmas dinner?" Chris said.

"You mean, like the English paper hats in poppers? Those hats?" I said.

"Oh, no. Hats. Dugi's hats. Big hats,

baseball hats, straw hats, fishing hats . . . you name it and my grandma brought them out and had us all wear them. Insisted."

I looked to Trudi, expecting she'd be mortified at this disclosure. But she was laughing.

"Oh that's right. I forgot about that. But, Chris, I think the dementia had already set in then, we just didn't know it."

"The hats were a big clue. Or should have been."

I don't know what would have been more difficult for me, the hat Christmas or the jersey Thanksgiving. I have hats, so I would have had a selection, but then I would have had hat hair too. It didn't matter though. I was there, charging forth in my Charger jersey.

"Well, it's fine," I said. "I'm just glad everybody else really is in jerseys."

"Did you worry we were playing a joke on you?"

"I did. A little."

"Oh, no. No joke. This is for real."

"Well, at least I don't have to worry about spilling anything on my blouse."

I helped carry dishes from the kitchen to the dining room, and once we were all seated I made small talk and recalled, I believe, which utensil to use when, all while keeping my elbows off the table. I made it through dinner and began to relax.

After coffee and dessert, Chris asked how I was doing.

"I'm good. Surprisingly good."

He smiled. "I told you so. And everybody likes you."

Maybe so, I thought. Maybe so.

We stayed late playing cards and a dice game around the dining room table that comfortably sat eighteen. I came close to winning one round of the game, and I happily noted several family members rooting for me. I didn't mind when a six-year-old cousin won instead and I gave her a high five. We had been among the first to arrive and were nearly last to leave. No one was more surprised than me.

"That may have been one of the nicest Thanksgivings I've had in a long time," I said to Chris on the drive home. "It's nice that you can all get together in one place. In my family we would have made three different stops by now."

"See? I told you. Nothing to worry about. They loved you."

"Well, I don't know about love, but they weren't avoiding me. Your cousins made a lot of effort to get to know me, and Ed mostly was interested in the fact that I had gone to law school. So I gathered I was all right by him. I like a low standard."

"Ed's standards are not low at all, but yes, he cares about education. My mom spent a fair amount of time talking to you, too."

"Yes, she did. That was nice. She wanted to make sure I was comfortable and had met everyone. So that was good, I suppose. She wasn't hiding me or claiming I was the help."

"Very funny. But it's over. You did fine."

"Thanks. Still, I'm looking forward to us being home with the beagle." In the car ride home, I was even able to catch up on a little sleep.

The next day Dr. Gilbert called. The surgery was a success. The margins came back clear — according to both the surgeon and now the pathologist. Now Seamus just needed to heal enough to start chemotherapy.

At my mother's house, Seamus had been subjected to the cone again since he'd resumed biting his stitches. Back home with Chris and me, in his efforts to remove the stitches, he'd taken to scooting his rear end on the carpet, sometimes leaving trails of blood. But I was deliriously happy with the surgery results and so once again followed Seamus around repeatedly shouting "Seamus, no!" and spraying stain remover.

On Saturday Chris went to his parents' home for their annual family Christmas photo. I stayed home with Seamus. I had laughed when he told me that he had instructions on how to dress (he was thirty years old!) and that they'd done this every year for as long as he could remember. I couldn't fathom that. I doubt my family had ever been together in one photo, let alone every year. Part of me wanted to go, just to watch. A bigger part of me wanted to be home with the dog, the fireplace, and a good book — the part of me that won. It was an easy argument for that part of me to win, however, since I hadn't been invited to photo day.

I was asleep on the couch — fire going, book on my stomach, Seamus asleep beside me — when Chris returned home earlier than I expected.

I sat up, and he plopped down on the couch between me and Seamus, causing Seamus to stand up and move, cone and all, over Chris to settle down between us. Seamus always needed to be in the center.

I maneuvered over the cone for a kiss from Chris but settled for kissing Chris's cheek as he stared straight ahead.

"You're home early," I said after a few

minutes.

"So you were right," he said, standing up. He headed to the bar and reached for his bottle of Maker's Mark whiskey.

I was pretty sure there was nothing I'd said lately that I wanted to be right about. And there was an intensity and strain on Chris's face that I'd never seen before. "We should have worn USC jerseys?"

"That wouldn't have helped." He sat back down, glass in hand. He moved the glass toward me in a mock toast. "I've been instructed to break up with you. Apparently my parents think they raised me better than this." He extended his arm, sweeping it across the expansive view of my sleek and elegant cougar den. "They think they raised me better than you."

My stomach churned and dropped. My jaw simply dropped. "I thought they liked me?"

"At this point, I don't think they fucking like me."

But Thanksgiving had gone well! Hadn't it? How could I have been so wrong? How could I have let my guard down and opened myself up to this sucker punch? How could I have been so stupid again?

"What happened?" I couldn't imagine —

I didn't want to imagine — such a conversation.

"It doesn't matter."

"It kind of does."

"No. It doesn't. They're fucked up. I'm not listening to them."

It was my turn to head to the bar. I stood up, but I only made it halfway across the room before I turned back to face Chris. "I knew this would happen. I fucking knew this would happen. Every. Single. Time. This always happens to me."

Chris's face fell. And then it tightened. "You know, this isn't about you."

"How is it not about me? We've been together for a year and a half now. They must have just thought you'd grow out of this. That somehow, I'd just go away, and in the meantime they'd fake being nice to me. All along they were thinking you're better than me? They're better than me?"

"Trust me. It's not about you. It's about me and my parents. You could be anyone and they'd be objecting."

"They wouldn't be objecting if you were dating someone of your own kind."

Chris ran his hand through his hair and then leaned forward, toward me. "That's the thing . . . you are my own kind. You're the only one who is my kind. They just don't

understand that because they don't understand me. I'm not breaking up with you.
You need to know that."

CHAPTER 7
TOXIC

I busied myself buying new toys for Seamus, feeding him anything and everything he wanted to eat, sharing all my food and then some, cleaning up the carpet, and ignoring, as best I could, the holiday season and a certain looming issue. I was also rapidly becoming an expert in mast cell tumors and cancer treatments as I researched and prepared for Seamus to start chemotherapy. Chemo scared the bejeezus out of me but was still easier to think about than Chris's parents' wholesale rejection of me — that, I tried hard not to think about.

At the Veterinary Cancer Clinic, I had been assured Seamus would not lose his fur and that medicine could control much of the nausea. The most likely side effects would be loss of appetite and a decrease in energy. This was hard to imagine. Seamus could lose four-fifths of his appetite and still consume the daily food intake of a linebacker mid-season. How would I know if he lost his appetite?

Within the first few months I had Seamus, my sister-in-law Jennifer sent a package to me, which the mailman delivered by tossing over the fence into the courtyard. By the time I came home, all that remained was blue, green, and yellow cardboard confetti bits and a few telltale plastic wrappers. I found one wrapper that had something in it: four shortbread cookies with the Girl Scout logo. Jennifer had mailed me the boxes of Girl Scout cookies I'd ordered from my niece in Missouri. Seamus had eaten two and a half boxes of them and was in the process of burying the rest of the stash when I interrupted. Thankfully, I don't eat chocolate so none of the cookies consumed were of the dangerous chocolate variety. I had to call Jennifer to find out how many boxes had been sent so I knew how much digging I'd have to do to find Seamus's stash. Jennifer was incredulous (she'd sent five boxes), but my niece McKinzee thought it was hilarious and promised to send Seamus cookies every year.

It wasn't that long ago that Seamus had climbed onto the back of the couch, jumped from there onto a barstool, walked from there onto the kitchen counter, and strolled over to the stovetop to lick out the hardened bacon grease left in the frying pan from that morning's breakfast.

And now the oncologist was telling me Seamus's appetite would decline in chemotherapy? I wasn't sure I'd be able to identify this side effect. Would he now eat only a box and a half of Girl Scout cookies? Just a box? The peanut butter sandwich cookies but not the shortbread? And I suppose a lack of energy would make the bacon-flavored obstacle course off limits?

I read the paperwork the clinic had provided. The patient information contained the following notes: "Chemotherapy for cats and dogs causes very few of the symptoms seen in people. If Seamus refuses to eat after a treatment, try bland but well-liked foods such as white rice or pasta, flavored with cooked chicken, lean hamburger, low-fat cottage cheese, or nonfat sour cream. . . . If diarrhea occurs, add white rice to Seamus's regular food. For vomiting, remove all food and water for four hours, then offer small amounts of water or ice cubes. Switch to the bland foods listed above." In light of Seamus's usual appetite, this was hard to imagine, but I memorized the information nonetheless. Then, I studied his pathology report. Some of it was overwhelming. I

144

struggled to glean any information from the reports.

From Seamus's immunohistochemistry report:

"The AgNOR value in this case (2.1) is intermediate. In one study . . . no dogs were euthanized due to mast cell disease with AgNOR counts less than 1.7. In another study . . . mast cell tumors that did not metastasize had a mean AgNOR count of 2.3, and those that did metastasize had a mean count of 2.8."

This seemed good: 2.1 is less than 2.3, so this says that chances are this hasn't metastasized, right? I kept reading.

"This pattern of KIT expression (pattern II) has been associated with a 14% rate of local recurrence, 31% rate of distant metastases, and 25.6% mortality due to mast cell disease."

I tried to find comfort in these statistics. To me, these odds were in his favor. Not great, but in his favor. So the chemo was necessary. The chemo would be good, I told myself. The chemo will give him his best chance at survival. These were just odds. Nothing was certain. We could still beat this.

Then, I turned to the Internet.

I read that pumpkin pie filling can ease constipation in a dog, which is also a possible side effect from the steroids given to prevent the nausea of chemo. Then I read that mast cell tumors like Seamus's could be fed by carbohydrates and it was best to limit the dog's diet to mostly proteins. This one sent me reeling. Seamus and I had established a morning routine in our year together. We woke and walked, he got breakfast, I got coffee, and then we shared toast. Seamus's favorite food in the world was toast. The moment he heard the toaster lever slide down, he began his toast dance at my feet. And when the toast popped up, he howled and continually bayed and herded me to hurry and sit and commence with the crust distributions. I don't like crust (blame my grandmother and her crustless dainty sandwiches while I was growing up), so it was a nice symmetry; I tore off the crusts and fed them to Seamus and enjoyed my crustless toast with no cleanup required. I've since watched enough *Dog Whisperer* to figure out that I'd probably merely taught Seamus the basic school math of toast = guaranteed crusts for Seamus. Hence, to Seamus, toast had become like the trashy girl in high school who puts out. It might not have been his actual favorite, but toast was a sure thing.

I'd been feeding Seamus crusts nearly

every morning. And this was feeding his tumor? And the Girl Scout cookies? Death in brightly covered cardboard! The sourdough loaf? Yeasty baked cancer! I'd given my dog cancer! My spiral of guilt was launched, sucking me down into the vortex. I went back online and did more research to find an all-protein kibble and fed him that, even though it cost more than twice what I'd been spending. I stopped giving him toast. Then, when I could no longer take the whimpering pleas, I stopped eating toast myself.

I could research canine cancer treatment on the Internet. I could not research "what to do when your boyfriend's parents object to your very being" or "how to become undivorced and younger" or "how to prove you are not trailer trash." I focused on what I thought I had control over — the cancer attacking my dog, rather than the attack on my relationship. Somehow, the odds against Seamus seemed more favorable. But I had little control over Seamus's treatment. While I knew he was to start chemotherapy, and he had recovered well from the surgery, I had yet to be able to schedule the chemotherapy. I left several messages for Dr. Sorority Chick and finally got a call back.

"We're waiting on the pathology report,"

she said.

"We have the pathology report. We had that two days after his surgery. It said the margins were clear."

"I know that. I'm not talking about that report. That report is a preliminary report. I need the report back from New York." She said this as though we were waiting for the latest fashion news and of course that could only come from New York. As though California didn't have pathologists (or fashion) and everybody knew we had to hear from New York. Everybody but me.

"Preliminary? What's preliminary about it? The surgeon said the margins were clear. The pathologist said the margins were clear. Why is that preliminary?"

I heard her exasperated exhale. I don't think she was trying to cover it. "We need the report from New York. The New York lab is the best there is. That report will tell us everything we need to know."

She was not moving without the New York report. I gave up pressing her. "How much longer?"

"A couple of days."

Three days passed without word from Dr. Sorority Chick. I resumed my game of phone tag with her, becoming victorious when she called not my cell phone as I'd instructed but my office at 6:40 p.m. (no doubt hoping for voice mail) and I answered.

"There's been an unexpected delay," she said.

"Yes, I know that. It's been over a week now, and we haven't even scheduled his first chemotherapy session."

"I mean with the New York lab. The mail is taking longer than usual so we won't have the results until early next week."

"Early next week? It will be Christmas by the time we start his treatments! This is ridiculous. Aren't we just wasting time here? Shouldn't the dog's treatments begin as soon as possible? I told you I wanted to give him the best chance possible, and it just seems like we're wasting time waiting for some mythical pathologist in New York." I admit I mocked the way she said "New York" with such reverence.

"He's not mythical, and a week isn't going to make any difference at all." She spit back at me the *myth* in *mythical.* "This is the top lab in the country. This report will tell us everything we need to know."

"Yes. I know. You've said that. Repeatedly. But what else, exactly, do we need to know?" It's not that I was looking forward to chemotherapy for poor Seamus. It's just that the anxiety of waiting for something as horrible, as frightening as chemotherapy was nearly unbearable. The unknown, I hoped, was more frightening than the known. Plus, I couldn't help but envision these big, bad cancer cells coursing through his body, attacking and trying to kill him while Dr. Sorority Chick sat around waiting for the fall issue of *Vogue.* "The Los Angeles pathologist said clear margins. From everything I've read — from everything you've said — the protocol is chemo. Why can't we just schedule the chemo? What's the downside?"

"If the report came back that this was metastasized and chemo was contraindicated, would you still want to proceed?" She said this with the same tone an eight-year-old uses when she thinks she's won an important battle. The "neener-neener" tone. Not the tone a doctor should use when suggesting a patient might die.

I resorted to the same tone in my reply: "If it would give him a chance at surviving, yes, I might do that. You're the one who said dogs tolerate chemo really well."

At home, I repeated the conversation to Chris and then stormed around the house, slamming cupboard doors and yelling, "She is the worst fucking doctor! What a bitch."

Chris was sympathetic but also storming around the house yelling about his parents. "Fuck them. Seriously, just fuck them. Who do they think they are? Fuckers!"

And not to be outdone, Seamus was also regularly howling, *Fooooooooooooood! Fookers! Get me fooooooooooooood!! Toooooooooooooooast! Where's my fookin' tooooooooooooooooast?*

This was, of course, the worst possible time for Chris and me to further discuss what his parents had said. But I couldn't help myself.

In our talks before his mother outed him, Chris and I had contemplated a number of scenarios about how his parents might react. I could certainly understand that a twice-divorced, forty-something woman who lived sixty miles away in Dowdytown was not the first choice any self-respecting Newport Beach parents of a private-schooled, Princeton-educated, oldest child would make for their son, and I assumed this would be the focus. And that things would not go well. I'm generally a glass-half-empty kind of person.

Chris, at least initially, thought that his mother would appreciate my sense of style, my education, and my extensive community volunteer credentials. He thought, or rather hoped, his father would appreciate that I was a lawyer and businessperson. Chris is generally a glass-half-full person. Neither one of us anticipated that his parents would set forth an edict. We had amusingly enough thought the choice was his to make. Not being parents ourselves, we had underestimated the parental instinct for protection of their young. And of course, we had failed to understand that a thirty-year-old could still be considered "young" to his parents.

But when they'd staged what I referred to as "the intervention" after Thanksgiving, it weighed heavily on Chris. And on me. I didn't have faith he'd stand up to his parents. I'd lost out to both of my mothers-in-law in battles large and small and had extremely low expectations as a result. Chris needed me to believe in him so he could believe in himself. I like to think that had the intervention come at another time, at a time when my dog did not have cancer, when chemo was not looming on the horizon, when I had a tighter grasp on my sanity, we would have handled it better. But that was not the case.

We argued.

And argued.

"Look, your mother says that she will never — NEVER — get over my two divorces. So, that's it then. There's nothing I can do about it. I don't even have to fight. There is absolutely nothing I can do to erase my two divorces, so there's nothing I can do to change her mind."

"You're missing my point. I told them I wasn't going to break up with you. I just need to know you are going to support me. That we're going to stand together against them."

"I'm not going to have anything to do with them!"

"Well, you can't take that position. They're my parents."

"What happened to 'fuck them'?"

And then we'd repeat variations of the same script.

I redirected my anger to the Veterinary Cancer Clinic. When I called again to follow up on the New York lab report, I didn't even bother to ask for the doctor. I spoke to the receptionist.

"It's been two weeks. We're waiting for the New York lab test results. Are they in?"

"Two weeks? It doesn't take two weeks," she said. "Let me check." After a short time she was back on the line. "The slides weren't sent until just a few days ago so we should have the results in another day or so."

"The slides were sent a long time ago.

They apparently took a long time in the mail."

"I don't know. This is a new thing. We haven't sent a lot of these out, but I don't think we mail them. They're slides and all, so I don't think they go in regular mail."

"Can you check and see exactly when these slides were sent out?"

She left me on hold for a few moments again. "Okay, so we overnight the slides by FedEx. That way we can track them. And yours went out four days ago."

That's when I remembered the FedEx charge on my bill. So Dr. Sorority Chick had forgotten to even send the slides and then just blamed the US Post Office. And this is a new thing — this New York lab. Did I even need the New York results? Did I need to pay for that, or was I just up-sized in the sale of veterinarian procedures?

"Please let the doctor know I called and ask her to call me immediately about that FedEx package."

The doctor did not call for two more days. She did not mention the delay, the late mailing of the slides, or in any way acknowledge that I'd called. She gave me the lab results — clear margins, precisely what the other results had shown — and nothing else. I tried to understand what this information gave us that we didn't already know and to find out if this was an "optional" report. She dodged me again. Which, in a sense, was all the answer I needed. I hoped whatever research Seamus had just participated in was worthwhile. At least we could now schedule his treatments.

Seamus would start chemotherapy on December 17. It seemed inevitable to me that I would have another crappy holiday, filled with doctors and medication and looming heartbreak. I filled the prescriptions for prednisone and doggie Benadryl. I stocked my household with chicken, rice, cottage cheese, high-protein dog food, dog toys, and pumpkin pie filling. I cooked and stored chicken for Seamus. I let him sleep on my bed, on the couch, on my lap. I talked incessantly to Seamus but almost no one else — until Chris came out to my house five days before Seamus was to start chemotherapy and we picked up our discussion of his family and our holiday plans.

"I'm not going anywhere. My parents are both out of town for the week, and I'm obviously not welcome at your parents' house," I said.

"They didn't say that."

"Uh, they kind of did. I'm not welcome in your life."

"Okay, fine. I'll just go over there for Christmas Eve, and then I'll be back here with you and Da Moose for Christmas."

In hindsight, I can see I wanted his parents punished for daring to not approve of me. And I can see I was angry about a lot of things. Perhaps I was feeling a tad sorry for myself. "Seamus has his second chemotherapy on the twenty-third, but sure, you go spend Christmas Eve with your family and leave us here alone. That will certainly show them! Boy, they'll know you can't be pushed around."

"That's not fair."

Fair? Fair? When did fair enter into anything?? And around we went again. Until finally we agreed to take a break from arguing. Chris tossed and slept in fits in my bed upstairs, and I cried, silently and alone, on the couch downstairs. Seamus, only days away from starting chemotherapy, moved between us all night — up and then down the stairs and then up again. A little before six in the morning, Chris came downstairs to me.

"I need to go," he said.

"You're going home?" I stared up at him.

He was holding his overnight bag and another bag filled, I knew, with the items he'd begun to leave at my house. "I need to figure things out for myself. I need to be alone to do that. I don't know what I want, and this is the hardest thing I've ever done. But I think I just need to be alone."

"You're breaking up with me?"

"I don't know. I guess I am. I don't know. Do you want me to stay?"

Many Decembers ago I was a front-seat passenger in a vehicle that drove off a freeway embankment and rolled down a hill, landing upside down. It is true that events like that are experienced in slow motion. My instinct, as the ground slowly rose up to meet the corner of the car roof right above my head, was to dive. I turned to the left away from the earth and rolled, a half-somersault of sorts; the back of my right shoulder took the brunt of the crash and I landed on the ceiling of the now upside-down car toward the back and clear of the front seat — where the roof had slammed in on the seat, tearing through the fabric where I'd been sitting only a moment before. The paramedic told me this was the one-in-a-million car accident when not wearing a seat belt saved my life. So did my instinct to dive and cover. That instinct was returning now.

Chris stood before me waiting for my answer, waiting for me to reach out to him.

I wanted him to stay. I wanted this relationship. I just couldn't step over my own baggage to get there. All I could think was that Chris's mother's style put my two former mothers-in-law to shame in the intimidation department. Her methods were ingenious — a combination of pure aggression and passive-aggression that kept us off balance and defenseless. She'd been so kind to me at Thanksgiving; she was so polished and polite. I had no idea she objected to me or the relationship in the slightest. And yet forty-eight hours later she sat Chris down and demanded he end his relationship with me. Frozen by my fear, I couldn't even muster the strength to go down fighting.

"I want you to do whatever you want to do. I don't want you staying here because you feel like you have to. But I don't want you leaving just because your mom says so, either." Dive. Cover.

Chris's face tightened. "See, just saying that tells me you don't understand what I'm going through. I'm trying to make my own decisions here, but I need to know you're on my side. It doesn't feel like you are. You can't even tell me what you want." He paused and stepped back, away from me. "I think I need to do this alone. I need a break. I'll figure things out, and maybe we can work things out. Maybe later. I don't know. I just think I need to go."

He picked up his bags and leaned down to kiss me. I turned my head, contorting my face to stop the tears. He kissed the top of my head.

"I'm sorry," he said. "I love you."

My face flooded with tears. I couldn't speak in response. How can you say you love me and then leave? Through my tears, without saying a word, without saying any of the things I wanted to say or should have said or needed to say, I watched him walk out the door.

Seamus raced out the door after Chris, howling. I watched through my tears and the glass doors as Chris stopped and bent down to Seamus. Seamus quieted, sat, and stared up at Chris, those big brown eyes pleading. He curled into Chris and tried to climb up into his lap, pawing at him. I could hear the howl turn to small, pleading whimpers.

I knew what Seamus was feeling. When I was about six years old, my parents separated, not for the first or last time. I stood in the driveway of our home watching my father pack suitcases and a few bags into his small convertible. When he went back into the house for another item, I took a bag out of the passenger seat to make room for myself. My dad came back outside and put the bag back on the seat. I reached to move it out again, telling him I needed a place to sit. He placed his hand over mine and put the bag back down in the seat. "I'll come back for you," he said, "as soon as I can." Weeks later, he did come back, but I didn't know that as I stood alone in the driveway watching as my crying father drove away.

Chris stayed in the courtyard petting Seamus and talking to him for several minutes. I doubted he was telling him he'd be back. He put his forehead to Seamus's for a moment, kissed the soft top of the dog's head, and then walked out the gate.

CHAPTER 8
ALPHA FEMALES

My sobs were not only alarming the dog; they alarmed me. I could not recall ever crying that hard. I woke in the middle of the night, gulping in air as I sobbed big, heaving, painful sobs. Seamus leaped up onto my bed and sat next to me, nervously looking up at me and sniffing my wet face. I petted him until I was calmer.

I hadn't cried this hard over either of my divorces. I'd cried a lot during the last days of my first marriage, but the sadness didn't last long and it wasn't the same. That husband had been a drunk and a cheater, which made the marriage much more difficult than the divorce, even though the divorce took over three years and left me with $50,000 of debt I hadn't known "we'd" incurred. (The great state of California decreed that debt he incurred supporting his girlfriends, expanding his alcohol and drug habit, and buying more cars than anyone could possibly drive was "community debt," by which they meant my debt since by then I was the only party gainfully employed.) Anger dried my tears quickly.

I also cried during the last years of my second marriage, but I didn't sob. I was sad at the end, of course, but had come to realize my mistake. I'd rebounded into a marriage with someone who would never drink to excess, never cheat, never use a charge card (let alone ones I never even knew existed); I married someone who would stay in a safe, comfortable, compact world. Which worked very well until I recovered sufficiently from my first marriage and divorce to want to leave that small world where I'd sought refuge and begin to explore a larger and more meaningful world. I left my first marriage thinking about the past — about what I didn't want to repeat. I left my second marriage thinking about the future — about what I wanted and what options were available to me. I left intending to pursue life. I did not leave crying, let alone sobbing, which is all I seemed to be doing now.

In the middle of the night, Seamus by my side, I tried to think about the future. In one moment I'd be thinking, I'll go back to my alphabet life. I'll be alone and I'll be fine. And then I'd think, no, the problem wasn't dating; it was that I'd moved too fast again. I never should have dated Chris. He was too young. It was all wrong. I should be choosier. Or just date for fun. That's it — I'll date all sorts of guys and really analyze what I was looking for. Don't just go on a date and a week later land in a relationship. And at all costs, do not meet the parents!! In fact, I'll date orphans. Only orphans. At my age that can't be too difficult, can it? Date men whose parents — well, at least their mothers — have already passed on. Oh, and no kids. He can't have kids either. In my state of mind, I didn't know if that was setting the bar high or low.

I gave up trying to sleep and got out of bed at sunrise. I could use a few extra hours in the day. Seamus dutifully followed me downstairs to the kitchen. Among the things I unfairly blamed Chris and cursed at the universe for was the timing of his breakup. In the five days ahead I had to host my office Christmas party alone, attend three holiday parties, and take Seamus to his first chemotherapy treatment. By Monday morning, the thought of the holidays moved me to the next stage of my grief — anger.

Fuck him. I am woman. I am strong, independent woman. Fuck him. Fuck his mother. Fuck them all. I can handle this all. By. My. Self. Fuck everybody! I will do it all!

Well, not all. I called my friends Tom and Kris, who own an Italian restaurant in a neighboring town, and got them to cater our office Christmas party in my home, since Chris was no longer available to cook. I asked my law partner Jane if her husband Francis, who makes a wicked martini and is the most charming man on earth (not unrelated traits, in my book), would bartend, and she said he'd be delighted.

I then decided that I could use the "my dog has cancer" excuse to get out of two holiday parties. Some non-dog people of course would look askance at this, but I didn't care about that. Hell, I didn't care that even a dog person might know that the dog — having fully recovered from surgery and not yet started chemotherapy — was not showing any signs that he was sick. I concluded that if I just appeared at the biggest, toniest, and most coveted invitation-only holiday party in town, I'd be seen by enough people that I'd look like I'd participated in all the horrendous holiday cheer. Plus, there would be booze. Copious amounts of free booze.

My friend Sheryl, an intelligent, beautiful

brunette a few years older than me, who'd been single for fifteen years, agreed to be my date to the party.

"Are you sure you're ready to go out?" she said.

"I need to do this. I'll be fine."

"Well, I've always wanted to go to this party. It'll be fun."

I dressed like a woman recently dumped — high heels, low-cut "his loss" red dress, smoldering eye makeup — and stormed off to the party.

Standing in the line at the bar, I noticed a man watching me from another bar line a few feet away. He smiled when he caught my eye. I barely remembered to smile back, but then I noticed how tall he was. And handsome. Very handsome.

"Who is that?" Sheryl said.

"I don't know and I don't care," I said, turning my attention back to the drink menu.

"I do. And you should. There are not that many single, good-looking men in these parts. He's gorgeous. And he's definitely checking you out."

"The only man I care about right now is standing behind that bar."

"Well, at least you're not bitter."

In an effort to fake festive, for Sheryl's

sake as much as my own, I ordered a candy-cane cosmo. It was that or a mistletoe martini. Oh, how I wish I were kidding. Normally, I can't stand my martinis to be violated by anything more than a bleu cheese-stuffed olive. But everyone seemed to be holding green or red or sparkly drinks. Insult was added to my injured drink when the bow-tied bartender, the current man in my life, hung a small candy cane from the side of my glass.

The drink tasted worse than it looked — which was saying a lot since something acidic in the drink was very quickly curdling the sprayed "snow" topping of whipped cream. As I sipped and winced at my drink, I again caught the eye of Mr. Tall, Dark, and Handsome. He was chatting in a group of people not far from where I was, but since both of us stood taller than most of the folks in the room, we easily made eye contact. He raised his glass in my direction. I was impressed to see that his drink had no garish holiday adornment.

Another friend approached, mistletoe hanging from her glass. "Isn't this ridiculous?" Michelle said, motioning toward it.

"I'm not sure which one is worse," I said, touching my candy cane to her mistletoe.

"But I hear there's a wine bar in the next room."

"Good to know," she said. "So, how are you? How are things with the cub?"

Once I let my friends know I was dating a man twelve years younger than me, the cougar jokes had flown fast and furious. Chris was quickly dubbed "the cub."

"Um, well. Not so good. Or, I don't know. Maybe this makes me a good cougar. Or good at being a cougar. I don't know. Anyway, he broke up with me." I set my curdled cream drink down on the tray of a passing waiter. "It's over. Fun while it lasted though." I was not feeling flip, but it was that or bursting into tears in the middle of a large, cheerful holiday party with everyone in town as my witnesses.

"Oh, no! I'm shocked. You were my hero! You got divorced after me but were right back out there and dating a younger man even. I was so impressed. I'm devastated on behalf of us all!" Michelle said.

"Sorry to disappoint. Wine, anyone?" I headed in the direction of the wine bar, and Sheryl quickly followed. Michelle hung back, no doubt preferring to enjoy the party with someone more festive.

"You sure you're okay?" Sheryl said.

"Probably not. But I'm trying."

My "trying" involved a few glasses of Chardonnay and whining to several friends in a pathetic attempt at sympathy. This is how I'd learned that several of my friends never did think Chris was good enough for me and always wondered what I saw in him. Jane thought I'd blown it again? I have no taste in men whatsoever? Zee and Sue thought I should have been warned off merely because he voted Republican? And Karen thought I'd jumped in too quickly when it took me a year to even admit I was dating him? This is not useful information for a drunk, brokenhearted, humiliated, middle-aged woman to learn during the holidays! Fookin' December!!

Later in the evening Sheryl and I again encountered Mr. TDH standing in a group of four or five people whom I knew. As if on instant replay, our gazes met across the tops of other people's heads. I looked away, but I couldn't help smiling. He was very, very good-looking. And I was very, very Chardonnay-ed.

"Okay," I said to Sheryl, "he's talking to Barbara. Let's go ask Doug who his wife is talking to. See what we can find out."

"So now you're interested? Brava!"

"I'm sure it's the wine talking, but sure, let's go find out."

Doug knew who Mr. TDH was, of course. The running joke in Riverside is that there are actually only two hundred people here, all attending each other's events and parties. You can't have six degrees of separation here. Two or three would be the maximum.

"You'd like him, Teresa. Great guy. Been in the commercial real estate business for years. He's very successful. Very."

"How come I've never seen him before? It seems I would have met him at some point."

"Well, he spends a lot of time in northern California, for business and personal reasons. He's divorced. Single, but divorced. His former wife and kids moved up to northern California so he bought a second home up there to be near his kids. Which tells you what a great guy he is."

It did? Kids? I should have backed away then, but I was concentrating on being open-minded. And Mr. TDH was being very handsome. "So he has kids. Any idea how many?"

"I think three. It might even be four." Doug was smiling. I was speaking to a man who had been married to the same woman for nearly fifty years and they'd happily raised four kids together. From his vantage point the information he was providing me was a glowing review.

I felt a small scream welling up inside me. Then Doug continued, "I'll tell you what a great guy he is: he brought his eighty-year-old mother as his date tonight. Isn't that the sweetest thing?"

"Oh. Shit." The scream was escaping. I needed to flee. "Thanks, Doug. Never mind the introduction." I backed away, nearly spilling my drink in my hurry. Shit! Shit! Shit!! His mother? As his date? Lord, I can sure pick 'em. I turned to Sheryl. "It's clearly time for me to go."

Sheryl snorted laughter as she followed me back through the crowd: "I can't believe you found the one guy who brought his mother!"

"As his date!! At least I know up front what that relationship is like and I can avoid it right away. See what progress I'm making?"

"Maybe his mother isn't all that bad."

I stopped and turned back to Sheryl. "Sure, now. But she will be a heinous bitch the moment she meets me. I am every mother's worst nightmare, this much I've learned. No more mothers. I will date orphans only." As I said this I saw over Sheryl's shoulder that Mr. TDH was making his way toward me, looking determined to introduce himself.

I'm sure he thought I'd seen a ghost. My face froze, my eyes widened, and every nerve in my body screamed "RUN!" I turned my back on him and left the party.

As Sheryl and I drove home, we discussed plans to go speed dating together. I had this candy-cane-cosmo-soaked idea that if I met eight or ten men together in one evening, I would at least be able to compare and contrast and perhaps figure out exactly what it was I was looking for. I might choose better, as Jane had encouraged. Sheryl teased me that an opening question of "Is your mother dead yet?" was not going to make me a big hit. I didn't care.

Again I couldn't sleep. I tossed around and flopped from my back to my right side, to my stomach, and then to my left side. I thought about speed dating, which seemed absurd at my age. I'd have to call Sheryl in the morning and tell her it was a bad idea. I wouldn't even know what I was looking for. Did I even want a relationship? Could I choose better?

I tried to think of something that would be better than what I had with Chris. I tried to complete the sentence, "Next time I'll find somebody who . . ." And everything led me back to Chris. Someone funny of course. Someone who got my sense of humor. (Like Chris.) Someone smart. Smarter than me. (Like Chris.) Someone I could rely on in a crisis. (Like Chris.) Someone who loved literature and art and travel. (Like Chris.) Someone with day-to-day compatibility. Someone like Chris. I'd marveled at how easily Chris and I moved through a day together. We were both late-night people, both preferred hot weather to cold, both loved food and wine, reading, writing, and board games, could talk all day or not talk at all, could keep a joke going on a riff — taking joy in topping each other — for hours. I'd never known that kind of compatibility. I'd never even known it existed, so I had no idea how important it was. I wanted that kind of compatibility back. I couldn't think of a single thing to look for in a man that would be better than what I had with Chris.

Except a deceased mother.

And then I realized it was like letting the genie out of the bottle. As long as I thought relationships were like my marriages, it was easy to think the alphabet life would sustain me. But now that I knew how good things could be, now that I knew love like that . . . now I could see how incomplete my alphabet was. I needed the letter L. I needed someone who really understood me and loved me anyway, even if his mother didn't.

I'd never even given Chris the chance to prove that last part.

This time my sobbing caused Seamus to scurry off my bed and return to his own. I got up and wrote Chris a letter. I mailed the letter later that day.

Seamus's chemo infusions would be done at the Orange County clinic of the Veterinary Cancer Center, which was only thirty miles from my home. I was now thankful I wasn't driving into Los Angeles, closer to Chris. Also, I hoped by switching locations a new oncologist would be assigned to Seamus's care.

I would be taking Seamus in every Friday at first, then every two weeks, then every three. If I timed it right and missed the traffic, I could be home by two or three and still be able to get a little work in, too. Assuming Seamus was doing okay. The chemo effects would be felt most strongly in the second or third day following chemo, so by choosing Friday I could be home on Saturday and Sunday when the side effects hit. My plan was set. My focus was clear. It was all I allowed myself to think about.

I slept fitfully. Seamus regularly jumped off my bed after I'd tossed and turned and woken him one too many times. I'm rarely early for anything, yet I arrived early for the first chemo appointment.

The Orange County clinic was newer than the LA one, but it had the same great artwork, tinted concrete floors, and, most importantly, bowls of dog cookies placed liberally throughout. I signed Seamus in, and the vet tech showed me how to complete Seamus's weigh-in. Once I finished his weigh-in (31.2 pounds) and marked the number down on the patient information sheet, I took a seat. Seamus alternated between jumping up into my lap and pulling me in the direction of the bowl of dog biscuits on the counter.

I watched the other people and animals in the waiting room as they came and went. A golden retriever with a shaved hind quarter that was an angry shade of red, a mewling tabby cat in a crate whose human was dabbing her eyes and sniffing, a mixed-breed dog with three legs but a lot of energy, and, sitting contentedly at the feet of a preppy, middle-aged couple, a basset hound with no discernible signs of cancer. But, I thought, this is a cancer clinic. Like Seamus, that dog was here because of cancer.

Cancer. I swallowed hard and turned my attention to a stack of magazines. I picked up a yachting magazine in which I had no interest and flipped pages without focus. I put the magazine back down and encouraged Seamus to jump up into my lap. I cuddled him close as I looked around the waiting room again, unable to think of anything else: all of these animals had cancer.

Cancer.

I fed Seamus more biscuits. I waited silently, not making eye contact with any of the other humans. I wanted to pretend all of these animals would be fine, and I didn't want to hear anything different. Talking would have been too dangerous.

"See-mus?" A young woman in turquoise scrubs approached us.

"It's pronounced Shay-mus," I said. Seamus leaped from my lap and, tail wagging, approached the girl.

"Oh. Shay-mus. That's a great name." She too wrote the phonetic spelling of his name on the chart and then gave him a biscuit. Seamus looked like I'd brought him to Disneyland for dogs. So far he'd experienced lots of other dogs, sitting in Mom's lap, plenty of treats, and bottled water. He didn't even seem to notice that his human, who in the past eighteen months had been divorced from one man and dumped by another, lost two dogs, spent thousands of dollars on veterinary treatment, and now would take numerous days off work for more time at the vet, was barely holding it together. No amount of treats was going to help that. But that was not Seamus's concern. His concerns reached no further than the next pocket full of dog treats.

The vet tech took us to an exam room. The sign on the door read "Seamus" in bright orange felt marker. Seamus sniffed out the jar of treats in this new room immediately and started howling in its direction. The tech laughingly indulged him with another biscuit.

"He's so cute." She bent down and rubbed his ears. Seamus turned around to give her more to rub and looked at me with eyes that said this was the greatest place ever.

"The doctor will be with you in a moment," the tech said, smiling as she left us alone in the exam room.

The door opened, and my face fell. It was Dr. Sorority Chick, still on the case. She was down to business immediately. No cookie. No eye contact with me or the dog. She focused on the chart in her hand as always.

The other veterinarians that were part of the Cancer Center all seemed to make concerted efforts to connect with Seamus — whether by petting or the tried-and-true "get to a beagle through his stomach" method. And then they were equally intent on showing compassion to me. Except Dr. Sorority Chick, who seemed intent on getting out of any room I was standing in as fast as she could. When she gave me his prognosis, her tone of voice was no different than it was when she told me the restroom was down the hall on the right. We didn't seem to be able to communicate with each other. And then there was the fact that she had lied to me about the New York pathology report — a simple fact we were both aware of. Now I was supposed to endure Seamus's entire chemo protocol with her?

She examined Seamus without saying much and then, "The tech will be in to get him, and they'll take him back to draw his blood. Then we'll give him the infusion. You can wait here or in the waiting area out front."

Not wanting to be with people and other pets sick with cancer and possibly dying, I said, "I'll wait here. How long will it be?"

"About twenty minutes, depending on how he does." And she was gone. Depending on how he does?

Moments later, Missy, a short, blond, heavyset tech, came into the room and immediately bent down to pet Seamus. And she slipped him a cookie. "Do you want me to take his blood draw here? So you can stay with him?"

I hate needles. And the sight of blood makes me nearly pass out. "Yes. I'd like to stay with him. Can I stay with him during the chemo?"

"It's usually best if we do the chemo in the back hospital area. We need to keep him calm and still, and if he sees Mommy, he might not be." She got the needle ready and positioned Seamus on the floor. "Here, just hold his head toward you and pet him or talk to him. This will be quick."

I didn't watch. I held Seamus's head so that neither of us had to look at the needle.

"Okay, give him a kiss and we'll take him back now. Are you going to wait here?"

"Yes. I'll wait here." I tried to be brave for my dog. "Bye, Seamus. You'll be fine. Cookies when you come out." I'm pretty sure he understood the cookie part. I'm also pretty sure he was a lot braver than I was.

I thought chemo would take hours. I don't know why I thought that, but it seemed so serious. And yet in just about a half hour, Seamus came bouncing back into the room, tail at full mast and swaying. He was pulling Missy along behind him.

"He did great," Missy said. "We had to shave his leg there a bit to get to the vein we needed. The bandage is from where the butterfly catheter was inserted. You can take that off tomorrow." The bandage was neon green. Seamus looked a little jaunty wearing it. I gave him his green cookie, and he ate it quickly.

"So far, no appetite loss."

"That might not start for a few days." She handed me his leash and gave Seamus a head rubbing. "He's a sweetie." Seamus sniffed her face in appreciation.

We made our way to the front desk, Seamus trotting along beside me, stopping to sniff at every doorway that might have a jar or a trash can with some treats in it. The Vinblastine chemotherapy, blood draw, evaluation, and all of the prescription medications, together with the ominous-sounding "hazardous waste disposal" charges, came to $236. And we had nine more treatments to go.

Seamus and I headed home to spend a Friday night alone . . . waiting, with my instructions in hand. Since much of the information was conflicting — chemo caused a lack of appetite, but the steroids he'd be on to control nausea may increase his appetite; chemo could cause diarrhea, but steroids caused constipation; chemo would make him tired, but the steroids might give him an energy boost — I had every possible product, supplement, and home remedy for every possible reaction. There was nothing to do but wait. It was not unlike going to a horror movie where you know the bad guy will show up and terrorize the main character, you just don't know how or when. But this was real — Freddy was not an actor; Freddy was chemo.

Once home, Seamus drank water (with me anxiously watching to see if he drank an unusually large amount or not enough), ate his dinner, and curled up in his bed for a nap. Which is pretty much what he did on every Friday night until Food Guy arrived.

There would be no Food Guy that night. Instead of cheese and crackers and wine, I made a late-night snack of boiled chicken and rice especially for Seamus and only Seamus. I got the fireplace going and curled up on the couch with a good book and a great dog and stayed there until early morning.

Chris called on Saturday afternoon. "I got your letter. And I want to talk about it, very

180

much. But first, how is Seamus?"

"He is doing really well so far," I said.

"Good. I'm glad. And how about you? How are you doing?"

"I don't think I'm doing as well as the dog, actually."

"Me either. I was hoping we could talk in person. I was hoping I could come out tomorrow."

I petted Seamus and blinked back tears. "Yeah. I think that would be good."

It had been a long eight days.

CHAPTER 9
BATTLE ON

Seamus picked his head up, eyes widened. He leapt off the couch, raced through the laundry room, and slipped out the doggie door charging full speed to the front gate. His frantic howl calmed in seconds, and I heard him grunting and whimpering in pleasure.

Chris was in the courtyard, bent down petting Seamus, who had curled his body into Chris's lap.

"Welcome back," I said.

"Hi." Chris stood, and we looked at each other over Seamus for an awkward moment.

"Come on inside."

We settled on the couch in the den, facing each other but not touching.

"I'm glad you sent me the letter."

"Me too. And I'm glad you called."

Another uncomfortable silence.

"I guess I should start . . ." I said.

"Maybe."

"I should start by apologizing. Again, I guess. I mean, I hope you understood my letter was an apology."

"Part of it was. And part of it was asking me to explain."

"Yeah. That's true. I'm sorry and I'm confused. I was going to start with the part where I'm sorry."

"We can start with where you're confused. Because I really need you to understand something. This has nothing to do with what my parents told me to do. I did not come over that night intending to break up with you at all. I was not — I am not — listening to my parents or doing as they instruct. This honestly had nothing to do with what they want."

"Okay. The timing just made it even harder to take. I have mother issues; I know that. It's hard for me to think I'll ever win."

"I understand that. I understand what it looks like. But really, everything just started snowballing out of control, and before I knew it, I felt like I had no choice. Like my parents were demanding I be one kind of person — this corporate drone with a perky little wife and kids, spending weekends with them at their club — and that isn't me at all. And you were demanding I be something else, or, I don't know, accusing me of being something else. And I realized I didn't know who I was or what I wanted. I thought I should be alone to figure things out for myself, with no one pressuring me."

"I didn't mean to be pressuring you. I was scared, so I got defensive." I wanted to touch him — to hold him — but I didn't.

"I know. That's what I mean. You didn't believe in me either. You're so caught up in all the shit from your past that you don't give me any credit. You just assumed I'm like everyone else. And that kinda hurts. I couldn't take everybody telling me who I am. And everybody's wrong." He adjusted his seat, turning toward me but moving farther away. "But I don't know what's right."

We sat, looking at each other, still deep in our own misery. I wanted to work this out. I wanted our relationship back. I wanted Chris back. Was he saying he still wanted to be alone? Did he still need to figure things out?

"You're right. You're right. You didn't deserve that. I wish I could have been there for you, and I acknowledge that I wasn't. I'm really sorry. I am."

"I appreciate that."

Again, we quieted, still inches that felt like miles between us on the couch.

"I know that it isn't fair that I just assumed you'd be like everyone else in my past. It's really, really hard for me. But I learned a lot in this last week. I learned what I had to lose." I took a deep breath, sucking in air and courage. "I don't want to lose you. I can do better. If you'll let me try again."

An hour passed. Maybe two. Or just minutes. I didn't know.

"I'm sorry I freaked out," Chris said.

"Freaked out and made the bad decision to break up with me?" I smiled, hoping he'd understand I was trying to lighten the mood, not confirm my dictatorship. And hoping I was right.

"Yes. The really bad, no-good, terrible choice to break up with the best thing that ever happened to me." He looked straight at me.

I moved my trembling hand to his thigh. "So, maybe we can try this again?"

He put his hand over mine. "I'd like that very much." He leaned in and kissed me. I never knew there was such a thing as tears of relief until then.

Soon though, Seamus howled to break it up. At least he gave us ten seconds.

We both laughed, and Seamus took that as his cue to join us on the couch. He wiggled his way in between us and leaned back, exposing his belly for a good, long rub.

"He looks good," Chris said.

"Yeah, he's done better than I have."

"Better than me too, I'm sure." Chris kissed the top of Seamus's domed head.

"If you need to talk more, I promise to just listen."

"Maybe later tonight."

"In the hot tub," we said in unison.

That evening, we agreed to a few ground rules, starting with better communication and no assumptions. We'd stand firm as a team in the battles we knew we had ahead with his family and Seamus's cancer. We also agreed that the holidays would have to be carefully handled. I was not welcome at, nor was I willing to go to, his parents' home. I wasn't up for the sort of frosty politeness that would occur even under the best of circumstances anyway. We agreed Chris would be spending Christmas Eve with his family and I'd stay home caring for Seamus. Christmas Day would be all ours, but we hadn't made any specific plans. Everything was tentative.

In the days following, I was able to take Seamus out for his normal morning walks. He still raced out to the garage with me and loudly howled his insistence that I not leave him alone. He still inhaled his kibble in mere seconds, and each evening he mashed up against me, reared back, and pawed at me until I rubbed his belly for a sufficient amount of time. Even though from all appearances Seamus underwent his first chemotherapy with no more side effect than a voracious appetite that resulted in some weight gain and, conversely, a little diarrhea, I was still anxious about taking him to his next chemo appointment.

His appointment fell on December 23.

This particular December had already been a heartbreaking disaster for me. December 23 and a second round of chemotherapy could not be a good combination. Common sense told me that the side effects would be cumulative. Just because he was fine the first time didn't mean the second time would be easy.

As I left with Seamus for his appointment, Chris left to meet his mother at her therapist's office for therapy of another sort, something he'd agreed to in our week apart. His mother felt this would improve their communications, and Chris felt like he should try, though he was every bit as leery of his appointment that morning as I was of mine.

At the veterinary oncology center, I still could not look at the other pets in the waiting room. I knew now that the bassett hound I'd seen before that didn't look like he had cancer was probably just like Seamus was now — a chemotherapy patient with poison coursing his veins, battling for his life. This time, I took Seamus outside to wait, letting the receptionist know where we'd be when they needed us. I paced up and down the strip of lawn by the sidewalk with Seamus alternating between sniffing the grass and looking back up at me expectantly. Through the glass doors I saw the receptionist waving at me to come back in.

The visit improved immediately when I was told Dr. Sorority Chick was on vacation and Dr. Roberts, the owner of the clinic, would be seeing Seamus. The weigh-in showed Seamus now weighed thirty-four pounds — a four-pound gain since this all began.

After liberal dosages of cookies, fifteen minutes in the hospital area without me, a neon orange bandage on his leg, an extra green cookie, a prescription for Tagamet and Zantac, and $190.55 in airline miles, we were finished. There wasn't even traffic on the way home. The second round of chemo was over, and the drive was longer than the procedure. I pressed the garage door opener and let out a deep breath as I pulled into the garage. The moment I put the car in park, Seamus began his happy howl: *I'm back here! Don't forget me! I'm here! Take me with you! Aaaaaarrrooooooooo!! Nooooooooo-ooooooooow!!!*

When we were back in the house I fed Seamus, adding a little lean hamburger and cottage cheese to his high-protein dry kibble. Together we curled up on the couch and napped as we waited for Chris to join us.

Chris arrived home two hours later. Even if Seamus hadn't nimbly jumped up off the couch and ran howling to greet Chris, I suspect Chris's mood would have woken me right up anyway. Chris flopped down on the couch next to me, pale and strained, while Seamus continued to howl and run around, tossing his squeak toys in the air and asking to play.

Chris petted Seamus to calm him, but he wasn't looking at the dog. He stared at the floor. After several minutes he looked up.

"So the good news is I won't be going to my parents' for Christmas Eve," he said, running his hand through his hair.

I inhaled slowly. "I take it your therapy was worse than Seamus's?"

"And more toxic, apparently."

"That's not good."

"No, I think it is. I think it had to happen."

I tried to focus on listening and supporting him as he described how the three-hour marathon therapy session had gone completely sideways. His relationship with me was not the only decision he'd made that his parents were determined to re-make for him. His career and his weight were among the hurtful topics dissected. Both, it seemed, were unacceptable (the first was too small and the second too large). I managed not to jump ahead with my own fears as I'd done previously, though it was difficult. He'd stood up to his family, and that was good enough. I was learning to take small steps.

"How did it end?"

"Not well. I'm not talking to them ever again. My parents are dead to me."

I started to protest a hundred different ways — they hadn't even given me a chance; they had no right to judge him or me; why couldn't they see how good we were together? But I held back. He needed my support, not my anger and certainly not my baggage. I did not want to be what came between Chris and his family, but I'd learned — Chris needed to handle this on his own.

And, I had to remind myself, this wasn't about me. This went much deeper than who he was dating.

By the end of the evening, we became enamored of the fact that it would just be the three of us for the weekend. These words don't usually form in my brain or come out of my mouth, but I was beginning to think, "Maybe this holiday won't be so bad." I just had to overlook, momentarily, how it was we came to be alone for the holidays.

On Christmas morning we opened presents by the fire. Seamus received a spectacular number of squeaky toys, which he gleefully began to gut. We lounged around reading with constant squeaking noises as background music for hours. Our only contact with the outside world was phone calls from both of my parents. The day passed peacefully.

When Chris began to prepare dinner, I sat at the kitchen counter with a glass of wine, and Seamus sat as close as he could get to Chris's feet in case any morsels dropped. As night fell, the three of us sat down to a delicious meal of chateaubriand, potatoes dauphinois, creamed spinach, and Yorkshire pudding. And of course Seamus got his own little plate of everything, though we did draw the line at having him sit up to the table, if only because I would not be as fast as he would have been in grabbing my share. Suffice it to say, no one had a decreased appetite.

I made it through the holidays — not unscathed, but perhaps undamaged. I needed that day to gather my strength.

By chemo number three on December 30, Seamus's weight had gone up to thirty-five pounds No, his appetite was not a problem. After three rounds, although I still frequently came home from work to check on him and had mostly eliminated any evening commitments so I could be home, I was beginning to believe Seamus would tolerate chemotherapy just fine. It was, as they had said, not as hard on dogs as humans. Whether that was the dosage or the type of chemotherapy or some biological reason, I didn't care. I was just happy to know he wasn't suffering and wasn't nauseous. Chemo, it was turning out, was something we could handle.

Chris went with me to the fourth treatment. He held Seamus when they did the blood draw this time and then held me while I waited through the infusion time when Seamus was taken into the hospital area without me. This was always the difficult part since there was nothing I could do except nervously bide my time pretending to read magazines or flipping the pages of a book. Having Chris with me eased the wait. Soon enough, once again Seamus came jauntily bouncing into the room, flinging his back right leg behind him with the paw barely touching the ground. Chris had once pointed out to me that Seamus sometimes ran or trotted as though he only had three legs. The back right leg was like a spare tire — there in case of an emergency but not really necessary. He didn't always do this of course, but enough that we noticed. I smiled when I saw that particular gait come trotting into the room.

When she joined me in the exam room, Dr. Sorority Chick informed me that Seamus would have two weeks off before we'd need to return for the next chemotherapy drug.

"The next one? This will be a different drug?" I asked.

"Yes. This one he takes orally."

I did not remember hearing there would be more than one drug. I didn't know there was more than one chemotherapy drug. "But if we know he tolerates the one he's been taking, why not just finish with that one?"

She gave me that "I'm trying to be patient with you but can't you just let me do my job and not ask any questions" look that I'd become accustomed to ignoring. "We need to throw everything at it that we can. In order to give him the best chance of survival we give different types of chemo."

"So there is a chance he will survive?" I had felt this somehow must be the case, but it didn't ever seem she talked about survival in the sense of beating the disease but rather only surviving for that year.

"Well, whatever amount of time we can get for him." And there it was again. The limitation.

We went around and around with me questioning whether survival in the sense of a cure or remission was a possibility and her dodging and dancing to not have to give what she apparently thought would be false hope.

"Really? So no dogs with mast cell tumors on the anal sac have survived?" I said.

"Of course they have."

"Okay, so he must have some chance."

"I'm just trying to be realistic."

"Yes, so am I." We glared at each other over the exam table. I'm not even an optimist, let alone a fantasist, and here this sorority chick of a doctor couldn't even bring herself to tell me, $5,000 and two months later, that Seamus had, oh, I don't know, a 10 percent chance of survival? It was ludicrous to me. And frustrating.

That night's tub talk with Chris was all about my combative relationship with this doctor.

"You can be honest. Do you think this is some sort of alpha-female drama being played out where she and I are both determined to be in control?" Apparently, where this doctor was concerned, I could maintain outrage and indignation even soaking in hot water, wine in hand, and sparkling city lights in the horizon.

"Well, that might be a little of it. I think your styles might be clashing. She clearly needs to be in control and just isn't a very warm or communicative person. And you want a lot of information, and um. . . ."

"I need to be in control, too."

"Yeah. That."

"And I'm not warm or communicative either?"

"Well, we're working on that."

"Okay, but I'm the customer here. If I ask a question and want to understand the treatment and what I'm paying for, don't I have that right? Why does she just act like I'm annoying her? What am I supposed to do, just hand her my dog and my credit card and say 'do what you want'? I'm not going to do that."

"Well, I imagine some people do."

I stared at him. Sure, maybe some people do. I looked over at Seamus on the patio chair, stretched out, head resting on his crossed front paws, big brown kohl-lined eyes staring at me. "I guess I'm not some people. I just want to understand the choices and be sure I'm making the right choices. I had no idea we'd be switching up chemo and dealing with a whole new set of possible side effects. I should have been told that before. I haven't even researched this new chemo."

"Maybe you should ask for a new doctor. They've got a whole facility full of them. Ask for another doctor."

"I think I will."

Thus braced, I gave myself a pep talk on the drive in for Seamus's January 20 appointment. I was going to make Dr. Sorority Chick explain the new chemo to me, what its risks were, and what it would do that the other wouldn't, and by god if she didn't respond, I would demand a new doctor.

When I arrived, I was surprised to see a couple I knew from Riverside waiting in the lobby with their bassett hound. They were also volunteers at the Mary S. Roberts Pet Adoption Center, we had the same regular vet, and I saw them and their dogs (they also had two beagles) frequently at events. I'd always thought of them as a happy, content, mild-mannered couple that seemed unruffled by much of anything. Their bassett, Molly, had the same kind of cancer as Seamus. And the same doctor.

"Isn't she great?" they both cooed.

"Dr. Gilbert?" I said, refraining from calling her Dr. Sorority Chick.

"Yes, she's been so wonderful with Molly."

"Um. Well. I'd say she's been less wonderful with Seamus. Or with me at any rate."

"Really?" They seemed as astonished to hear this as I was to hear "wonderful" expressed in a three-mile radius of Dr. Sorority Chick.

"Well, basically, I can't get her to talk to me about anything other than Seamus having only a year to live."

"Oh, no." They looked at each other. I'm no good with married-people speak, so I have no idea what the glance expressed. I imagine it was "oh poor Teresa — her dog is dying and she's losing her mind and blaming the doctor."

"And I know that she doesn't want to give false hope, but it seems like some hope would not be out of the question, don't you think?" I was probably pleading with them — strident and desperate. I'm sure they wanted to change appointments so as not to encounter me again, and indeed, I only ran into them one other time.

"Oh, of course. You have to have hope." They smiled encouragingly. As in, encouraging me to leave them and their happy bubble alone.

By the time Seamus and I were called back into the exam room, I was completely subdued. Of course it was my fault. I was being too aggressive and demanding. I should just be friendlier with the doctor and let her do her thing without question. I should be like the nice couple.

Seamus weighed in at 36.20 pounds (later, I noted his treatment report said "Body Condition: overweight"). I handed over my credit card and my fat dog and obediently sat and waited, feeling like I had curled up with my tail between my legs.

CHAPTER 10
CRASHING DOWN
AND FIRING UP

I pulled three bottles of pills — steroids, pain medication, and the chemo pill — from the bag I'd been given. I reread the chart setting forth when each pill should be given over the next twelve-day period. As I again read the instructions on each bottle, I set them down in a row, next to the chart on my kitchen counter. The instructions for handling the pills stated that they should not be stored near any open food or drink, the pill should not be broken or cut, and if I was pregnant, nursing, or planning to become pregnant, I should be very, very careful when administering the drug as fetuses and babies are particularly vulnerable to the toxic effects. What about a thirty-six-pound dog?

I reached into the bag for the rubber gloves I'd been instructed to use when handling the chemo, and I set them down next to the pill bottles. Gloves. How much clearer could it be that I was poisoning my dog?

I poured kibble into Seamus's bowl along with some beef broth. After he finished his breakfast, I called him to me and petted him for a long time, rubbing his ears, scratching his back, and apologizing in as many ways as I could. Then I donned the rubber gloves, stuffed a quarter of a hot dog with a pill, and, tears in my eyes, handed the hot dog to my beloved beagle. Seamus swallowed it in one bite, wagged his tail, and looked up at me for more. I gave him another piece with another pill hidden. He ate that too, and the third piece.

By evening, he seemed unaffected. That would all soon change.

I often wonder how people who live alone without a pet explain all the weird noises in their house. Generally, Seamus follows me around the house and is close enough that I figure any noise that isn't me is him, and this helps me sleep at night. And I like his little sounds — the cheap aluminum tags jingling together slowly when he's moving about and more quickly when he's scratching his ears with his back leg, the little grunts and harrumphs when he sleeps, the circling and scratching to get all the blankets and pillows arranged just so before he lies down, the incessant sniffing of the air for any whiff of possible toast, his nails tapping across the wood floor as he trots off outside, and the little swoosh of the plastic doggie door behind him. A dog is a presence in a house.

Seamus is not always right by me at home, but if I'm upstairs, he's upstairs. If I go downstairs, he's downstairs — of course, the kitchen is downstairs, so that would explain that. He will be in another room apart from me but usually within eyesight of me and definitely within hearing distance.

That's why I was immediately concerned eleven days after the new chemo was administered, when Seamus did not follow me downstairs for my morning coffee. My morning coffee comes first, but once the pot is brewing, Seamus gets his breakfast. I poured a cup of the high-protein kibble in his bowl. The sound of kibble hitting the tin is like a mating call to a beagle. And still, there was no Seamus. I made toast and poured myself a cup of coffee. The toaster lever going down should have been another trigger — a noise that can usually get Seamus down an entire flight of stairs and through two rooms in what seems like negative time. I've been known to hit the toaster lever just to get Seamus downstairs for a walk. It didn't work this time.

I hurried back upstairs, coffee and toast in hand, and found Seamus still in his bed. He raised his head and sniffed at the air in the direction of my toast. When I held out some crust for him, he sniffed and then took it from me but didn't sit up. He ate a little, chewing slowly, and when I returned to my bed he eventually followed me, sitting at my side and waiting for more toast. As I finished getting ready for work, Seamus curled himself up on my bed and slept.

This must be the tiredness they were talking about, I thought. His next blood check was three days away, since that's when his white blood cell count was expected to be lowest. From the looks of Seamus that morning, this chemo was having more of an effect than the others. If the white blood cell counts were the ones that give a body energy, they were waving white flags, weakly. I added up the number of days or half-days of work I'd been out of the office for all of his treatments already and mentally ran through the stack of files on my desk. I had to go into the office. I figured I'd just come home for an early lunch and if he didn't seem better then, I'd call the vet. When Seamus didn't follow me down the stairs as I left for work, I hesitated. I went back upstairs and petted him, kissed him on the forehead, and promised I'd be back.

I was home again three hours later. Seamus didn't greet me outside or even as I walked in the front door.

I raced up the stairs and found him lying in his bed, awake, alive, and looking at me, but not even lifting his head. He was barely keeping his eyelids open.

I called the cancer clinic.

The conversation seemed to take hours. I wanted to hear either "that's perfectly normal, give him a baby aspirin and take him for his blood test as scheduled" or "bring him in immediately." I wanted to be told what to do. I wanted not to be in charge.

"You should probably have him looked at," said the receptionist at the veterinarian cancer clinic.

"Should I bring him to you right now?"

"Well, you could bring him to us or to your regular vet."

"But if this is related to the chemotherapy, shouldn't I bring him to you?"

"You can. Or you can take him to your regular vet. You were scheduled for a blood test with your regular vet, weren't you?

"Yes, but that's three days away. Should I wait that long?"

"Probably not."

"So I should bring him in to see you now?"

"You don't have to bring him to us. You can bring him to your regular vet."

I wanted to scream at her. It seemed clear I needed to bring the dog in, but the way she kept mentioning my "regular vet" was confusing.

Did that mean this was not something requiring a specialist? This was not related to the chemo? What would my regular non-emergency vet do with a lethargic chemo-beagle?

"I don't want to go to my regular vet. I want to bring him to you guys."

"If that's your decision you can do that."

"Well, isn't that what I should do?"

"You just need to get him some attention. I wouldn't wait."

"Are you saying I don't have time to drive him in to see you?" The drive usually took me about forty-five minutes.

"No. It's completely up to you. Wherever you would like to take him."

Frustration was seeping from my pores. Why couldn't she just give me instructions like "bring your dog in immediately"? And why couldn't I just say, "I'm bringing my dog to you right now"?

"It seems like this is something for you guys to handle. Why would I take him to my regular vet? He's not a cancer specialist."

"We just don't like to interfere with your relationship with your vet. It's your choice."

Only later did I understand that, of course, as my vet had been the one to refer me to the veterinary cancer center, they were careful not to return the favor by proceeding to steal all further veterinarian care. Great, that works for their relationships, but what about the care Seamus needs? And needs now!

"I'm bringing him to you right now. I'll be there in a half hour."

I forgot to call my office to let them know I wouldn't be coming back in, and I cursed every other car on the freeway as I sped past, well over the speed limit, but I arrived at the clinic in a half hour. I lifted Seamus out of the car and carried him in. He didn't even lift his head to sniff for the cookies. He leaned his head against my shoulder, and I could feel all thirty-six and a half pounds of him, slack and heavy in my arms.

"Oh, Seamus!" The receptionist came around the desk and rubbed his head. "Let me take him right back. We'll get him set up, and then the doctor will see you."

I don't know if the receptionist was the

same girl on the phone, but now at least someone was giving him the attention he needed. The attention I needed him to have. She took him from my arms, and they were gone. I didn't even get to say good-bye. I felt a shot of panic that I hadn't felt since they first told me he had cancer. Just as I'd relaxed and begun to think he'd make it — he'd survive not just the chemo but the cancer — WHACK! Seamus was being rushed into doggie intensive care.

I retreated to the waiting room. This time I cried and I didn't care who saw me. Every seat in the room could have been filled and I would not have been able to hold back the tears. I would have contorted my face and sniffed and gulped air, but inevitably, I would have lost it anyway. I was frightened. I felt horribly guilty that I'd not rushed him in immediately that morning. I felt responsible that I let Dr. Sorority Chick change the chemotherapy. I'd given Seamus the very pills that were causing this! I wrapped the poison in a hot dog and tricked him into eating it. Everything was my fault. My dog was going to die, and it was my fault. There wasn't even a small part of me telling myself I was being ridiculous.

When I finally got to see the doctor, it wasn't, mercifully, Dr. Sorority Chick. It was Dr. Roberts again. But Seamus wasn't with her.

"Seamus is a sick boy. It's a good thing you brought him in," she said.

"Is he going to be okay?" That has to be the question most asked of a veterinarian. I wonder how often the answer is the same as the one I got.

"We hope so." She leaned across the exam table, resting on her forearms but making eye contact. "He's febrile and has a very low white blood cell count. We've got him on IV fluids, antibiotics, and we gave him an injection of Neupogen to help build back up his white blood cell count."

Okay, so maybe I got him here in time. "What happens next?"

"We're going to keep him overnight. Maybe for a few days. We'll recheck his white blood cell count tomorrow and reassess. The concern is infection. He doesn't have enough white blood cells left to fight off an infection, so we need to be very careful."

"Can I see him?"

"It's best if you don't right now. He's resting and getting his fluids, and that's exactly how we need him to be."

I left with assurances that Dr. Sorority Chick would be checking in on Seamus and

I could call and check on him at any time. That evening the doctor would call me to report on Seamus's progress, I was assured. I drove home with the empty dog crate rattling in the backseat, replaying in my mind how exuberant Seamus had been the night before and trying to decipher whether there were signs I should have picked up on. Then he was still howling and stealing food and demanding belly rubs. Now, because of the "cure," he could hardly lift his head and he was on doggie life support. It was hard not to think I'd made all the wrong choices in his care. It was particularly hard when there was no phone call from the doctor that evening. I left a message on the clinic voice mail.

The next morning and on into the afternoon, my only information on Seamus's condition was provided by the receptionist, who continued to take my messages. I wasn't hungry — what was the point of eating if Seamus wasn't there demanding his share? I didn't want a glass of wine — alcohol is a depressant and that was definitely not going to help. I didn't talk to anyone about what was going on since it seemed most folks thought I'd already spent too much emotion, money, and time on this dog. I suspected that even Chris was beginning to think I was a little obsessed.

I'd stopped talking about Seamus and his cancer treatments at work. There wasn't anyone else in my office who was a "dog person." I'd noticed they all looked at me like I'd lost my mind when I said anything about my visits to the vet or my worries about Seamus. Many of my friends were the same way, and some mere acquaintances offered up their own unsolicited and horrifying opinions.

Dog people know that somehow in this world it's perfectly acceptable to spend thousands upon thousands of dollars on fancy cars, big televisions, gaudy jewelry, and even plastic surgery, but if you choose to spend your money on your pet, no matter how important that pet is to you, some people will frown in disgust. People will judge. And people will call you insane and make horrible suggestions like killing the dog. But I earned the money. I could spend it as I chose. And I'd always choose my dog over a newer car, more clothes, and, at the rate we were going, over a vacation. I didn't care. I wanted Seamus to live.

I tried to reach the doctor again at four in the afternoon but got an answering service. I left a message asking that the doctor call me with an update and then chastised myself for not driving in and demanding to see how Seamus was doing. Never mind that at this rate I'd be working extra hours and retiring years later just to pay for his care, I still should have taken the afternoon off to drive to the clinic and check on Seamus. It's what any good dog owner would have done.

Late that night the doctor finally called. But it wasn't Dr. Sorority Chick. This was a new doctor. Her name was Autumn Dutelle, and she was everything Dr. Sorority Chick was not — kind, caring, compassionate, and not in a hurry to get away from me. She also had been the one caring for Seamus since I brought him in. She apologized that no one had called me, and I gleaned that updates to me were Dr. Sorority Chick's responsibility.

But Seamus was doing fine. He had his appetite back, and his white blood cell count had returned to normal. I think that's when my heart rate and breathing also returned to normal.

Dr. Dutelle called me again the next morning to let me know Seamus was eating, barking, and back to his same old beagle self. She saw no reason he couldn't go home that afternoon. As long as he had a normal bowel movement, he'd be ready for me. Maybe that's an unusual thing to hope for, but that's what I was hoping for all afternoon. Come on, beagle bowel movement!

When I was reunited with Seamus, he did indeed seem back to himself. He was howling and sniffing out the treat bowls, still preferring the green bone-shaped cookies. The tech left him with me in the exam room and informed me that Dr. Dutelle would be in soon, and indeed she was.

Dr. Dutelle could easily be mistaken for a teenager — a happy, smiling, bright teenager. She was freckle-faced, with jaw-length light brown hair and short bangs cut straight across her forehead. Her eyes were large and green and compassionate. I could see that she genuinely cared about Seamus and was nearly as happy as I was that he'd pulled through. She sat on the floor with him, stroking his back, rubbing his belly, and holding his muzzle in the palm of her hands as she spoke to him. He crawled into her lap, pawed at her for more petting, and worked her over for more cookies. She obliged.

She may as well have been rubbing my belly, for all the comfort I felt. She was empathetic, and I could tell she'd been watching Seamus and caring for him, and even worrying about him, for the time he'd been there. And finally, I had the conversation I'd been needing to have.

"This was all because of the new chemo, right?"

"This rarely happens, but yes, this was a reaction to the chemo. His white blood cell count dropped dangerously low. Unfortunately, chemo doesn't just attack the bad cancer cells; it attacks the good ones too. Usually, the good ones can regenerate faster."

"But not this time? Not with Seamus?"

"Not with this chemo. It happens in less than 5 percent of the patients."

"We're not giving it to him again, right?"

"No. Definitely not. We'll change the protocol."

"Why not go back to the old chemo? Why do something different?" I didn't know if I could give him another chemo. What if it happened again? What if the cure was worse than the disease? Was that even possible?

"Here's the thing: Seamus has — or had — an aggressive type of cancer, given where it was located. We want to give him the very best chance, so we need to fight it with everything we have. The first chemo may have worked, but it may not. We have no way of knowing yet. Another chemo gives us another weapon."

"What if this happens again?"

"The protocol we'd like to switch him to has much less of a chance for a reaction."

"But there's still a chance he'll react badly again?"

"I know you're worried. I understand. It's a lot to go through. There's always a chance of a bad reaction, so I can't say there isn't. He did really well with the first one, so chances are very good he'll do well with this next one. It's what we recommend, but it's your choice."

At least she was acknowledging that I had a choice.

When the time came, I made two choices.

When Dr. Roberts came back in to see me and Seamus, I agreed to try one more chemo.

"But I have a condition. I want Seamus's care assigned to Dr. Dutelle. I don't have any faith in Dr. Gilbert, and frankly, I don't care for her style. I can't go through this again if Dr. Gilbert is involved."

"That's fine. Not everyone is a good personality match. That's why we have several doctors here you can choose from."

"It's not just a personality problem. She has not been looking out for my dog's best interest."

Dr. Roberts nodded, but I could see that she was not agreeing with me but rather choosing not to engage. "It's your choice, of course. I have no problem switching you to another doctor."

"Now that I understand what good care should be like, I choose Dr. Dutelle."

Instantaneously as I spoke, I was relieved to be done with the cold, uncaring, unresponsive veterinarian. I was also satisfied that I'd finally taken control of the situation. Bring on the teenage wonder vet! Dr. Roberts then advised me that Dr. Dutelle had just completed her residency and was brand new. So in fact, Seamus's care would be assigned to Dr. Dutelle but overseen by Dr. Roberts. Even better.

Many more airline miles on my credit card later, Seamus and I both bounded out of the clinic. The total count of toys and treats I showered on Seamus that weekend may have run into the thousands as well. If I was going bankrupt saving the life of a diabolically cute beagle, we may as well have fun with it. Seamus tore around the house throwing his peach, mint green, and lavender lobster into the air before catching it and attempting to rip its guts out. Just for good measure, he also rifled through every trash can in the house to see if anything had been left behind in his absence. His appetite was back.

I called Chris.

"Seamus is home with me now and doing really well."

"Glad to hear it. I'm telling you, the dog is indestructible."

"I'd rather not keep testing that theory."

"True."

"And I finally dealt with Dr. Sorority Chick."

"You saw her?"

"No, of course not. But I did ask to have Seamus reassigned to the doctor who treated him this last weekend. She's really wonderful."

"I'm glad to hear it. That will be better for both of you."

Yes. Yes, it would.

I checked on Seamus every couple of hours throughout that night and the next. When Chris came for the weekend, I noticed he too checked on, petted, and indulged Seamus more frequently. And on Saturday morning, Chris cooked all three of us scrambled eggs and bacon.

CHAPTER 11
THE RED ZONE

Each morning I donned the rubber medical gloves to handle the chemotherapy medication, and each morning I wondered if I was killing Seamus. Then I would remind myself: the pills were killing cancer. I was trusting Dr. Dutelle and doing what I had to do. I stuffed the pill into a chunk of cheese and held it out to Seamus. He sniffed at it and gently took it from me, not with a bite. Instead he held it in his mouth, walked away from me, set the pill-stuffed cheeseball on the floor, and began to disassemble it.

"Seamus, buddy, I'm sorry," I said, picking the cheese back up and stuffing the pill farther down. I tore off a piece to make it smaller in hopes he'd swallow it all more quickly. I handed it back to him.

The newest chemo regime involved the Vinblastine given intravenously at the cancer center, alternating with Cytoxan given at home in pills, every two weeks.

Seamus was also still on the prednisone steroid, which I also gave him in a pill. Although true to his beagle nature, Seamus would eat just about anything, he was now on to me. His nose was strong enough to sniff out the pill smell no matter what I hid it in. He'd deconstruct the food, spit out the pills, and then gobble up the treat. I'd changed up the food I hid his pills in every third or fourth dosage so that his excitement over new food would cause him to simply inhale, rather than dissect, the new pill-stuffed treat. But after two or three pills, he'd know that the hot dog, the ball of cream cheese, the roast beef slice, the American cheese, all held a nasty, bitter pill, and he'd return to his investigative techniques.

"It's for your own good, buddy. I promise." I held his muzzle, forcing him to swallow the pill. His eyes demonstrated the betrayal he felt, and I'm sure mine looked as sad as his.

But Seamus did not react badly to the Cytoxan chemo pills. Instead, he seemed to have an increased appetite and energy. I worried that he was gaining too much weight. And, it seemed, he had too much energy. I was walking him every morning and usually in the evenings as well. But still, he would run around the house frantically chasing his toys, or sit, rocking back and forth, letting out frustrated sighs, signaling he needed attention. No amount of attention seemed enough.

One evening, a month into the new chemotherapy protocol, I finally felt Seamus was doing well enough (or more likely, I was doing well enough) that he could be left alone in the evening. Chris and I went out to dinner and pretended, as best we could, to be a normal couple out on a date.

When we arrived home, there was a voice mail message. Chris hit the play button while I petted and talked to a wiggling, howling Seamus.

"Teresa, I'm so sorry to call. I really am. I love dogs, but your dog has been barking at the gate since six this evening."

I looked up at Chris. We'd left for dinner at six. Chris was shaking his head slowly as the message continued.

"He's still barking . . ." The message was left at quarter to eight. "I'm so sorry, but we just can't take it anymore and we thought you should know, it's not the first time. It's been going on when you leave for work as well."

This was not the neighbor who had originally complained and whom, we were fairly certain, had left the note on my gate. This was Judy, the quiet neighbor on the other side of us — she and her husband were home and working in their yard (her) or garage (him) most every day, best we could tell.

Barking all day? I lay down on the floor. "I give up. This dog is going to be the death of me."

Clearly, I had created a monster. The dog might well survive the cancer, but now he'd gotten so used to my constant attention and instantaneous response to any and all howled demands that he'd developed a severe case of separation anxiety. I'd been doing a nice job of ignoring that problem, having convinced myself the howling was only as I came and left and only when the dog was recovering from some sort of medical procedure. The phone call made it hard to maintain that denial.

"I'm sorry, baby, but you knew this was coming. You need to stop spoiling the dog and get in control of him. I think it's obvious he's going to beat his cancer. He probably just needs more exercise."

I had begun to think Seamus was going to beat the cancer, but I had yet to voice that thought. My relief at Chris's opinion of Seamus's survival allowed me to overlook his (obviously correct) statement that I was spoiling the dog. "Okay. You're probably right."

"To start, the three of us can start walking these hills around here. A longer, more intense walk will do us all good."

We began a regular walking routine, and Chris began staying most of the week at my house, taking Seamus for additional, longer walks. We also tried various treats to distract him when we left, hoping that would eliminate the howling. Sometimes we left him with a chew stick, sometimes it was a peanut-butter-stuffed Kong toy, and sometimes a steak bone.

We came home from grocery shopping one afternoon to Judy's husband, a retired Marine, standing at our front gate looking none too happy. He politely but firmly explained that my dog was preventing them from enjoying their yard. They couldn't be outside because of the nonstop racket from the dog. I, humiliated and cowering, took the still howling, frantic dog into the house while Chris tried to explain that we were trying to deal with the problem. The neighbor held firm that we were failing in our efforts.

I knew what I had to do. Because the dog had not yet cost me my entire life savings, I hired a dog trainer for help. And not just any trainer. Oh no. One who had been trained by one who'd been trained by none other than Cesar Milan. The Dog Whisperer himself, twice removed.

The moment Nicole walked into the house, Seamus knew there was a problem. Normally he happily howls, run toward the visitor, jumps up (bad, bad dog), and sniffs around waiting to be petted or to rifle through the visitor's purse. When Nicole walked in the house, Seamus stopped, backed up, and returned to his bed in the corner of the living room. The one with the pile of toys and several blankets. He glared at her from the safety of his turf.

Nicole and I sat down on the couch.

"So, is this how Seamus lives?"

I looked around the room. He had a comfortable bed, a pile of toys, and another bed in the laundry room (a mere twenty feet from the other bed). There was a canister of treats on one counter, a collection of pill bottles on another, and there was a baby (read: beagle) lock on the kitchen cupboard below the sink, where the trash can was. I was sure I didn't like where this was going.

"Yes. Pretty much. Well, he's been sick. Remember, I mentioned he has or . . .

well . . . he had . . . cancer? He's in chemo right now? So, um. Well, yeah. This is how we live."

"And these blankets?" She patted the blankets on the couch — two of them, folded up to be the size of, for example, a beagle. "Does Seamus come up on the couch with you?"

"Sometimes."

"When he wants to?"

Um, yes. Those times.

Seamus also could see where this was going. So just to embarrass me further or to have his say, or both, he joined us on the couch and snuggled in next to me, paw thrown across my leg.

"See that?" Nicole said, pointing to the paw on my leg.

"Yes. He does that all the time. Most of my other beagles never cuddled like Seamus," I said, beaming. My dog is absolutely the cutest. She surely could see that. He'd melt that icy exterior of hers.

"That's a claim. He's claiming you as part of his pack. He's the boss here, and he's letting you know that."

It's not cute??!!!

She went on to explain some pack leader/follower thing and something about my lack of leadership skills, while I rubbed Seamus's belly, cooed at him, and was generally dismayed that Nicole could overlook how totally adorable Seamus was. It's a good thing I didn't have children.

Nicole made it clear she was training me, not the dog (and Seamus and I both balked at the concept that he was merely a dog). First, she ordered me to remove all comforts I had been providing Seamus except one bed. Apparently four beds and two couches in one small townhome was more than any dog needed. The theory was that I had allowed Seamus the run of the house, and it was time to make him earn his rewards. No toys, no time on the couch, no human food, no jumping on my bed, only one dog bed, and worst of all, no petting until he had done something that deserved a reward or occasionally when I felt like it, but only at my own instigation and only very occasionally. Seamus had a lot to learn. And, she seemed intent on telling me, so did I.

"But he had cancer. Cancer! And he's still in treatment. He's on chemo. Even right now."

"Yes, and if he had only that year to live, I'd probably agree with you. Spoil away. But, he likely has another ten years or so, and this behavior cannot continue."

Seamus skulked off to a corner. I briefly

considered moving to the country, but I live in a townhome for a reason. (Or several, namely I'm not big on yard work, housekeeping, maintenance, and dark, scary places with no neighbors. Also, I need a Starbucks nearby at all times.) This training regime looked like it might prove more deadly than the cancer.

Other than turning my home into what appeared to Seamus and I both to be Guantanamo Doggie Bay, our training consisted of a lot of exercises that involved rewarding Seamus with treats when he did what I was instructing him to do — sit, stay, come, follow me without straining on the leash. And walking. A lot of walking.

I was to walk Seamus for at least an hour in the morning and an hour in the evening, and at all times I was to have complete control of the dog — he was not to be sniffing, pulling, howling, smelling, "marking" territory, or in any way . . . well, enjoying the walk. Or that's how it seemed to us. I was not getting any enjoyment out of the walks either. I was nowhere near an hour in the morning (let's call it twenty minutes) and only getting about a half hour in the evening. But it felt like more. A walk spent tugging, barking commands, and battling for control was no fun for Seamus or me (and we took turns doing each of those things).

This wasn't supposed to be fun, Nicole assured me. The fun would come later. This was the exercise and discipline parts. The parts that had been missing from Seamus's life and the reason he was terrorizing my neighbors.

I did pretty well, for me, getting up and walking Seamus each morning. My townhouse was about one-third of the way up a very steep hill. I walked Seamus to the top and then stood trying to catch my breath and breaking the rules by letting Seamus sniff and enjoy the grass in the small park at the top of the hill. Then we followed the road up and around, circling the tree and boulders several times, which I told myself amounted to a real walk without having to leave the safety of my townhouse complex. Plus, if I dropped dead from cardiac arrest, someone would see me, and Seamus could easily find his way back home.

I told myself that Seamus was in chemo and didn't have much energy and thus the twenty-minute morning walks should be fine. But after about the tenth time we arrived home and Seamus ran howling and racing through the house, stopping at my feet to howl and herd me toward his empty bowl, I had to be a bit more honest with myself. He was having no trouble with this chemo. The steroids seemed to be the only pills affecting him, as he was now a solid thirty-seven pounds with the usual voracious beagle appetite.

Nicole's suggestion was a backpack. Luckily, she meant for Seamus. I bought a cute little dark green "Outward Hound" backpack and, as instructed, put a full twelve-ounce water bottle in each side pocket. This added three pounds to Seamus and was supposed to make him work harder and burn extra energy. And of course, I was supposed to increase that walk to at least a half hour. At least.

On weekends, Chris took Seamus for serious hour-long walks up and down hills throughout our neighborhood. It was a testament to my leadership that when Chris reached for the backpack, Seamus ran to hide behind my legs.

I worked up to a half hour in the morning and about the same in the evenings. Eventually, over a few months, I also lost ten pounds so I felt I must have been doing something right.

I wasn't.

The neighbor complaints continued to roll in. If Chris and I went to dinner or a movie or ran an errand, however short, I was constantly checking my cell phone to see if the neighbors had called. I dreaded coming back home. As I approached my garage I'd slow up the car, roll down my windows, and listen for the inevitable howling. If I didn't hear it, I could breathe again, but then as soon as the garage door opener was pressed, the frantic howling would begin and I'd know Seamus was at the gate. I'd race out of the car and into the house, hurrying Seamus inside. Next I'd check the answering machine — if the light was flashing, I knew the neighbors had called. I called them back; I left notes; I emailed them. I implored them: *I'm working on it, I swear. I've hired a trainer. We're trying everything. But for the love of god people, call me on my cell phone so I can come home and stop the dog! I can't do anything about it if I don't know it's happening. And if he's howling, it's because I'm not at home. You see how leaving a message on my home phone does not help??* But, I was learning, my neighbors are of a generation that doesn't use cell phones. And my dog was driving them more in the direction of pitchforks.

The answering machine message light continued to flash.

I phoned Nicole desperate for more help.

Nothing seemed to be working. She returned for more training. This time when she came in the house she called Seamus out from his bed where he had retreated the moment her car was parked. He came to her, tail tucked, ears back. I couldn't see that she was doing anything in particular. Sure, her voice was firm and her demeanor calm, but I did not sense whatever it was that Seamus sensed.

She ordered him to sit. He looked at me, eyes huge. *Do something!* I looked away. Seamus sat.

Then she made him lie down. This was accomplished by showing him a treat, bringing it down to floor level so that his eyes — when not pleading with me — followed. She then brought the treat out a few inches so that Seamus extended himself forward, eventually reaching a prone position. She gave him the treat and ordered him to stay. He stayed.

"Wow," I said.

"This is a very stubborn dog," she said.

"Yes, I know. He's a beagle."

"It's not just the breed. Are you walking him?"

"Yes."

"An hour in the morning?"

I looked down at Seamus, and he immediately began to get up. Without looking at him, she ordered him back down. He looked at me. I looked at her. Seamus slunk back down.

"Um, no. I don't have an hour in the morning."

"Then you shouldn't have a dog."

After everything I've done for this dog? Are you kidding me? If I didn't have this dog, he'd be dead twice over! He was a street beagle with cancer, for godssake!

"I'm doing the best I can." That's all I could muster. I looked as pathetic as Seamus. She may as well have ordered me down.

"Seamus is still very much in control in this house. He's a real problem, and you've got to learn to handle this. Watch."

She used her boot-clad foot to roll Seamus over onto his back. Seamus curled his lips back. I'd never seen those canine teeth before unless food was being pried from his mouth. And I'd never heard a growl like that one. She held him in place.

"You see that?"

"Yes. I do. Let him up!"

"No. He needs to know he's not the leader here. He needs to learn respect."

The growls increased, and Seamus snapped at her boot.

"Oh my god! I've never seen him do anything like that!"

"This is a red zone dog," she said, still calmly holding down what was now an enraged, fangs-bared, snapping beagle under a boot. "This is not acceptable behavior, and if you do not do anything about this, you will have a much bigger problem on your hands than just the howling."

Yes, I would. If anyone broke into my house, rolled my dog onto his back, and held him there under their boot, my dog was likely to bite them. I'm not seeing the problem. He's a beagle. A beagle! Snoopy? Shiloh? A beagle!

"Let go of him. Let him up. This is ridiculous."

"No, it isn't. I'll let him up when he stops fighting." She then explained that "red zone" meant a dangerous dog. A dog out of balance. A dog that could become a serious problem. And if his dominance continued, he may . . . And that's where she lost me. He may keep howling? He may be completely ornery? Sure. Okay. But that's not a vicious, snarling danger to society. Or me. Or even himself.

"Don't hurt him. He's been through enough."

"I would never hurt an animal. I'm not hurting him."

I couldn't even watch. I walked away while she said something to me about my energy level and a dog's ability to perceive emotions or stability or mental health. Something like that. Then she called me back into the room.

Seamus had stopped fighting. He lay, exhausted, under her boot, not looking at her or me.

"That's submissive behavior. That's what you want to accomplish."

"I'm not sure it is." I was pretty sure it wasn't. Seamus looked miserable.

She took her foot off the dog. "Stay." He didn't get up.

"This whole thing seems to take all the fun out of having a dog."

"For now. You have to get . . . stay . . . in control of the dog . . . stay . . . first." Seamus had made a few lame attempts to get up. Again, without looking at him, she had given commands that he obeyed. It was just sad. Hadn't this dog been through enough?

Finally she said, "Okay. Up." Seamus got up slowly, not trusting that there wouldn't be another command. He slunk over to me, and, of course, I went to pet him.

"Don't."

"Don't pet him?"

"He didn't do anything to deserve petting."

"Are you kidding?"

"No. Petting should be a reward for now. He was a very bad dog. Did you see how long it took him to submit? That's not behavior you reward. Tell him to sit. When he sits and holds the sit, you can pet him."

This was perhaps the perfect storm of bad behavior — Seamus's stubbornness, my unwillingness and inability to discipline him, and an overly strident, unreasonable trainer. I was at a loss.

At Chris's suggestion, we began watching *The Dog Whisperer* on television. I even read his book. Chris, who had never been a dog person, decided that the training made sense and he began to seriously follow the techniques. Seamus and I decided the Dog Whisperer was Satan himself.

Chris became a freelance writer full time, which allowed him to spend more time at my place. (It also made his Los Angeles apartment unnecessary, but I wasn't focusing on that just yet.) That also meant he was taking Seamus on longer walks, which did at least burn up some of that beagle energy. Chris also learned the training exercises from Nicole, and we took Seamus to the large lawn in front of the townhouse complex and practiced. I figured it couldn't hurt if the neighbors at least saw how hard I was trying. And I was trying. No matter what Nicole thought.

I bought a thirty-foot lead and used it to teach Seamus to sit, stay, and come when called. On the large front lawn at the entrance to my townhome complex, Seamus sat, on the leash, with me thirty feet away circling around him. If he tried to come toward me, he was ordered back. When he sat long enough that I could walk a full circle around him, I was allowed to call him to me and reward him with a treat. This was supposed to use up some of the dog's mental energy as well as physical. And, of course, it was to assert my dominance. We practiced regularly. Eventually, Seamus figured out the game and merely sat, looking bored and not even following me with his eyes, until I returned to my original spot, at which point he'd perk up, wait for me to say come, and then charge at my hand that held the treat. He'd give me tolerance, but not submission. *Fine, lady. You've got me on a leash. I can wait you out.*

I was certain we were not making progress on the separation anxiety and howling front, but I had to keep trying.

When I wasn't walking Seamus, exercising Seamus, running Seamus through boot camp drills, and avoiding anything as harmful as petting him or letting him on my bed or couch or other couch or any of his extra beds or feeding him table scraps, I was marking off days on the paper calendar and checking the boxes after giving him the correct tapering dosages of steroid, and then the Cytoxan itself on days eight, nine, ten, and eleven only (and wait, does the day of the appointment count as day one or is that day zero?), getting his blood checked, and then driving back to the cancer center for the IV chemo only to start the process over again. This went on for four more months. Other than a weight gain that pushed him close to forty pounds, there was no evidence Seamus was in treatment for cancer. He was full of energy, howling, eating voraciously, and feeling fine.

Still though, I was cautious and a bit apprehensive about the state of my life. Seamus's health may have been improving, but the problems with Chris's family were not. True to his word, Chris had not spoken to his parents for several months. While he seemed unaffected by this, I was worried.

CHAPTER 12
ANY OTHER DOG

The three of us fell into a pattern of sorts, isolating our trio and spending our days walking, training, and drugging (Seamus only, and all prescription, I swear). On those walks and, of course, in the hot tub, Chris and I began to talk about moving in together.

Without paying rent on his apartment and driving 120 miles round-trip a couple of times a week, Chris would have the chance to focus more on his writing. He now wrote two monthly wine columns and was working on a novel, in addition to the freelance copywriting work he did for his prior employer. And I found I liked having Chris around more than I liked being alone. Seamus liked having Chris around, too. That was obvious.

Seamus was coming to the end of his chemotherapy, we were not actively battling Chris's family's opinions, and my friends who had voiced disapproval had, if not changed those opinions entirely, at least stopped voicing them. It was a peaceful time for us. We felt ready to move forward. Though I still worried about the situation with his family, I couldn't deny there was a certain freedom that came with having no outside opinions or negativity to contend with. We decided that he'd move in at the end of summer. I silently wondered if he'd contact his parents with his new address, but I didn't ask. Our living together was only going to add insult to that injury.

Emboldened by our decision and Seamus's improving health, we went out one evening after Chris had taken Seamus for a particularly long walk and we were convinced the dog was tired enough to stay calm. When we got home, Seamus happily greeted us at the garage door, wagging his tail and putting his front paws up on my thighs, the better to reach up and inhale my scent when I bent down to pet him. He seemed fine. Not anxious and not spinning in circles or howling into my face. Nonetheless, I trudged upstairs to the master bedroom to check the answering machine.

The dreaded red light was blinking. I hated to push "play," but I had to. At the beep the original complaining neighbor launched into a plaintive wail describing Seamus's reign of terror.

"Here, listen, it's horrible. It's just horrible. We can't take this. Listen!" She held the phone out and recorded, from her home, Seamus's incessant, frantic, and distinct whiskey howl. Even played back on tape the howling was intolerable.

Point made — and made well.

I hung my head. "I don't even know what to do anymore. We just can't win."

"We'll figure this out," Chris said. "We've got to figure out what triggers it. He doesn't howl every single time we leave. That's impossible."

"I don't know that it is. He's a pretty stubborn dog."

For the next several weeks, we tried to map out when or what set off the separation anxiety. It seemed that the morning walks were at least keeping Seamus calm and quiet during the day. Or maybe that was the medication. But by evening, once I was home, he was not willing to let me leave again. We were also able to tell that if I left and sometime later Chris left, the dog did not howl. But if Chris left and then I left, the dog howled. And if Chris and I left together, the dog howled.

On the evenings we wanted to go out

237

together, I started to leave the house before Chris, drive down the street, park, and wait for Chris to come fifteen to twenty minutes later. Soon though, Seamus caught on to that as well and began to howl when Chris was only twenty feet or so away from the house. And I could never leave the house at night if Chris was not there.

Feeling trapped, I turned to Dr. Davis, Seamus's veterinarian for all things non-cancer. Dr. Davis suggested what we came to call "doggie Prozac," but I hesitated to add more drugs to Seamus's system. Instead, I stopped working with the trainer I could no longer afford and hired my friend's teenaged son to come over and sit with Seamus. It seemed like an easy enough job for a college kid — bring your homework, your girlfriend, whatever you'd like, just be there so my dog doesn't bark.

The first evening he dog-sat, Mitchell brought his girlfriend with him. We ordered pizza for them, heated the hot tub, told them to feel free to use it, and showed them how to work the television. Enjoy, kids! We'd just like an adult evening out, whatever it takes.

When we returned home the teenagers were still on the couch, right where they'd been when we left, only looking a lot less relaxed. Seamus had barked so much they had to keep him in the house with them, blocking his access to the doggie door and the outside. Mitchell's girlfriend, an accomplished singer, tried singing lullabies to calm Seamus. That didn't work. They filled his bowl with kibble — that did not distract him. They petted him and brought him up onto the couch between them — that didn't last. Nothing worked for longer than a few minutes. Seamus clearly did not feel that a pair of teenagers was adequate companionship, and he voiced that opinion all night.

On subsequent evenings my twenty-something single office assistant dog-sat. Seamus liked Kelly well enough and seemed to remain calm, but soon Kelly's schedule got too busy for a beagle-sitting job. A single friend who at the time had no dogs of her own also occasionally babysat as well, but I felt ridiculous calling an adult who refused any payment to come simply sit in my house with my neurotic dog while I went out for drinks with other friends or dinner with Chris.

Just as I thought that after giving up nearly all of my savings for this dog I was now going to have to give up any social life for him as well, a solution presented itself. I learned that a client of mine was opening a doggie day care business right down the street from me.

Seamus and I were first in line to be "interviewed," and when that day came, I was no calmer than a parent with a toddler in need of the perfect Manhattan private preschool. The truth was, I didn't really know how Seamus got along with other dogs. Most of his interactions with other animals took place in clinic waiting rooms. And would they take him knowing he needed medication regularly? Would he howl and cause hysteria among the other dogs? And in the back of my mind also was the obvious fact that this was not going to be cheap.

For once, my worries were overblown. Seamus passed his doggie civility test and became the first overnight guest at Ruff House Pet Resort. Since 6:30 p.m. was the latest pickup time, it would be necessary to leave him overnight any night we were going out to dinner or a movie or any of those things normal people with normal dogs did. Any date Chris and I had would have an extra $35 tagged on — the price of an overnight stay for Seamus.

The first time I tried out Ruff House, Chris and I attended a fundraiser for a battered woman's shelter on whose board of directors I served. I checked my phone for calls or urgent messages every fifteen minutes or so, fully expecting a demand that I come get my dog. I could almost hear the "we can't take it anymore" complaint.

My phone did not ring.

Waking on my own the next morning with only Chris beside me, no beagle face in mine, no urgent howling, and no pressure to get downstairs and into the laundry room where the kibble was kept, was unsettling. I suddenly had all this time on my own. And such quiet! But I had only one cup of coffee before leaving the house to pick up the dog. I didn't need the quiet nearly as much as I needed to know that Seamus was okay.

"He did great!" Denise, the owner, said.

"He did?" I said.

"Yes. He's wonderful. I've never seen such a cuddly beagle. We didn't have too many dogs, and he was the only one staying the night, so Karen, our overnight staffer, just let him sleep on her bed with her."

Uh oh. "She did? All night?"

"Yes. He loved it."

"I'm sure he did. How was he during the day? Did he play with the other dogs?"

"He did for a bit. But every time he saw me, he howled until I came over. He's so funny!" She seemed to be laughing, but I had a suspicion this was not going to end well.

"He is definitely a funny dog. Sorry for the howling."

"Oh, no worries. We're a doggie day care. There's going to be noise. I just went and got him, and he hung out in my office with me, followed me around. He's great company. He's a cuddle monster."

Thus did Seamus complete his dominance. While I had found a solution — a thirty-five-dollar-a-night solution, but a solution — to my problem with the neighbors, every time Seamus stayed at Ruff House he howled his demands that he not be left with the other dogs and his demands were met. I'd arrive to pick him up and he'd be sitting in the receptionist's lap or lounging on a dog bed in Denise's office. Occasionally he'd be running in the yard with the other dogs, but on those times, always, he'd be running the fence perimeter howling. Everyone knew he was battling cancer, so everyone spoiled him. Everyone. Even other dogs' owners, if they knew of his battle, would give him treats, pet him, and mention how the howling was understandable. Sure, as long as you aren't our neighbors.

I told myself that once the treatments were

over and we knew he was cancer-free and not dying within the year, we could really dedicate ourselves to breaking the codependence. I'd find a new trainer with more realistic techniques — after all, this was not an exercise problem. Just one more round of the two chemotherapy drugs, and we'd start anew. I also told myself we'd deal with Chris's family after Seamus's treatments finished as well. One crisis at a time, we'd move forward.

On June 2, Seamus trotted into the veterinarian cancer clinic, flinging out that back right leg and looking fit, if not trim. He was now at 38.5 pounds. He'd gained nearly 20 percent of his body weight. No matter how much walking and how much training we did, Seamus gained weight and kept howling. Maybe it was me who couldn't get it right. Maybe I did lack leadership skills. Maybe I fed him too much. Sure, he was on steroids and weight gain was a common side effect, but it's a common side effect of toast, burritos, cheese, pizza, bacon, potato chips, and fried chicken, too.

Dr. Dutelle greeted Seamus with her usual cheery hello and handful of green cookies. She didn't seem concerned about his weight gain. The last round of Vinblastine was administered intravenously, and Seamus got his last bandage — bright green again — wrapped around his right front leg. All that was left were the Cytoxan pills on days eight, nine, ten, and eleven, and it was over. I was feeling giddy. The finish line was in sight.

"His next appointment will be in a month, and that's when we should do his re-staging," Dr. Dutelle said.

"Re-staging?"

"What we recommend is an aspiration of the liver and spleen, a complete blood workup, and an abdominal ultrasound. This way we can see whether there are any signs the disease metastasized. They will give you a patient care plan with the estimate of costs at the front desk when you check out."

Estimate of cost? We're not done yet? The finish line was slipping away.

I could estimate the cost myself — a lot. More than I could spend. As I paid for that visit, I was handed the estimate anyway: $1,059. About $2,000 more than I could afford.

When day eight came, I put on the rubber gloves to give Seamus the first of the last four Cytoxan pills. I felt a moment of relief. Whatever these future tests and costs meant, at least Seamus was through the treatments. I was determined that we'd finish up and enjoy a summer without medical worries.

A week later Seamus jumped on my bed, walked between Chris and me, and put his face up into mine, making sure I was awake and knew it was time for breakfast. Immediately, I noticed a bump on his eyelid. The bump was small, black, and mole-like, but it was definitely new. I pointed it out to Chris.

"How does a new cancer appear in the midst of all of that chemotherapy? How is that possible?" I said. "Maybe I gave it to him wrong?"

"Whoa. Hold on a minute. You don't know that's cancer. Just have Dr. Dutelle check it when you bring him for his next checkup," Chris said.

"That's two weeks away." Despite all I'd done for the dog already and despite all he was doing to ruin my life, I was still willing to drop everything, put him in my car, and drive off to the veterinarian cancer specialist, particularly when the dog cuddled up and snuggled into the blankets with me as he was doing then.

Chris played the role of rational thinking adult. "I don't think that's cancer. But even if it is, you just finished his last chemo pill a few days ago. What else would they do for him right now? You can wait for his next appointment."

I spun anxiously and considered my options. Chris was probably right, but then I'd nearly waited too long to bring Seamus in when he'd had the white blood cell crash. What if time was of the essence here again? What if he needed surgery immediately? And if he did, how would I pay for more surgery? And more chemotherapy? Because of course I'd do that. Wouldn't I? Could I? Could Seamus tolerate more? Could I tolerate more?

A reasonable compromise, somewhere between overreacting hysteria and cold, heartless bitch, is what I settled on. I took Seamus to see Dr. Davis for another blood test to see how his white blood cell count was doing and to have the eyelid bump examined.

"I don't think this is cancer," he said.

I didn't respond. I just stared at him.

"Don't look at me like that. I know you're thinking that's what I said last time, but this is different. And he's been in chemo for how long now?"

"Six months. Or a hundred years. I can't really remember."

"I'm going to give you a prescription for an ointment. And Valium."

"Valium?"

"For you. And I'm kidding."

I managed a laugh. Dr. Davis and I had always joked around. I hated to think I was losing my sense of humor along with my savings. "Okay, I deserved that. I might be a little stressed."

"Put the ointment on his eyelid twice a day. If it doesn't clear up, we'll excise it."

I knew excise meant biopsy, but I appreciated that he was choosing his words carefully.

I was not optimistic. At $13.80 the ointment seemed almost silly. How could something that didn't cost thousands of dollars possibly help this dog? Not this dog. This dog only gets very, very expensive care. What chance did a little tube of goo have?

A week later, I took another afternoon off work and returned to the cancer clinic for Seamus's follow-up appointment.

Dr. Dutelle sat on the floor facing Seamus. She petted him and rubbed his head, scratching behind his ears as she did so. She remembered to give him his green biscuit, and he howled at her for another.

"How'd he do?"

"Great with the pills. No issues at all. Except, as you can see, the weight gain."

"That should start to go down as we get him off the steroids. He's almost done."

I liked the sound of that so much; I hesitated to point out the new bump.

"Yeah, that will be great. I . . . uh . . . I . . . wanted you to look at that growth on his eyelid."

"I see that. Let's take a look."

Dr. Dutelle lifted Seamus onto the exam table. Seamus immediately turned away from her and sat down. He was not letting her anywhere near his rear end. Dr. Dutelle and I both laughed. Smart dog. I held him while she looked at his eyelid.

"Dr. Davis prescribed an ointment. I've been applying it for about a week. I think it's getting better." I wanted that to be true.

"If this were any other dog, meaning a dog that did not have a history of mast cell tumor, I'd tell you this was likely a meibomian gland inflammation. But we need to be sure this isn't a recurrence."

"So this could be another cancer?"

"I really don't think it is. But I'm going to recommend that we do a fine needle aspiration and a cytology workup."

I stroked Seamus's head. "I don't know how I'd pay to do this all over again."

"No, no, no. I'm not saying this is cancer and we have to do everything over again. Not at all. I just want to make sure we know what we're dealing with."

Fifteen minutes and $240.75 later, Seamus and I returned home and awaited the results.

Dr. Dutelle called me at work the next day and used a lot of big words like "probably meibomian hyperplasia versus meibomian gland adenoma," which, she explained, meant the tumor was benign. She wanted me to continue to use the ointment Dr. Davis had given Seamus and if that did not resolve the mass, she recommended removal. If Dr. Dutelle had been any less caring and sincere and genuine, I would have begun to think she had a lot of student loans to pay off, and Seamus and I were going to be helping for a long, long time. I decided not to think about whether another surgery might be necessary, however minor.

A week later, as Seamus snuggled up against me and I rubbed his belly and petted him, I felt a lump. Jelly-like, and not big, but definitely palpable and under the skin. I felt around to see if it seemed attached to anything, but I couldn't tell — nor did I know what it might mean if it was attached.

Our regular checkup (and yes, by now, I was a patient too — this was every bit my health issue as well) was a week away, on Chris's birthday. For both reasons, I'd already scheduled an afternoon off work.

This time Seamus weighed in at 38.6. He'd only gained one-tenth of a pound. After she examined the eyelid bump and declared improvement, I showed Dr. Dutelle where I had felt the new lump.

"That's great that you found that. It's good that you examine him for bumps and lumps and changes."

I pet Seamus. A lot. He insists on it. It's good to know there's a medical purpose to all that petting. I'm Seamus's first line of defense, I suppose and it seemed he needed a lot of defending.

"So what do you think?"

"If this were any other dog —" I no longer heard what followed this statement. I knew that what followed meant more expensive tests and treatments.

This time the cytology and ultrasound-guided aspirate, along with a re-staging cytology, got me $503.25 in airline miles on my credit card. Attached to the bill was a notice that nutrition consultations with a certified clinical nutritionist were now available. In case I hadn't done enough, I could now get a customized dietary plan to address Seamus's specific nutritional needs.

Dr. Dutelle called promptly, as was her custom, and gave me the news.

"It's a fatty tumor. And his eyelid is fine. His test results came back perfect. Congratulations. Seamus is in complete remission."

Complete. Remission.

I couldn't believe I was hearing the words. I hung up the phone and squealed in excitement. I annoyed Seamus that evening with all of my hugging and kissing on him. Chris was equally excited and grilled steaks for all three of us, though only two of us had champagne. In honor of Seamus's remission, we did not retire to the hot tub out of reach of the dog. We stayed on the couch, with Seamus happily between us.

In the days and months to come, of course, I still worried. I checked his skin constantly and monitored his behavior, watching for a decreased appetite, increased thirst, decreased energy — any change at all. He never changed. He was steadfastly Seamus.

When I came home from work late one evening and saw that he was limping, I refrained from rushing him to urgent care. The next day I took him to Dr. Davis and together we decided for once we would treat Seamus like "any other dog." We'd see if the limp resolved itself in a few days with Seamus on anti-inflammatory medication

251

before we x-rayed and tested for bone cancer. Seamus was walking normally in less than twenty-four hours.

And later, when Seamus scooted his rear end on the floor, eventually I recognized he needed his remaining anal gland expressed (thank goodness for groomers) and was not signaling the return of cancer. Cancer, it should be noted, does not itch.

Not long after, Chris moved in with me. I was confident this would last. This thing we had, whatever it was we called it or anybody else called it, had a future. I felt that most strongly when I found myself referring to Seamus as "our dog." When Chris had picked up Seamus from his surgery, he was picking up my dog. When he took him for checkups in the months and year after treatments were completed, he was taking our dog to our vet. Despite my plans for that alphabet life, "L" for love had leapfrogged to the front of all else. Chris and Seamus and I were a family of three, happy together in our sleek and elegant cougar den. We thought our largest problem was Chris's damaged relationship with his parents.

We couldn't have been more wrong.

■ ■ ■ ■

PART II

■ ■ ■ ■

CHAPTER 13
HIGHLY SUSPICIOUS
OF MALIGNANCY

Seamus's lump was discovered in a doggie spa. Mine was found in the shower.

My left hand brushed over the upper side of my right breast while I was shaving my underarm. Something felt unusual, thick.

If I were a better cook, I would have known that something thickening will soon harden. But ever since Chris moved in, he'd taken over doing all of the cooking in our house. When I got out of the shower, I put my right breast in his face.

"Does this feel strange to you? Like a lump?"

Undaunted by my approach, Chris spent several minutes in careful examination of the specimen presented, while I tried to focus him on the upper right side in a less preferred area near my armpit.

"I can feel what you're talking about, but it doesn't feel like a lump."

"No, it doesn't. But it's weird. I think I

better watch it."

"Probably a good idea."

Over the next couple of weeks, I watched it. Every so often in the shower and in the morning lying in bed I'd run my fingers across the area. I pressed. I poked. And I hoped it would go away, but I knew that it wasn't. I tried to focus on work, particularly since the last quarter of the year is typically the busiest in my practice. And my law office was particularly important now. Having a happy and stable home life had given me the courage to take a huge step professionally earlier that year. I'd left my law partnership and opened a new solo law office. The first ten months had been exhilarating and the office looked to be a success. I couldn't afford to be distracted. But however determined I was to stay focused, my thoughts ricocheted from the logical "I should get to the doctor's office" to the classic "I'm way too busy right now" to the reassuring "I just had a clean mammogram less than four months ago."

That was in early November. By December the thickening was an unmistakable hard lump. No chefs were needed. I was going to the doctor. In December.

The first appointment I could get was December 18, the same day as my office

Christmas party (and one day off from the anniversary of Seamus's first chemo treatment, I couldn't help but note). I had a certain atmosphere in mind for this dinner, and it didn't include a dark cloud of disease.

My new solo law office had opened on January 2 of that year. My plans were big and modest at the same time. I called it "The Teresa Rhyne Law Group, A Professional Corporation" even though it was just me, Michelle (my extremely capable administrative assistant), Laureen (my part-time, very efficient, and sharp paralegal), and the ever-flexible Chris to help with the bookkeeping and manly stuff (lifting water bottles, moving furniture, scaring off door-to-door solicitors, and even, for a while, taking out the trash). And of course there was Seamus, who could now come to work with me on most days. He had a bed and toys in one corner near my desk, although he preferred curling up in the guest chairs directly across from me, as though he had an appointment and urgent matters to howl about. (*More fookin' food! Seriously, people. I need more foooooooooooooood!!*)

I loved my office. For the past year, I'd worked long days and nights and weekends establishing an estate planning practice in just the way I wanted. It had been a pretty good start, but I had a lot more I wanted to do. A whole lot more.

While my former partners, in the splintered groups we had become, had moved into nice offices with much of the same customized furniture and artwork of our old offices, I had chosen to start small and build slowly. I rented a less than "Class A" office space with four simple rooms on a ground floor so my elderly clients could reach us easily. My furniture came from Staples. We painted the walls a vivid green and tangerine orange in an effort to give some personality to our little box. My one splurge was a painting for the reception area — a dog coming in a door, stepping jovially over a "Welcome" mat.

When one of the splinter groups of my former partners gave their law firm a new name that resulted in the acronym RCK, we quickly dubbed them "The Rock." My office had the acronym TRLG. Looking around our tiny, bright, happy ground-floor office that was no longer downtown and much, much smaller and simpler than our prior space, I dubbed us the "Trailer Law Group." A joke among ourselves of course. We generally tried not to say that in front of the clients we were trying to impress.

Two clients of mine — a married couple

— own a successful tile and granite business with customers like the Ritz-Carlton. I remember them telling me how they started in a pickup truck hauling tile around themselves. I liked that image, and I liked what they'd done with their business. Instead of a pickup truck, I had my trailer law group, and instead of tiles I had my books and my documents and my training — over twenty years at that point. And I was just about to make our first expansion move. I was in discussions with the landlord to double my office space to include the recently abandoned space next door at a now much reduced rental rate, thanks to the sinking economy. I was talking to another lawyer, a Georgetown law school graduate, about joining the firm as my first associate. The Christmas cards that held the staff's holiday pay bonuses said "Deck the Double-Wide" — a reference to our expansion plans. It was a heady time, but for this one gathering cloud.

I wanted this office holiday dinner to be memorable. Although sentimentality, at least as far as humans go, is fairly foreign to me, I wanted my staff to know how much I valued all they'd been through with me in the past year and that I knew how hard everyone had worked. Spouses were joining us for the dinner. I wanted everyone to pause, relax, have fun, and really enjoy ourselves and our accomplishments. For once, I had actually wanted to celebrate the holidays.

I went to my doctor's appointment alone without telling anyone but Chris and my assistant, Michelle. Chris offered to accompany me, but I declined. He needed to be home with Seamus, whose separation anxiety had only increased as he got used to Chris being readily available to him. Besides, if Chris came with me, that would mean this appointment was a big deal, and I was still hoping it wasn't.

I lay on the exam table with my paper gown opened, still thinking about the office dinner that evening and reminding myself to sign the bonus checks. The physician's assistant pressed around my right breast with her fingertips, concentration visible in her wrinkled brow as she looked ahead, above me.

"It's over here," I said, placing my own left index finger on the far right side of my breast, near my armpit.

She placed her fingers over mine, and I removed my hand.

"You have to press in a bit, but it's there."

She pressed. "Ah, yes. I feel it. You did

well finding this."

"Except I sort of wish there was nothing to find."

She quieted, palpated my breast, and said the words that launched me out of my denial. "I don't like this at all."

Right. Me neither.

On the exam table, in my paper gown, with the jars of cotton balls, posters on medical issues, and sterile containers on laminate countertops, I recalled Dr. Davis's "we really weren't expecting this" comment after Seamus's diagnosis. Does anyone really ever expect cancer? Is there ever a good time for cancer to appear? And was it not enough that I'd been through this with Seamus already?

Apparently not. I was given a referral slip and told to schedule a mammogram and an ultrasound immediately.

Back in my office I called the facility and learned the next available date was nearly two weeks away. I pressed further, insisting this was an emergency, but to no avail. Fortunately my doctor's office intervened and got them to squeeze me in . . . or, more to the point, squeeze my breast in. A mammogram was scheduled for the following day, a Friday, with an ultrasound on Monday; it seemed even for the doctor they couldn't fit me in for both procedures on the same day.

I went to my office party thinking I could keep my mind off the tests, the look on the P.A.'s face, or the lump itself. And I tried, although my closed office door earlier that afternoon was probably an indication something was up. I hoped they thought it had to do with holiday gifts. At the dinner everyone got a laugh out of the Airstream trailer wine-stoppers and charm that they got with their bonuses, and I don't think anyone was aware anything was wrong (except my assistant Michelle, because she always knows what's going on with me). But it wasn't quite the dinner I had in mind. My mood had shifted.

I drove to the imaging center the next day for the mammogram and endured a painfully slow weekend until I could return again on Monday for the ultrasound. Neither was a particularly difficult procedure; in fact, the weekend between with plentiful time to overthink and worry was more difficult. But I could sense that both the technicians performing the procedures knew they were looking at cancer. There's a distinct lack of eye contact. And no one ever said to me "85 percent of these things turn out to be nothing" as I've heard is frequently said to women who have irregular mammograms. No one ever said "cyst" or "fatty tissue" or "it could be nothing."

No one said anything to me, except that my doctor would be calling me. I began to wish Chris was with me, talking and teasing me away from the precipice.

And the doctor did finally call — at 3:45 p.m. on December 23. I could have guessed the results just from the date. By then I was prepared for the news. As I like to say, my expectations are low and generally met.

"I'm sorry, but the results are highly suspicious of malignancy. I'm going to send you to a surgeon. You need to have the lump removed. We're not even going to bother with a biopsy. This needs to be removed immediately," the doctor said.

He gave me the name and number of a surgeon and told me to call the following morning. In the meantime they'd fax my records to the surgeon's office.

I paused briefly. My thoughts went something like, "Wow. Okay, cancer. Probably. So there it is. First Seamus, and now me. A surgeon? Call a surgeon. Tomorrow . . . I don't want to wait to call tomorrow, I want an appointment tomorrow. Tomorrow is Christmas Eve. No way will I reach a surgeon's office on Christmas Eve. I'm calling right now." And just about all of that thinking was correct.

I picked up the phone.

"Hello. Doctor Riverside Surgeon's office."

"Hi. I've been referred to you by Dr. Primary Care Guy. My mammogram and ultrasound were HIGHLY suspicious of MALIGNANCY and I need an appointment ASAP. I'd like to come in tomorrow."

She didn't bother to contain her chuckle. "We're not open tomorrow. Or the rest of this week."

Thanks. Thanks for your help. This marked the first moment I wanted to say "I have cancer" in a way that, oddly, uses it to my advantage. I didn't. I said, "When can I get an appointment?"

"January 12 is my first opening."

"I need something sooner. This is supposed to be ASAP. It's HIGHLY. SUSPICIOUS. OF MALIGNANCY."

"That's all I've got."

"Then I'll need to get another referral. I can't wait that long."

" 'Kay," said the heartless, unhelpful, evil receptionist. And I could swear I heard her crack her gum. But that might have just been my brain exploding.

I called my doctor's office, angry that he

hadn't given me more than one surgeon's name in the first place, annoyed he didn't know the surgeon they had sent me to wasn't even open for the rest of the week, and fairly certain that at 4:15 p.m. on December 23, I was not going to reach him or a surgeon. I explained the situation to my doctor's receptionist, and then again to the doctor's exchange a half hour later, and again, the next morning, to a different person who answered the phone in the doctor's office. No one called me back.

I left my office at noon on Christmas Eve and went to my hair appointment (oh, the irony). I was situated in the styling chair with the cape draped over me and my stylist behind me asking how much I wanted cut when my cell phone rang. My doctor was calling, at last. His office had been calling around to find a surgeon who could see me "stat." The best they could do was a surgeon in the next town over with an available December 30 appointment. I took the appointment, with only mild trepidation as to how far down the list of "recommended" surgeons they went. Thus, Kelly, my hairstylist, became the next person to know what I was dealing with. Her best friend's mother had recently passed away from breast cancer, so Kelly also became the first person to cry when she heard the news.

I chose not to tell anyone in my family what was happening, since most of them felt the same way I do about Christmas, and at this point there was nothing definitive to tell. I had an appointment with a surgeon, but that's all that was certain. Besides, this year my family had a chance at a nice holiday.

My brother Jay and his wife, Jennifer, with their daughter, McKinzee, and son, Lucas, took a motor home trip to California from their home state of Missouri, and we'd all be together on December 26. This was the same brother who had been in the December motorcycle accident that put him in a coma and intensive care for weeks, but since he had no memory of that and, I'm sure, because he had children, he still enjoyed December. And we were all excited that his two kids and my younger sister's two kids would be meeting for the first time.

Before that family get-together, though, Chris and I had another dinner to get through. Less than three hours from the doctor's phone call, Chris and I were headed to Christmas dinner with his parents.

Christmas dinner would not be the first

time we had seen Chris's family since the blowup, but that didn't mean I'd be comfortable — not under these circumstances or any other.

Chris and his parents had matched each other in stubbornness — neither had picked up the phone or even emailed for more than a year and a half. When Chris moved in with me, I asked if he was sending his new address to his parents. He said no, but he did send the information to his sisters and one of his aunts. And it was through that same aunt and, to a lesser degree, his sisters that there was any contact with his family.

As I had once gone nearly two years without speaking to or hearing from my mother, I knew how these things could happen. In both cases there was not a point where someone had yelled, "I'll never speak to you again." Rather, each side fumes silently and determines to "show" the other side until weeks, and then months, and then more than a year has passed. And how do you reconcile from there? How do you then pick up the phone? What do you say?

For Chris, it was his father who made the first move with an email asking to talk. After a series of emails between them and eventually Chris's mother, too, the four of us agreed to meet.

Chris and I discussed the ground rules between ourselves one evening. Chris insisted that we meet them together. And since it seemed clear to us that much of the problem was his parents' inability to see Chris as an adult, we thought the meeting would go better if they came to our home and saw for themselves that he was, in fact, all grown up. And that it wasn't a bad life he'd chosen, whether they agreed with his choices or not. We also decided that wine or alcohol of any sort was a bad idea — we needed every wit we had to be at full attention, but also, I knew I'd need to watch what I said carefully.

The day of the meeting was an uncomfortably hot August day in Riverside (where temperatures often exceed one hundred degrees), and making matters worse, they had trouble finding our townhome. When they arrived, they were perhaps ruffled from the drive, but I could see they were as stressed about this as we were. I showed them around our home, and they expressed surprise at the view we had and the size and airiness of the condo, which everyone does, but I still figured they were thinking, "So it's not a meth lab in a trailer!"

Eventually we were all seated in our living room, Jim and Trudi on one side and Chris and I on the other, with Seamus seated in the middle of the room, facing Chris's parents but looking nervously from them to us, eyes wide. He seemed to know I needed a buffer. It couldn't hurt to have a cute buffer.

To their credit, Jim and Trudi began the conversation by saying that they realized they had treated Chris like a child and that they had been slow to realize he was an adult entitled to make his own decisions. It was less to their credit that in explaining the "shock" they initially felt at Chris's choice of a girlfriend, Chris's father compared me to a snarling Doberman ready to pounce on their little puppy. He said this while gesturing to Seamus, sitting innocently in the middle of the ruckus. It's tough to say whether Chris or I (or possibly Seamus) was more offended by the analogy, but both of us set it aside after exchanging startled glances. The discussion was difficult and personal and, as I finally came to fully understand, had nothing to do with me — this was a matter between parents and their firstborn. For those reasons, I won't repeat the discussion here.

Eventually the meeting concluded with a form of "agree to disagree" about how things were handled and a resolution to try to move forward. We'd all have to get to know each other as people and not labels; that much we could agree on.

So from August to December we'd been working on the relationship. We'd seen them a few times, and I could see they were trying hard, but I found it difficult to trust their actions or motivations. I continually expected that there'd be trouble once again, as though they were merely gathering evidence against me. I could not get out of my mind how kind and considerate they'd been to me a mere forty-eight hours before instructing Chris to leave me. My relationship with them was thus cordial but distant. I had told Chris that I would appear at the obligatory events — birthdays, holidays, weddings — but that he'd have to attend the voluntary, informal family gatherings alone.

Christmas Eve dinner, with many of the same aunts and uncles I hadn't seen since that fateful Thanksgiving, was on the "obligatory" list. I considered bowing out but couldn't figure out how to say "I can't be there because I'm pretty sure I have cancer even though the doctor hasn't said that yet" in a way that sounded less than pathetic or just an outright bad lie. Staying home alone with Seamus sounded appealing at first as well, but staying home alone with my thoughts echoing around an empty house did not.

And Seamus was another unresolved issue. Chris had kept up a regular walking routine with Seamus, walking him farther and faster than I ever had, but it never helped. The more we gave, the more Seamus became entitled to. We now never left him alone, both out of courtesy to our neighbors and fear they would take their complaints to animal control or the homeowners' association. If Chris and I both needed to be gone, we hired a dog-sitter or took him to stay overnight at Ruff House, which by then had a new owner, but luckily Marti was as adoring of Seamus as Denise had been. But I didn't want to leave Seamus overnight on Christmas Eve because we wouldn't be able to pick him up until the twenty-sixth. The one part of Christmas I'd come to enjoy was the morning alone with Chris and Seamus, a fire, a strong cup of coffee, and a stack of books that were our usual gifts to each other. I didn't want to give that up, especially under these circumstances. I needed my support group of two.

We decided to take Seamus with us.

Chris's parents' neighborhood was not, however, one that would tolerate a howling beagle. For that matter, their home décor was not one that would tolerate a hyperactive beagle with a penchant for luxurious beds that bordered on obsession. Although they were "dog people," Chris's family's dogs tended to be like them — beautiful, tidy, well-behaved, and from small, tight-knit packs. My family's dogs were like us — big (in size or personality), unruly, prone to bad behavior, and running about in large packs known to assimilate strays. They were willing to have us bring Seamus along, but there would need to be some rules. We put him in his crate in their garage while we went to a restaurant for dinner.

Without even being present at the dinner, Seamus was once again my buffer. I elicited laughter from the entire table by reporting on how Seamus had earlier that week eaten nearly three pounds of gourmet cheese, courtesy, once again, of the deliveryman's failure to read the note "do not throw packages over fence" posted right above the "dog in yard" sign on our gate. That led to many more stories of Seamus's food escapades, including the now legendary sourdough escapade. I found it easier to not think about the lump or the "highly suspicious of malignancy" message if I engaged in conversation, rather than sitting alone with my concerns, which is what I generally did around his family.

Once we returned to Chris's parents' home, Seamus was released from his crate and allowed to join the festivities. Chris made sure my wineglass was filled and Seamus was occupied with toys. I sat on the floor of the formal living room with Chris's sister, Courtney. Courtney is the youngest child in the family by several years, and she plays that role well. She is perpetually the center of attention. In other words, she was the perfect person for me to spend the evening with. She kept up a steady stream of conversation about I don't know what with no need for me to reply much more than to occasionally nod. Seamus ran in and out of the room, sniffing around the table and approaching me to see if I might have any handouts. Finding no food available, he'd run from the room chasing after Chloe, the small, adorable cockapoo that had been Chris's parents' family pet for fourteen years and reminded me of my childhood dog Tippy.

We left at ten that night, with Chris driving and Seamus exhausted and resting in his crate for the hour-long ride home.

"Well, that went better than I thought with Seamus," I said.

"It did?" Chris said.

"Well, yeah. He didn't seem to be too much trouble. And your parents seemed fine with him."

Chris turned to look at me, astonished. "He took a dump in the middle of the living room."

"He did?"

It's fair to say I was distracted. I don't know that I could have managed knowledge of cancer on the horizon and dog shit on the ivory carpet simultaneously. I also don't know how Chris, or his parents for that matter, managed to keep that odiferous fact from me, but I'm glad they did.

The three of us got our quiet Christmas day home alone. Chris and I both splurged on books for each other, food for the three of us, and new toys for Seamus, with each of us trying to outdo the other on the latter. Yes, by then we knew it was wrong — very wrong — to spoil this dog in this way, but it was endlessly amusing to see Seamus toss the newest toy in the air, chomp it in his jaws, and hear the frantic squeaking noise repeatedly until we chased him around the house. He had no use for the toys that did not squeak. No rubber toys or cuddly toys for Seamus. Just toys with squeakers for hearts — all the better to rip them out, leaving a trail of stuffing.

The following day we drove to my father's home that he shared with his wife, Nancy, in the desert near Palm Springs. There were fourteen of us together that day. And two dogs. Seamus, of course, and Max, my dad's Australian shepherd.

My Christmas gift to everyone was a family photo, shot by a professional photographer friend of mine. At the time I planned this it served two purposes — I didn't have to shop for everyone and it would be a once-in-a-lifetime gift everyone would enjoy. Now, the photography session would nicely serve a third purpose — it would record for all posterity the final moments before cancer invaded our family and it would distract me nicely from that fact.

We had four more days to muddle through before I could finally see a surgeon.

CHAPTER 14
DR. GOOD KARMA

"This cannot be the place," I said.

"Check the address again," Chris said.

I looked at the paperwork in my lap, then I handed the referral sheet to Chris.

"It doesn't even look like a medical clinic," I said.

"I was thinking that. It looks like an old real estate office or something."

"And it was a gas station before that."

We stared at the gray, cracked-stucco, two-story building at the end of a mostly vacant strip mall.

"Well, let's go in. Maybe it's better inside?"

Chris held open the door of the clinic for me. I stepped inside.

The waiting room was filled to capacity. Each patient seemed to have three or more children in tow. A man brushed by us, not waiting to be all the way outside before lighting up his cigarette. Three feet from the door was good enough for him.

I turned back to Chris. "I have insurance."

"Apparently this is what's available during the holidays," he said. "Look, we're here. It's just a consultation. At least talk to the surgeon."

"It looks dirty. I don't want to be in a dirty surgery center."

"Well, let's hope this isn't where surgery is done. Go check in. Maybe they send you off to a different place after you check in."

"Your optimism is astounding."

At the reception desk I was handed a clipboard full of paperwork and told to take a seat.

There was no seat available.

We leaned against a wall while I tried to fill out paperwork until finally one patient was called back and two children trailed after her, opening up a row of seats in the far back corner of the room.

Seated, I concentrated on the paperwork and kept my head down.

"Is that actually Astroturf?" Chris pointed at the bright green grass-like flooring.

"Maybe just industrial carpet?"

"There's no padding."

"How do you know?"

He pointed to the corner of the room. The Astroturf carpet had peeled back and disintegrated, exposing the concrete floor and a few candy wrappers. "Did you tell them you had insurance?"

"I'm going to see the surgeon. But I don't think I can be treated here. This is awful."

The man who left to smoke returned and took the seat next to Chris, bringing his tobacco smell and cough with him.

We waited forty-five minutes — through the smoker's throat clearing, the children's tantrums, and several loud, mundane cell phone conversations — before I was finally called back to an exam room. Chris followed me and sat with me for another fifteen minutes while we waited for the doctor.

By the time Dr. Tamil entered the room, I was anxious and angry. Why was it so hard to get medical care even with a "highly suspicious" condition? I recalled Dr. Sorority Chick and her cold, uncaring attitude and tried to steel my resolve. I would get some answers, whatever it took.

But Dr. Tamil was reserved and quiet. Despite her surroundings, she had a dignified air, and her opening remarks disarmed me immediately.

"I am sorry for your wait. I understand this is difficult, and we are, unfortunately, severely understaffed this time of year," she said.

"That's because you are the only clinic open during the holidays, apparently."

She nodded, resignedly. "I'm afraid that's close to the truth."

She had, however, already read my charts and reviewed my mammogram and ultrasound. And she did not rush through our appointment.

I lay back on the exam table while she palpated my right breast.

"It's very good you found this."

"So I've been told. But somehow, I don't feel good."

"I understand. It is a problem. But I do not recommend surgery first. I disagree with your primary care physician. You are young. There is no reason to have more scars than necessary. I would recommend a biopsy first, to be certain we know what you are dealing with. Then we can proceed to surgery, if necessary."

"Meaning if this is cancer?"

"Yes."

"We don't already know this is cancer?"

"Not for certain, no. I don't want to mislead you. It does not look good, but a biopsy would be recommended before surgery."

I sat up and closed my gown. "Okay. When can we do that?"

Dr. Tamil sighed and slouched up against a counter. "If you were in a specialized cancer center, the biopsy would take place in the next couple of days, most likely. If the biopsy showed cancer, we'd schedule an MRI and then surgery, and this would all occur in a week to two weeks."

"Two weeks?" That seemed both quick (to be in surgery) and interminably long (to have cancer hanging out in my body).

"Two weeks if you were at a specialty cancer hospital. That is not here. Not in Riverside County. You have good insurance and you could go to City of Hope or UCLA or some such facility, and that is how things would proceed. I and some other doctors are working hard to get that out here, but it does not exist here. Not yet."

"So what happens here?"

Dr. Tamil now sat, her weariness as palpable as my tumor. She explained the long, through-the-looking-glass process ahead of me.

I met my friend Stacey for lunch a few days later.

"Um, wow. You look great. Nice suit. Are you losing weight?" she said.

"Probably."

"Shit. What's going on?" Stacey is the same friend who pointed out to me that when something is really wrong in my life she can tell because I always look really, really well put together. Her methods were tried and true.

Every year after Christmas, she and I got together to compare who had suffered the most through the holidays. I knew this year I would win the "whose holidays sucked more" contest. I told her about my highly suspicious lump and the visit to the Medical Clinic for the Holiday- and Hopeless.

She leaned forward. "You have to get out of town. Go to UCLA."

"No, it was okay. The surgeon herself turned out to be very nice. She seemed quite capable. I liked her. And the surgery won't be in that facility. Turns out that was a temporary space."

"So when's the surgery?"

"Well, that's complicated." I stirred the lettuce on my salad plate. "And a bit unbelievable. I'm still waiting for them to schedule the biopsy. I personally carried my ultrasound and mammogram films to the radiologist's office hoping to speed up the process. But no. I was told he'll review them, someday, apparently, and the scheduler will call me with the date for the biopsy. Right now, it looks like January 16. I'm waiting to hear if they can get me in sooner. And Dr. Tamil is trying to help with that."

She would not have been surprised to know I was in my immaculate Tahari black suit and black patent leather Cole Haan Nike Air heels as I drove around picking up and delivering my medical records to various offices overcrowded with patients, without once smearing my red lipstick or disturbing my carefully coiffed and recently highlighted hair.

"That's twelve more days. It's absurd. And that's just for the biopsy. Then what?" She stabbed her Caesar salad.

Yes. It was absurd. As Dr. Tamil explained, locally it was three weeks before the biopsy could occur, a few days to a week for the results. If the biopsy showed cancer, we'd then schedule an MRI, which would take another couple of weeks. Once we obtained the MRI results, we could schedule surgery, and that would be anywhere from three to six weeks later. All totaled, if this was cancer, it'd be hanging out in my body for another nine to twelve weeks. Unfathomable.

But what choice did I have?

I was already so tired. Ever since the

"highly suspicious of malignancy" call, I'd been unable to sleep or find medical care. No sooner did I make it through Christmas and to a surgeon than all medical offices closed up shop and stopped answering the phones for the New Year's holiday. By the time I was having lunch with Stacey, the dark cloud of cancer had been hanging over me for nearly two weeks, and I still didn't know if I had breast cancer. I didn't even have an appointment for my biopsy, let alone any surgery.

Once I shared that with Stacey, she became even more adamant. "Look, you can't stay in town for this. You can't. We don't have the specialists you need. We don't even have enough doctors. Obviously we don't have the facilities. I'm telling you, you need to get to UCLA."

"I don't know how to do that. Do I just call UCLA? And who? What do I do, just call the UCLA Medical Center and say 'Hi, I may have cancer. Can somebody there check it out for me?' to whoever it is that answers the phone?"

"Pretty much, yes. That's what you do. I'll get you the number. What kind of insurance do you have?"

"I have a PPO."

"So you can go wherever you want? You

don't have to stay in their groups, right?"

"Yeah, I guess so. The surgeon was telling me that with my insurance I could go to a cancer center and the timeline would be greatly compressed."

Until I said that, I didn't realize that Dr. Tamil may have been suggesting that I do exactly that. I didn't realize that maybe she knew that the timeline locally wasn't acceptable and was encouraging me in the only way she could to seek more timely care.

What an idiot I'd been! I needed to get out of town! Even the surgeon thought so!

"Exactly." Stacey stabbed at her Caesar salad again.

On my way back to my office I drove through Starbucks for a double latté. Caffeine for lunch was becoming a staple. Within an hour of my return to my office Stacey had emailed, forwarding the email from her own UCLA doctor.

Hi Stacey —

Is it a breast lump? If so, I can probably get her in to see someone sooner . . . but let me know the location of the lump, so I know who exactly she should see.

Hope you're well,
Jeannine

284

I couldn't reach my doctors by phone for days, and here Stacey had received a personal email from her physician within an hour. An email? From a doctor?

I responded:

Stacey (and Dr. Rahimian):
Thank you both for your prompt response.

It is a breast lump and it is continually described as "right breast 10 o'clock" – which is pretty accurate. It's most easily felt when my arm is lifted up because it's approaching the underarm area. I've been told it's not a cyst (this was after the ultrasound).

I'd appreciate a referral. Right now I'm scheduled for a biopsy on January 16. Thank you,

Teresa

The response came five minutes later directly from Dr. Rahimian, a gift from the universe, bearing yet another gift:

Hi Teresa,
I would recommend Dr. Amer Karam. He's a gynecologist at UCLA who has a specialty in breast biopsies and surgery as well. I trust his surgical skills and his

judgment very much. I just called the office and his next available appointment is January 8. The number to call to make an appointment is 310-xxx-xxxx.

Let me know if you need help with anything. When you see him, let him know that I referred you.

Jeannine

I called immediately and was given an appointment with Dr. Karam for January 8 at 2:00 p.m. Two days later.

When I told Chris, he was more relieved than I had been.

"I'm really glad you did that. I know you love and support Riverside, but it's obvious this time they don't have what you need."

"I guess I found that hard to believe. I think I didn't want to believe it."

"You had to leave town for Seamus's care. You should at least be willing to do the same for yourself. Remember how much time you spent demanding an appointment for Seamus? You called and cajoled until you found a place and a time that was acceptable."

"I forgot that. I'm more successfully aggressive about veterinary care, apparently."

Chris pulled me close and wrapped his arms around me. "Yeah, let's work on that, 'kay? Pretend you are doing this for Seamus."

The night before my appointment with Dr. Karam, Chris and I were both sitting up in bed reading. Well, he was reading. I was staring at the print on the pages of the book I was holding.

Though I had no official diagnosis, I knew I had cancer. The feeling had only increased with each medical personnel I encountered.

Chris looked over at me and put his book down. "You doing okay?"

"I'm trying to get used to the idea of cancer. Because I have a feeling this really is cancer."

He put his hand on my leg. "Yeah, I kind of think it is, too."

"You do? You? The eternal optimist?"

"Yeah. I hate to say it, but since you've said it . . . It just seems like the doctors know this is cancer."

Seamus was snoring in between us. I petted his head, and he yawned, stretched, and rolled over for a belly rub.

"At least we know how to handle cancer, right?" Chris said. "And, you know, I got to see another woman feel you up, and that's not all bad."

I threw a pillow at his head. "I'm sure that

was totally erotic."

"Actually, no. It nearly ruined any girl-on-girl fantasy I ever had. That's just not what I pictured it would be like."

"Dr. Tamil and I are both sorry, I'm sure."

"Do better."

I moved closer and snuggled in next to Chris, squeezing Seamus between us, since he wasn't about to give up any ground. I felt relieved — supported and relieved to have spoken the words and to have had an honest response from Chris that was without platitudes or false hope. He'd even made me laugh. We weren't as frightened as we might have been had there not been a thirty-pound, brown-eyed, food-stealing cancer survivor cuddled between us on the bed when we talked, giving us a living reminder that cancer isn't always a death sentence. Although the word *cancer* had now been spoken and was sitting there in bed with us, we were calm.

"Mostly, I'm worried about working through this," I said. "Whatever treatment I go through, I've got to keep the office opened."

"We'll figure it out. We can do this."

I liked the sound of "we."

Since Chris moved in with me, he had not

been back to Los Angeles as much as he would have liked. Sixty miles becomes a lot longer distance when there isn't a budding romance at the other end. Where he had lived was very near the UCLA Medical Center, so we made plans for dinner with two of his friends following my appointment with Dr. Karam. With a 2:00 p.m. appointment, there's no point in getting back on the freeway to drive home right after. LA traffic is its own disease.

We pulled into the UCLA Medical Center on the same campus where Chris and I had met many years earlier in a writing class. The Medical Center is a sprawling, gleaming white compound with three high-rise towers, one low-rise administrative building, and underground parking that could house a city, which must be why they charge eleven dollars per car, even if you're only there for an hour.

"You know another thing that's like finding treatment for Seamus?" I said.

"Driving to LA?" Chris said.

"Well, yes, but also the 'shit, this is going to cost a fortune' feeling." I pointed to the cars parked in the "reserved for doctors" spaces — Mercedes, Mercedes, BMW, Jaguar, Mercedes, BMW, Porsche.

"It's West LA. Those cars are required.

And leased."

We went to Tower 200 and walked down a gleaming, sunlit hallway with large, bright artwork. The sign outside Suite 240 said "Gynecology & Obstetrics," which stopped me for a moment until I recalled Dr. Karam's dual specialty.

Obviously, it stopped Chris, too. "I'm not going to lie. That sign is freaking me out," he said.

"Really? More than cancer?"

"Good point . . . I think."

I signed in, and we took our seats. There were seven women and one man waiting with us. I found myself wondering, were all these people cancer patients? Did everyone have a sad story, like the dogs I couldn't look at in that other waiting room? But no, that wouldn't necessarily be the case here. I wasn't yet a diagnosed cancer patient, and I suspected the whining, loudly complaining young woman with the sheepish man at her side was probably there because she was newly pregnant. I don't think cancer patients are really all that pissed off at having to wait twenty minutes. We've got bigger things to be pissed off about.

I was called back to the exam room almost immediately. Chris followed.

"You know Dr. Karam is a man, right?

This isn't going to be as much fun for you," I said.

"I have different reasons for being here this time."

The staff was friendly and efficient, and in no time at all I was dressed in the customary paper towel with sleeves, and Chris and I were alone in the exam room waiting for the doctor. I held the films I'd picked up from Riverside and all of the various medical records I'd gathered from the imaging center, the other surgeon, and the radiologist. We didn't have to wait long.

Dr. Karam bounced into the room, smiling and energetic. He was average height but thin, with a head of wild dark curls, the requisite white lab coat, trendy glasses, and clogs. And he was young. Really, really young. Still, he exuded confidence and intelligence. I liked him instantly.

"You look too well to be a patient," he said while shaking my hand.

I refrained from saying, "You look too young to be a doctor." I was twenty-three when I graduated from law school, and I had hated it when people told me I was too young to be a lawyer.

"I hope so. I don't really want to be a patient."

"That's true. No one really does." He

smiled warmly.

I introduced Chris, and the three of us chatted and discussed why we were there and the difficulty we'd had getting an appointment in our hometown.

"I'm sorry you had trouble. That's a long time to wait when you get news like this," Dr. Karam said. "Let's see what we have."

I handed him my files and films, and he studied them carefully, finally looking up and saying, "May I examine?" Which is a nice way of saying "show me your breasts" without also throwing Mardi Gras beads.

This would mark the fifth exam of my right breast (not counting Chris's exam) in the last month. I could find the lump in under a second by now, but if you were new at it, there was a little searching involved. Dr. Karam found the lump easily though and said simply, "I see."

"I was kind of hoping you wouldn't."

"You can get dressed. I'll be back in a moment, and we'll talk." He left carrying the records.

Chris and I looked at each other. "That was fast," he said.

"He seems so young," I said.

"He does. But he seems to know what he's doing."

I was glad Chris liked him, too. "He does.

I like him. Where is his accent from?" I had unending faith that Chris could, because he usually did, identify (and subsequently impersonate) just about any accent.

"Well, by the name, I'd say he's from the Middle East, but there's a western European accent as well. Interesting."

Dr. Karam was back in about five minutes, looking and sounding more serious. "If you can wait here, I'd like to go downstairs and see if I can get you in for a biopsy this afternoon."

"This afternoon? Today?"

"Yes. Is that possible?"

"Well, yes. We're here. It's just an afternoon procedure and I can drive back home and go to work tomorrow?"

"Yes, most people can. It shouldn't be a problem."

"This sounds serious." Of course, I knew it was, but I also knew these were my last few moments of pushing this away. Sitting in bed, safely at home with a beagle between us, and saying "It's cancer" to Chris was suddenly very different from sitting in a doctor's office waiting for him to say "It's cancer." The diagnosis is more serious when the person saying it is in a lab coat than it is when he's wearing pajamas.

"Let me show you," Dr. Karam said.

We followed him to another small room where my films were placed on a light board — the July mammogram that didn't show a thing, next to the December mammogram with a white mass. He pointed to the mass.

"This is what we are concerned with. As you can see, it wasn't there before. This is something we don't like. I would like to have it biopsied right away, and we can also schedule an MRI. If you don't need the MRI, we can cancel it, but if you do, we'll be ready to go."

"If I do? Meaning, if I have cancer?"

"Yes."

"And I take it you think it is cancer?"

He leaned his head to the right and focused on me. His voice was kind. "It walks like a duck and talks like a duck . . . We're going to treat it like a duck right now."

At the time, I wasn't able to laugh at the thought of a duck in my breast. I didn't make the "duck breast" jokes until later. "Biopsy it is," I said.

We waited in his office while he went downstairs. In twenty minutes, he arranged a biopsy while Chris and I discussed rearranging our dinner plans.

Dr. Karam returned, looking dejected. "I'm sorry, but they can't do it this afternoon. It's too late already. I've scheduled it for tomorrow morning. Nine a.m. Is that all right?"

I couldn't imagine saying no. "Yes. That's fine. We'll just have to leave at 5:00 a.m. to be here on time, but it's not like I'm going to sleep tonight."

After a few minutes of discussion, Chris and I decided we'd meet his friends and go out to dinner after all. Why not socialize while we still can? And always, there was the traffic concern.

Thus a few short hours after I'd been told the lump in my breast walked and talked like a cancer duck, I was in an Italian café in Brentwood meeting Chris's friend Ashley for the first time, along with his longtime friend Emily and her date that evening, whom neither Chris or I had ever met (and would never see again). I briefly wondered if I was allowed to drink wine before a biopsy and then ordered some anyway.

Dinner went on surprisingly normally with introductions and discussions of how the holidays had been until someone asked what we were doing in LA.

Oh, that. Right.

They were all in their early thirties and, I assumed, would be pretty unfamiliar with breast cancer. I suddenly felt very middle-aged as I explained how we'd spent our afternoon.

"Oh my god! And you're just calmly here having dinner with us," Emily said.

"Well, yes. You've all been a nice distraction, and it beats sitting on the freeway, right? Sorry to be a downer though. I'm sure that's not what you guys want to be hearing from a virtual stranger."

"My mom had breast cancer. I know all about it. I went to her appointments with her, so I know a surprising amount about breast cancer. Just let me know how I can help. Call me anytime," Ashley said, becoming the first of a long list of people offering help.

"Oh, I'm sorry to hear that. How is your mom doing now?" I said. Chris pushed his thigh against mine under the table.

"She died a year ago. I know you don't need to hear that right now. Sounds like you caught this early. You'll be fine. If you need any referrals, though, let me know. My mom had great doctors."

Shit. She died. From the very thing I likely had. I struggled for a response. What does one say? How does one make all this go away, just for one more evening? I was new at this. There was so much to learn.

"I'm sorry for your loss. And thank you for offering to help. I will keep that in mind if I need it. But for now, let's just forget I said anything and enjoy a nice evening ignoring cancer, shall we?"

The clinking of wineglasses was a nice transition and muffled the exhales of relief.

We were home by eleven, and although we went straight to bed, I couldn't sleep. I tossed and turned, wondering if I should be telling my family, worrying about the possibility of chemotherapy, a mastectomy, hair loss, nausea . . . a variety of possibilities, all horrible. I tried to stay focused on the biopsy — the thing immediately in front of me. That much didn't sound bad. Dr. Karam had described the procedure. I'd lie still for about thirty to forty minutes while they insert a needle into my breast tumor area. They use a tool that he described as a little "Pac Man" that extracts three to five chunks out of the tumor. And it's over. I'd have bruising and maybe some pain, but not much. And when it was over, I'd finally have some answers. I took a deep breath and curled myself up against Chris, spooning around him. I finally fell asleep just a couple of hours before my alarm clock rang.

I had no funny little beagle howling in my face and ushering me downstairs to give him breakfast. Seamus was at Ruff House, where it looked like he'd have to stay another night unless we were able to get back from the biopsy by six that evening. I hoped we would. I knew I'd feel better if Seamus were home with us.

Despite leaving the house at six, Chris and I got stuck in morning traffic. We arrived by 9:15 but as it takes a good fifteen minutes to get parked and get to the building, we were a full half hour late by the time we checked in at the imaging center.

"Teresa Rhyne," I said as I signed the check-in sheet.

"Your birthdate?"

"February 17, 1963."

"What month?"

"February."

"This says March."

I wasn't really sure what to do about that. I was nervous — you know, breast cancer biopsy and all — but I was still pretty sure I knew my own birthday. I'd had a few of them by then.

"Okay, well, it must be wrong." I showed her my driver's license.

"We'll get it fixed. Have a seat."

When I was called back to the procedure room, I had to go alone. No visitors were allowed in the surgery room. I kissed Chris good-bye, and he squeezed my hand. We probably looked like a Renaissance painting of a couple parting, their fingertips slipping apart as they look longingly back at each other. Or we did in my head anyway. I'd come to rely on Chris's cajoling me out of my pessimism and distracting me from the seriousness of what I was undergoing. I didn't want to be alone, but I was.

I was of course given a hospital gown to change into, but I only had to strip from the waist up. This was mildly comforting to me. No real medical procedure is performed on a patient still wearing jeans.

Once again someone in scrubs read from the computer screen and got my birthdate wrong.

"I'll get that fixed right away," she promised.

I smiled and made a mental note to continue to say my birthdate as "February 17 but your computer thinks it's March." I also noted that UCLA's computer system was not nearly as effective as the felt-tip marking of "SHAY-MUS" on his chart. I had visions of not being allowed surgery since my driver's license did not say March 17.

As I moved from place to place — gown change, blood pressure check, weight, temperature, another waiting room — the feeling that I was, in fact, a cancer patient increased. There was a woman who seemed to be one step ahead of me in each of the procedures. She was visibly shaken, distraught even. I wondered if she already knew her diagnosis, but I didn't talk to her. There seemed to be an unwritten "do not speak" rule followed even by the medical personnel. The only words spoken were instructions on what to do when. Move here. Wear this. Wait here. Sign this.

Finally it was time for the ultrasound, and I was led to a small room with a lot of complicated, computerized machinery. The radiologist was a resident who introduced herself as Dr. Koo. She too looked fifteen years old. Did UCLA only hire new graduates? Is there a special recruitment for child prodigies? After two years do they make them move on, citing their loss of youthful appearance? This was west Los Angeles, after all.

In the middle of the ultrasound of my "right breast ten o'clock," Dr. Karam poked his head into the room to confirm the MRI he'd scheduled. If it turned out not to be cancer, we could cancel the MRI, he reminded me.

"You seem to only be talking about this being cancer, so I'm guessing we won't be canceling that MRI. I assume you know already that it's cancer." I continued to push for a diagnosis — I needed something definitive. And I suppose I was still hoping the duck was actually a chicken or a goose or something not-duck.

"I'm 95 percent certain it's cancer," Dr. Karam said.

Dr. Koo exhaled. Clearly she also could tell it was cancer but couldn't say anything. When Dr. Karam left, Dr. Koo launched into a "survival rates are really high when you catch it this early" spiel. I was alarmed to hear this. Survival?? What does that have to do with anything? I've just got this little cancer thing; we'll deal with it and move on. No dramatics, please. Dr. Koo did not know that Seamus had already taught me what she was trying to tell me. She did not know that I did not hear "death" when the word *cancer* was spoken.

Then Dr. Koo said something even more absurd. She smiled shyly. "Your doctor seems really young." This, coming from Little Dr. Cindy Koo — who looked no more than twenty-two — still makes me laugh.

It was at last time for the biopsy.

The operating room for the biopsy procedure was large and well-lit, with one exam table, a tray of instruments, and heavy overhead lights. Several women in white lab coats and scrubs were present, and their general good moods and casual demeanors relaxed me.

My tumor sulking there at ten o'clock, and far on the side of the breast, near the underarm, meant that for the radiologist fellow Dr. Overstreet (another woman) to get to it, I had to lie on the table on my left side but with my top half twisted back to the right and my arm moved even farther back. This is remarkably similar to the position one assumes for certain chiropractic adjustments . . . which I've been getting from my father the chiropractor since I was five or six years old. I moved easily into position. The needle that goes into the breast to numb it for the biopsy, however — not a lot can prepare one for that. It stung. Dr. Overstreet held my hand and squeezed with me when the needle was poked in.

The numbing worked mercifully quickly, and when the Pac-Man instrument was inserted I didn't feel a thing. But I heard it. I heard it shoot and snap like a staple gun. When they numb the breast, they should do the same for the ears.

The process was quick. Five staple-gun shots and it was over. A cotton ball was pressed to my breast and taped down and then I was helped up slowly.

"How do you feel?" the doctor asked.

"Good, I suppose."

"Good. That's all we can hope for at this point."

"So no one hops off the table elated?"

"Hardly ever," she said. "You'll go with Dr. Koo again now. She's going to do a mammogram."

"A mammogram? Now? After that?" I could feel the bruise growing in my breast. And now they want that same breast pressed between plates of glass and squeezed until the sides touched?

"Think of it as before and after pictures."

And if you think a normal mammogram is painful, try it after Pac-Man has attacked your breast. Let's just say there was bleeding.

Chris was again allowed to join us. While Dr. Koo bandaged me up again, we had a Harvard (where she went) versus Princeton (where Chris went) supremacy discussion. UC Santa Barbara (where I went) won. After all, I was the one with a 95 percent chance of cancer and a bleeding breast.

CHAPTER 15
LIKE A DUCK

It was after business hours, my staff had gone home, and I was alone in my office when Dr. Karam called.

"I'm sorry to tell you this, but it is what we thought it was," he said.

"It's a duck?"

"Close. It's invasive ductal carcinoma."

"Oh. Duct-al. Your accent is worse than I thought." I could push this away with humor only a little bit longer before I'd be left alone in a room with cancer.

He did laugh, but only briefly. "It's what's known as triple-negative breast cancer, which is, unfortunately, an aggressive cancer. You are very lucky — it's very good you caught it early."

"I'm not feeling lucky right now."

"No, I understand."

"So surgery, of course. Will I need chemotherapy?"

"Most likely, I think. Yes. With this type of

cancer chemotherapy is the protocol. But we'll know more after the surgery, and then you will talk to an oncologist. I feel comfortable we can do a lumpectomy. We'll know more after the MRI tomorrow."

I already had it on my calendar. When I hung up with Dr. Karam, I called Chris.

"I guess we knew this was coming," Chris said.

"Yeah. Still feels a little weird to have it confirmed — to finally know I have cancer. Like, as I'm sitting here talking to you there's cancer running around in my body."

"Weird, I know. You okay?"

"I think so. We have to go back to UCLA tomorrow. And I guess I should start to let my family know."

"True. There's still time for that though. Maybe come home early tonight?"

I looked at the files on my desk, the papers in my inbox. "Not like I'm going to be able to concentrate anyway. But I do have a few things to finish up. I'll see you in a few hours."

"Okay. I love you. Lots."

"I love you, too. Kiss the beagle for me."

I hung up the phone and stared at the wall in front of me for a few minutes before going back to work. When work quickly turned to a shuffling and rearranging of papers and rereading the same sentence without even vague comprehension, I went home.

Chris poured me a glass of wine, and we talked about what I should say to my family. How does one drop the word *cancer*? It can't be done lightly, and since I hadn't prepared anyone, I was going to have to start at the beginning with each phone call. I suspected they were each going to question why I hadn't mentioned anything sooner.

I called my dad first, but I reached only his voice mail.

I called my brother next, and again I reached voice mail. Both times I struggled with what kind of a message to leave. How will I possibly sound normal? Maybe I should just hang up.

Beep.

"Hi. Um, it's me. Call me back." I hoped they'd realize I meant "tonight."

As I dialed my sister's number, my father did call back.

I was glad it was my dad. The child in me wanted to tell my dad first. I knew he'd be calmer than other family members, stronger, and more likely to respond in the logical manner I greatly prefer. He'd also likely have useful medical information. But I also needed my dad like little girls need their dads — to make the bad things go away. Or at least to make them better.

As an adult, though, I knew that regardless of his outward response he'd likely take it the hardest. I'm not what anyone would call a "daddy's little girl," but we are close and always have been. Also, he's suffered a lot of losses. His parents died together in a car accident when he was two years old. One of his sisters died in childhood. It was his wife who died on December 23. I saw how torn apart he was when my brother had that motorcycle accident, and I didn't want to be the cause of that kind of pain again. It can't be easy to hear that your child has cancer. Even if your child is forty-five years old. I was in that not unusual place of wanting a parent to care for me while also feeling I should be caring for him.

When I told him, he said he wanted to go to my doctor's appointments with me. I was sitting on my bed in my own home, still in a suit and high heels from work, glass of wine on one side of me, Seamus on the other, but I may as well have been in jeans and braces, sitting on my yellow canopy bed with a can of soda and Tippy beside the thirteen-year-old me in La Habra Heights — the last house my parents lived in together before their divorce. I smiled. I liked the idea of having my dad with me at my appointment, but I assured him Chris could handle it for now.

"He's going with you?"

"Yes, of course. He went with me yesterday, too."

"He's a good man. You tell him to take care of you. Doctor's orders." He paused, and I knew he was, as I was, gathering strength. "No. You tell him those are Dad's orders." He stopped again and in a softer voice said, "You sure he can handle it?"

"I'm sure. He's been really, really good. And he's been handling it fine for a few weeks now."

"I can't believe you didn't tell us sooner. You should have told us."

"Jay and the kids were there. It was Christmas. I wanted everything to be okay, at least for a while. Plus, I didn't know anything for certain yet. You would have done the same thing."

He only had to think of that for a brief moment. "Yeah. You're right. I would have."

I hung up the phone and immediately began to reconsider. Maybe I should have my dad come with me. Maybe this was too much for Chris alone. Was I being selfish? Having Chris, and only Chris, with me so far had been comforting and stabilizing for me. But should a thirty-three-year-old have to deal with his girlfriend's breast cancer? His friends were all married and having their first and second children. He'd be even more removed from their life experiences. He'd have no one to empathize with him.

I resolved to talk to him about that. Later.

Telling my mom was difficult for other reasons. I am not prone to drama. Mom is . . . let's just say "not like me." Making matters worse, she and my stepdad, Ted, had retired and moved to Missouri to be near my brother and his family, and the distance was likely to increase, not decrease, the drama. At the time of my diagnosis they were on a driving vacation, headed west. When I called my brother, I mentioned that I'd wait to tell Mom until I could tell her in person once she arrived in California.

"Mom's not going to California," Jay said.

"What? I thought they were driving out here."

"I talked to them yesterday, and they decided to just go as far as Arizona. California is too complicated." If a voice could put air quotes around a word, my brother had just done so with "complicated."

"What does that mean?"

"I don't know. She's your mother."

"Who drives all the way to Arizona from

Missouri but doesn't go another couple hundred miles to see her own two daughters?"

"Your mother." I could see his smile through the phone. Much like parents refer to a misbehaving child as belonging exclusively to the other parent, my brother and I did that with our mother. "Look, she said there were too many people to see in California and she didn't have enough time, so why bother. But you should call her. Obviously she'll come out now."

And there was the tricky part. Did I want her to come out now? Chris was taking me to the MRI, and my dad and I had agreed that he'd be accompanying Chris and me to the surgery consultation with Dr. Karam once we had the MRI results. That was enough support for me. And, thirty years after their divorce, my parents in the same room was still not a comfortable situation. I put off calling her for one more day, telling myself it would give her one more day to enjoy her vacation.

"You know, I've been thinking," I said as Chris and I drove to UCLA the next morning. "It would be the great irony of my life if Seamus lived, but I did not."

Chris knew more than anyone that I have

never been able to read a book or watch a movie, a cartoon, or even a commercial with a dog in it if there is any possibility that the dog suffers or dies. I once made him turn off the Disney movie *Underdog* because the opening scene has a beagle about to be used in a lab experiment. Note, the beagle was in fact Underdog himself, and since this was the beginning of the movie, it seemed fairly obvious the dog would survive. No matter. I could not watch even simulated potential suffering. Chris pointed out that this was a Disney children's movie and thus the dog was not likely to die or suffer. I reminded him what happened to Bambi's mother. Not that I could watch that either, but I had heard rumors.

"That's not funny," Chris said.

"Well, it's kind of funny. And that would be so typical of how my life goes."

"You're not dying. I forbid you to die. The dog lived, and you will, too."

"All we can do is hope I'm as lucky as Seamus."

"You will be."

"I'll do my best. And speaking of thinking I'm going to die . . . I'll call my mom now."

I reached my mother in her Scottsdale, Arizona, hotel room and asked her to put me on speakerphone so my stepdad could

311

hear, too. He's calmer. Much, much calmer. I thought he would help soften the news. But to my surprise, my mother was also quiet.

"I don't know what to say."

"I know, Mom. No one does. But I feel fine, and we caught it early so the prognosis is good." I already felt like this was becoming a canned response.

"What can we do?"

"Nothing right now. Chris is taking me to all of my appointments, and Dad is going to meet the surgeon with us. So for now, everything is under control."

"Well, that's good. Thank Chris for me. He takes good care of you."

"He does. He takes very good care of me."

"And I suppose it's good to have your dad there to meet the surgeon. That will be helpful. But I still want to come out. We're only five hours away."

The phone call was much easier than I expected.

She must have been stunned momentarily. Shortly after, it was her repeated return phone calls with new questions, concerns, and thoughts about whether to drive out to California now or later, among the calls from my younger sister and a few friends, that prompted Chris to say, "You should set up a blog."

"A blog?" At this point, I read only one blog — the one written by the writing instructor responsible for Chris and I meeting. This hardly made me a candidate to blog myself.

"Well, think about it. You write anyway. This way, instead of group emails, you can just post what's going on and whoever wants to check in can. You won't have to spend as much time on the phone, and you won't have to guess who you should include on the emails."

"Hmmm." I would have given more thought to it, but my cell phone rang again.

We arrived on time at the UCLA radiology department. I repeated my hospital mantra: "Teresa Rhyne, February 17, 1963, but you have it in the system as March 17," and waited while the staff person promised to fix the birthdate. Dr. Karam came around the corner, tousled, grinning, and holding a grande Starbucks cup.

"*Hola,* T," he said, all smiles and good energy.

"Sure, you can be happy. You have Starbucks and you're not getting an MRI," I said.

"This is true. Do you like Starbucks?"

"It's more like lust."

"Then you'll be happy to know there is one on campus. I'll show you where later."

"Don't bother showing me. Just bring me one when I wake up after surgery. It's that 'no liquids after midnight' rule I'm worried about."

"I will do that!" He said this in a way that made me believe him. Or at least gave me hope that the surgery would be simple and in the end, he'd be standing at my bedside with a cup of French roast. He was that comforting.

"So, what are you doing down in radiation?" We were two floors down from his office, and I wasn't expecting to see him. He's a surgeon, after all.

"I decided to go with you. I will watch what they do."

It did not occur to me to wonder why he would do this. I just thought he was an amazingly kind and involved doctor — which, of course, he was.

In the MRI tube, while Chris and Dr. Karam chatted outside, I planned out the blog. It made a lot of sense. I had anticipated calling friends to let them know what was going on but had a hard time getting past "Hi, I'm sure you want to know every detail going on in my life, so yeah, I've been diagnosed with breast cancer and this is obviously a big cry for attention." And where's the cutoff for who gets a call? People I'd known many years? A few years? Months? People I loved? Liked? Tolerated? And who has the energy for all those phone calls? A massive group email seemed the logical answer. But then, how do I continue to keep informed those who want to be kept informed, without perhaps oversharing with folks who maybe didn't want to know or didn't care?

A blog made sense.

I could set up the blog and send a mass email letting everyone know at once, and if anyone wanted any more detail, they could check the blog when and if they pleased. This seemed eminently sensible. The planning going on inside my head blocked out most of the loud gonging, ringing noise in the tube.

Just about when I started thinking I'd like to scratch my nose and maybe turn my head, the radiologist's voice came over the intercom.

"Great job, Teresa. You were really calm. We're going to bring you out now."

They backed me out of the machine, like a tray of cookies coming out of the oven (but let's hope I wasn't overbaked).

Dr. Karam had to leave before I was done

(what? For a surgery?), but Chris remained waiting patiently, tapping away at his iPhone.

"So, I decided you're right. I'm going to need you to set up that blog," I said.

"It's already done."

"What? Doesn't it need a name?" I'd come up with one during all my tube thinking.

"You're registered at thedoglived.blogspot .com." He turned the iPhone screen to me.

Yep. That was the name I'd wanted. "Thanks!"

"No problem. But the full blog title is *The Dog Lived and So Will I.*"

"So, no irony?"

"No. For once, you're going for positive thinking."

I smiled. "Seems like a good time for that."

When we were home, I posted my first blog entry and then sent the massive group email sharing the blog address. Seemed easy enough.

But a group email doesn't work for everyone.

On the night Chris was going to call his parents to let them know, his sister called him instead. Kati called to let him know that at that moment his parents were at the vet's office with Chloe, their family dog —

the one Seamus had romped and misbe-
haved with on Christmas Eve, the one that
looked like my Tippy. Chloe was severely ill
and needed to be put to sleep. When Chris
told me, I cried for the first time since I'd
found my lump.

Out of respect for Chloe and all she'd
meant to the family, Chris held off a few
days before telling his parents of my diagnosis.

With family and close friends informed, I
turned my attention to work. I was still waiting for the MRI results, but even in the best
of circumstances, it seemed I had several
months of cancer treatments on the horizon.
I worked later into the evenings to get ahead
and to distract myself. On one of those
evenings Chris called me at the office.

"I don't want you to be surprised, so I'm
calling to let you know ahead of time," he
said.

"I've been surprised a lot lately, so you're
kind of scaring me."

"Sorry. Well, you might be scared. My
mom is going to call you."

Might be scared? In the four years Chris
and I had been together, I had never had a
phone conversation with anyone in his family, and I think we all liked it that way. Even
though Chris had patched things up with

his parents, I still felt their disapproval of me had only been ratcheted down to disappointment.

I got no further work done but rather sat at my desk running through scenarios. I decided the likely reason for the call was to implore me to break up with Chris. Why should a thirty-three-year-old young man have to go through something like breast cancer with his girlfriend? It wasn't fair to him. And since I'd had that thought myself, I'd be hard-pressed to argue with her. The best I could come up with, sitting alone at my desk anxiously awaiting the call, was, "It's up to Chris." Pathetic.

The phone rang.

I let it ring a second time. I considered not answering.

I decided to be an adult. A frightened, vulnerable, defensive adult . . . but an adult.

Then I struggled with how to answer the phone. A simple "hello" when I answered my office phone would sound too casual and perhaps give away that Chris had called to warn me of her impending call. "Law office" sounded too formal. On the fourth ring, I answered with "Teresa Rhyne," realizing just a tad too late how stupid that sounded, especially the way I'd phrased it as a question. Teresa Rhyne? Maybe? Don't hurt me?

"Hi, Teresa, it's Trudi."

"Oh, um, hi." Ah, yes, there's the familiar conversational brilliance under pressure.

"I spoke with Chris, and I wanted to call to welcome you to the C Club."

Welcome me? Well, maybe she thought I would die and that would solve her problem. "Um, thanks . . . I think."

"No, it's not anything anyone wants, I know that. But it is a club, and you don't realize it until you go through it. I don't know if Chris told you this, but I'm a breast cancer survivor myself. Sixteen years now. So I know you can do this. You're strong; you'll get through this."

I'm strong? She thinks I'm strong? And she sounded genuinely concerned. Caring. I was able to do a little math, too. If she was a sixteen-year survivor, she was the same age when she got diagnosed that I was now. And she had three kids, the youngest of whom would have been eight years old at the time.

"Thank you. I think I will get through it. I don't really have a choice." Did I sound ungrateful? Remote?

"Chris will be strong for you, too. I told him he needs to go to every appointment with you. That's what his dad did for me, and it makes all the difference."

"Chris has been great. I'm very lucky there. He has gone to every appointment with me, and he's kept me laughing."

"Jim was the only husband in the chemo room most of the time. A lot of men can't handle this; it's shocking. But the Kern men can handle it. I told Chris he'd have his mama to answer to if he doesn't support you."

Wow. Had we progressed more than I'd given credit for? Maybe I'd been projecting my own fears a bit. "He's really supportive. He's even now set up a blog for me so I can update everyone without repeating myself all the time."

"You'll have to give me the address. I want to be updated. And the girls will want to follow, too, I'm sure. They're worried about you, too."

We talked for twenty minutes as both my surprise and skepticism decreased, when I finally realized cancer had given us the common ground to talk to each other as people, not obstacles. She told me about her surgery and chemotherapy and was careful to tell me how much better the treatment is now. She told me how important it was to her when she went through treatment that her illness not affect her children. She also offered to accompany me to chemotherapy. I assured her Chris would be going with me and, if necessary, my dad would as well.

While I couldn't quite yet conceive of she and I doing something as personal — as intimate — as going together to my chemotherapy treatment, I was grateful for the call. I felt a shift in our relationship in just those twenty minutes. No, not a shift. That's not quite right. Before this we had no relationship. And now we did. I was no longer the person who might be ruining her son's life, and she was no longer the person who might be trying to ruin mine. We were women who both had breast cancer and both loved Chris. This was solid, common ground. This was enough to build on.

Chris was as surprised as I was. I imagine his parents were equally surprised. And relieved.

I started writing more and more on my blog:

Breast Cancer silver lining number one: who knew I had friends that were optimists?! And then there is the fact that I don't think I've ever heard "I love you" so many times from so many people (well, sober people anyway). Plus, I've heard from lots of friends and family, including some I hadn't heard from in a long time. More silver linings: some people have suggested that there might be weight loss with chemo (I try not to think what they clearly think of my current weight), and there is a certain focus to my life suddenly (I have time for two things: work and dealing with "this," and hey, I can't spend any money on anything else either. . . . so that simplifies things greatly).

And then finally there is the "CANCER WINS" silver lining. No, really, it's a silver lining. Basically "I have cancer," while true, is also a fantastic way to get out of anything and everything!! Oh, and get my way on anything and everything! Who can say no to "I have cancer, can you do me a favor?" No one!! (Okay, except Seamus — he is completely unmoved by this.) I'll try not to let the power go to my head. I'm pretty sure I'm going to have to conserve it for when I really need help. Besides, Chris is on to me.

I had full confidence in Dr. Karam. But that is not to say I went without my panic moments before the surgery. And each time I panicked, he responded with equal parts humor, information, and tranquility. Although he asked me to call him by his first name, Amer, I began to call him Dr. Good Karma instead.

When I heard from a former secretary at my old law firm about a painful blue dye shot into the nipple for purposes of finding the sentinel lymph node pre-surgery, I emailed Dr. Karam as near tears as I had been yet in the process (save for the loss of Chloe, the cockapoo). The shot had been described to me as an eleven on a pain scale of one to ten, and I needed assurance (I needed denial!) from Dr. Karam. I sent the email just before I left my office at about seven in the evening. I should have just stayed put and waited for his response. I would have saved myself the agony of my overactive imagination for my entire fifteen-minute commute. Instead, although he'd responded almost immediately, I didn't get his email until I was home, pouring the whole story out to Chris and elevating the pain level to something like 426 on a scale of 1 to 10.

Dr. Karam's response to me from his Blackberry was this:

"The blue dye is the one I use in the operating rm when u r asleep so u won't feel it plus my skilled hands will keep any pain away ;-). u may get some staining of the breast that is temporary and ure urine turns blue and green for a day (the college kids I teach always get a kick out of that). The shot u get in the morning is for that tiny bit of radioactive material that also goes to the sentinel lymph node and that is not painful. I use both techniques so I can make sure to find the sentinel node."

I was amused by the shorthand texting language. It looked not unlike what my niece posted on Facebook or in her rare text messages to me, only slightly easier to decipher. I knew what he was saying: Anesthesia is my friend. As is Dr. Good Karma. For life.

Other pieces of advice, mostly unsolicited, came my way as well. Sometimes I ignored it, and sometimes I emailed Amer with questions. He always answered quickly and thoroughly.

My assistant Michelle was pregnant with her first child during this time. We compared stories of inappropriate comments from well-meaning (we hoped) people and both wondered why anyone felt that their own gruesome stories, be they of childbirth or chemotherapy, were going to be helpful. Michelle also let me know when one of my clients called inquiring after my health because she had overheard two men talking about my cancer diagnosis in a local restaurant one evening.

Although I had set up a public blog, I hadn't yet determined how I wanted to handle my diagnosis and treatment where my clients were concerned. Since I practice in estate planning, I am frequently discussing illnesses and death with my clients, but it didn't seem right to bring my own illness or mortality into the conversation. And, from a practical standpoint, it wouldn't do to have people thinking I was too sick to handle any clients or, worse, dying. Knowing that my right breast had become casual dinner talk made me realize I'd have to handle this head-on. I decided I'd be open and forthright about my cancer and the treatment — and I'd emphasize that I was still carrying on in my practice. I'd be that thing that I'd resisted for so long — perky and upbeat. Well, maybe just upbeat.

I went to the mayor's State of the City address on Thursday, my first public foray post-diagnosis. From this small but extremely scientific survey, I can tell you there are four basic responses a person has to encountering someone who has been diagnosed with breast cancer, to wit:

1. Person assumes serious, even pained, facial expression, grabs "cancer person" by hand, and winces in a barely audible voice, "I've heard about your situation/diagnosis/illness" (no one can utter the word *cancer*). "I'm soooooooooooooooooooo sorry." Then cocks his or her head to the side and continues peering at "cancer person" as if she is dying on the spot.
2. Person assumes stoic face, says, "Hi. How are you?" to cancer person while glancing furtively at cancerous breast but refraining from in any way outwardly acknowledging that they've "heard."
3. Person rushes over to cancer person, hugs, smiles, or just generally effuses and says "Oh my god, I read your blog. It's so great that you are keeping your sense of humor." And frequently there's the "If there is anything at all I can do, please let me know." OR
4. Person rushes up to "cancer person" and immediately begins a barrage of things "cancer person" must know, people who must be contacted, information that must be gathered, doctors' names, other "cancer people" who must be talked to, and graphic descriptions of things that cancer person may have to endure but is in no mood to contemplate at the moment.

Guess which response is my favorite? That would be #3. I think that if you know someone who has been diagnosed with cancer, and particularly breast cancer, there are a few things you should keep in mind. Early on, the person feels fine. I can't tell, physically, that I have a disease right now. Other than the yellow-green fading bruise from the biopsy, physically I feel fine. So why wouldn't I continue on with my normal life? So when you encounter a "cancer person," if you know this person at all — treat her the same way you normally would! For those who may in the future be in categories 1, 2, or 4 above, a few comments:

1. This response most frequently actually comes from men. I understand — men want to fix things and solve problems, and this is not one that most men can fix (Dr. Good Karma can, however!). But the response is awkward at best. Again, I still feel fine. And it makes me feel like I have to comfort YOU and assure YOU that everything will be all right. And hey, this is about ME!!
2. You're kidding when you look at my breast, right? Are you expecting to see something bursting *Alien*-like from my chest? I'd prefer "so I heard you've had some bad news lately" or something that at least opens the

door for me to say "yes" or change the subject or do something other than think, "Wow, this person is really uncomfortable right now; I wonder what I did?"

4. Um, wow. I can't carry that kind of information in my head. And while I know you mean well, every woman's situation is different, and I'm really, really squeamish so lots of the details need to be left out. I'll deal with it when I have to. It's better if you write something down or just say, "I know of a good doctor/someone who's recently been through this/a great website" etc., followed by, "Would you like me to SEND you the information?" Much, much better. Because then "cancer person" (who has very little control over the disease she is recently battling) can at least maintain control over information and decisions. And the information is available when it's needed. I can barely keep track of the number of doctor's appointments, restrictions, instructions, tests, results, etc., that I currently have, let alone things I may encounter in a few months' time.

I received a call about my stellar performance when getting my MRI. Or, at least, that's how I liked to think about it. UCLA called to ask if I was willing to participate in a research study being conducted by more of those genius twelve-year-old scientists who seem to congregate on the UCLA Medical Center campus. Research was being conducted to find a way to diagnose breast cancer through a magnetic resonance spectropscopy rather than the more invasive biopsy. They needed volunteers who'd been diagnosed with breast cancer and were willing to have this additional procedure done before surgery. They were having a hard time recruiting volunteers.

The time between diagnosis and surgery is a stressful time, and I understand that many folks need sedation in order to stay still in the MRI tube, so it was easy to see why getting volunteers might be difficult. But where others needed sedation, I merely needed a good idea — the blog — and I was set for an hour of confinement well spent inside my own head. I'm more frightened of those three-day cancer walks than I am an opportunity for a noble nap, so I agreed to participate in the study. Since Chris and I had already decided to stay the night at a hotel near the medical center the night before my surgery, the research scientists agreed to do the MRS that night as well.

We headed into Los Angeles on a cool,

windy January day with our suitcase packed for two days, a bottle of wine (for Dr. Karam), and reservations at the Angeleno Hotel, a high-rise, iconic round building with views of the city and the Getty Center, about a mile from UCLA. Shortly after we checked into the hotel and made our way to our room, Michelle emailed me a photo of flowers that had been sent to the office by clients. Later she emailed a photo of her and my paralegal wearing pink ribbon bracelets in solidarity and wishing me luck. Chris and I sat on the balcony enjoying the view for a few moments before the wind sent us back inside.

The MRS was scheduled for 8:00 p.m. The building we had been directed to was empty when we arrived. We cautiously made our way down deserted hallways until we were met by another young, white lab-coat-wearing doctor who introduced himself as Scott and thanked me repeatedly for agreeing to participate in the study. After explaining the study again and having me sign paperwork, I was once again dressed in a hospital gown, lying on my stomach in a magnetic resonance tube. The noise the machine made was quieter and I didn't have a blog to be creating in my head, but otherwise the procedure seemed similar to what I'd undergone before.

Dr. Good Karma even appeared again in person to follow my treatment and, as he said, see what the scientists were studying. I only knew this when he spoke to me through the intercom of the machine and woke me from my nap.

"How are you doing in there?" he said.

Even waking from sleep to a voice with no body present, I recognized his distinct accent and happy cadence.

"Well, I'm good so far. Thanks."

"We're out here discussing wine and France."

I knew these to be two of his and Chris's favorite subjects. "Well, just don't forget me in here. And speaking of wine, am I allowed to have any tonight? As long as it's before midnight?"

"One glass. But make it a good one."

He was gone before I was removed from the tube, but it was nice to know he'd stopped by to answer the really important medical questions.

Doctor's orders: Chris and I had a delicious meal of poached egg on frissee salad with lardons and croutons, steak with gorgonzola butter, and truffle fries at West, the restaurant on top of the hotel. I savored a glass of Chateauneuf du Pape. Calories consumed the night before cancer surgery cannot possibly count.

At five in the morning I was wide awake, but it wasn't because of the food.

CHAPTER 16
GOING NUCLEAR

We dutifully reported in to the surgery center at seven in the morning. So did about 163 other people. And apparently it was half-off-surgery-for-children day because they were lined up out the door. And crying. Children cry when confronted with surgery. I cry when confronted with 7:00 a.m. and no Starbucks. It was not a pretty or quiet scene. Again, I thought, the surgery center could learn from Seamus's veterinary surgery center. Since Seamus received green dog bones by the handful each and every time we went to the Veterinary Cancer Group clinic, he associated that drive and that building with nothing more than adoring fans and nearly unlimited cookies. He raced into the building, tail high and wagging. Perhaps the human surgery centers should hand out something equally distracting. Seamus had his green bones; I could do with a little green Starbucks cup. I'd be more willing to submit to medical procedures.

After they took everybody else back to surgery one by one and the family members dispersed, Chris and I were still huddled in the corner. When the clock ticked past 7:30 and then past 7:40, I approached the woman at the desk.

"Hi. I'm supposed to be in nuclear medicine at 7:30."

"That's not here."

"Okay, well, I was told to report here."

"For what?"

Wow. Okay. "So someone can take me to nuclear medicine before my surgery. I'm not entirely sure."

"Well, me either. I'm new here." She placed her palms flat on the desk and pushed herself upright. "Hang on. Let me go find someone who knows something."

This seemed like a wise idea.

Had I known what was ahead of me, however, I would have thanked her for the delay. A few minutes later she returned with an apologetic and fast-moving nurse, who insisted I sit in a wheelchair while she rushed me down to nuclear medicine through a series of long hallways and service elevators with Chris rushing behind me.

Nuclear medicine, we discovered, is in the

basement of the medical center. And it's a scary, cold place. Cold in temperature and demeanor. They hand out blankets in the waiting room, but we didn't know this initially. The nurse checked me in with reception, told me I could take a seat (she needed the wheelchair back), and then was gone.

In the waiting room with us was a swarthy-looking man in his early forties, unshaved and wearing a leather jacket and boots, and next to him was a woman who looked like "Mom" — just not his mom. Mom like Mrs. Cunningham or June Cleaver or any of those moms who did not have swarthy-looking sons. They took Swarthy back into the treatment rooms, and five minutes later a tech came out and said to Mom, "Mrs. Jones? Your son-in-law would like you to be with him for the procedure." Mom smiled sweetly (and knowingly) and followed the tech.

The fact that Swarthy needed support in the arctic nuclear zone scared me further. Also, I was hoping his procedure had nothing to do with his prostate.

Soon a large and tall man in an official-looking lab coat entered. I didn't catch his name, or if I did, I blocked it out. We'll call him Lurch.

The receptionist said to Lurch something to the effect of, "We have a such-and-such brain serious major procedure today."

Lurch responded, "Really? I haven't done one of those in twenty years."

These are not comforting words in a medical center. Please, do not let me find out my brain is in my right breast.

Lurch went into the exam area but returned in only a few minutes.

"Ms. Rhyne?"

I stood up. "Yes?"

"Come with me." Lurch turned and headed back from where he'd come, not bothering to wait for me.

I turned to Chris. "And you come with me." If he had not been available, I would have made Swarthy's mother-in-law come with me, too. Lurch was not a man one wants to follow into the bowels of nuclear medicine.

I caught up to Lurch in the hallway, and he said, still walking, "So you understand why you're here and what we're doing?"

I knew I was in nuclear medicine to get what Dr. Good Karma had described as the "shot of a tiny bit of radioactive material" that would later help him find my sentinel node as he snooped around in my underarm, but still, there was quite a bit of blind trust involved in these procedures. I wasn't too different from Seamus naively following a cookie right on into surgery. I mumbled, "Um, yeah, kinda . . . I just know it's painless."

And Lurch laughed at me.

He let out a big "Ha!" that echoed down the hallway.

I stopped following him. Just stopped. I stood staring at his back, slack-jawed and immobile.

He turned back to face me. "Oh, come on. It's four injections to your breast. It's going to hurt. There's going to be pain."

I don't know how I got the rest of the way down the hall into the treatment room. There isn't supposed to be pain. Dr. Karam said no pain. Had I been carrying my cell phone I'm certain I would have texted Dr. Karam right there: "U said no pain. Lurch says pain. Come quick."

In the treatment room I was relieved to find that Lurch the Ass was not the doctor. Lurch is not even a doctor. The doctor was a young woman (of course she was young) and far, far kinder. Lurch is just some masochist who's spent too much time in the nuclear zone where his empathy froze off.

Following Dr. Karam's original text about

this procedure, I did a little reading. I did understand a bit about what was going to happen, and a part of me (the part of me that stayed back at the Angeleno and was sipping coffee and resting comfortably) found it rather fascinating. Dr. Karam had given me a book written by his colleague, Dr. Chang. I followed along as I encountered each phase of my treatment.

"Doctors use the radioactive tracer as follows: They inject it in and around the cancerous area (or under the nipple) at the time of the initial cancer surgery. . . . In the operating room using a portable Geiger counter known as a gamma probe, the surgical team identifies the first draining node and removes it following the removal of the primary cancer. The pathologist then analyzes the node using a technique called frozen sectioning. He freezes the node by using liquid nitrogen and then cuts the tissue into thin slices and views them under the microscope. If he sees no cancer, no further surgery is performed."

I had four injections around the cancerous area. Unlike Seamus and his tender rear end, I thought that perhaps where my tumor was located was somewhat fortunate, if one has to have cancer in the first place. Three out of four of the injections weren't really much. But the one closest to the nipple . . . yeah, um . . . ow. Not painful in the way Lurch had seemed to hope, and certainly tolerable, but . . . ouch. The pain was enough to make me bite my lip but not draw blood.

Did I mention that Lurch is an ass?

Chris and I had two hours to kill while the radioactive material found its way through my breast before I was to return to nuclear medicine for "pictures." We chose not to hang out shivering in nuclear medicine. Instead we sat in a sunny window reading. We laughed when we realized I was reading David Sedaris's *When You Are Engulfed in Flames* and Chris was reading *Then We Came to the End* by Joshua Ferris. Perhaps we should have thought about our selections ahead of time.

With the hotel, dinner the night before, and the little sunny reading nook where we sat giggling at our respective readings, I could almost pretend we were on a mini-vacation. If we could just ignore the nuclear side excursion and the part where Dr. Karam was about to remove a divot from my breast. And cancer. We'd probably need to ignore cancer for a truly restful vacation.

When we returned to nuclear medicine, the place was no less frightening. There was an old guy asleep (or so I told myself) on a gurney in the hallway. His contorted bones were thinly covered with wrinkled, dry skin, and his mouth hung open. On the bright side, that eliminated any possible feeling bad for myself I could have mustered.

The "pictures" turned out to be not as simple as I thought, given that everyone so adoringly referred to them as "pictures." I was envisioning a quick little x-ray and I'm outta there. Not so fast. I was told to lie down on a rather ordinary-looking medical exam table, but then a panel came down on top of me (they asked again, "Are you at all claustrophobic?"). Two "pictures" that take five minutes each are necessary. The tech kindly pointed out on the screen what they were doing. So I turned my head to see the screen, pretending I knew what I was looking at.

Of course, this being nuclear medicine, everyone left the room while the pictures were taken. As I waited out the five minutes, I noticed there were actually three screens. The one he pointed to, a much bigger one in the middle, and then one in my periphery vision that I could barely see. But the big one in the middle, while difficult to see, was terrifying. It had a lot of red, some yellow, some pink, and a big ol' scary-looking jagged-edged black spot in the middle.

Wow.

I'd seen lots of scary pictures of my cancer by that time, but that one was the worst. Probably because of the red everywhere, and it was obviously extremely close up since they were looking for a little tiny lymph node, but it freaked me out. I kept trying to figure out where this famous lymph node was on the screen amid all that pulsating blood. I also wondered if cancer really was black or that was just how it was depicted on the screen. Finally I decided I just couldn't look at that picture anymore, and I went back to the perfectly harmless-looking black-and-white screen he had told me to look at. It had a nice little countdown clock on it, too, and that helped calm me. It wouldn't be too much longer before Dr. Karam removed that frightening, pulsating, jagged, black mass from my body.

The tech returned. "Good job. We found the node. I'm just going to mark it on you." He drew on my underarm with a Sharpie to pinpoint the node for the surgeon, which seemed very low-tech for a procedure that started out with a radioactive injection.

"You're all done now. You can sit up."

I sat up and immediately looked to the large, terrifying screen, ready to ask just how bad it all was. And there in front of me was the threatening computer screen . . . with a beautiful red, yellow, and pink sunset and the black silhouette of a palm tree sticking up in the middle of it. The words "Polynesian Spa Music" were displayed across the top.

When they insisted on wheeling me back to the surgery floor in a wheelchair, I couldn't argue. After all, I'd been seeing cancer in the sunsets.

I remember only this much from surgery: the anesthesia nurse was Steve, and he was very kind and good at what he does. The other anesthesia nurse (apparently there to supervise Steve) was an attractive woman with a really cute, colorful surgical hat — until I noticed it was images of coffee and had *latte, cappuccino,* and other such words all over it, which was just cruel to me in my then state. She was justifiably concerned I might rip it off her head when the anesthesia kicked in and I lost the last two inhibitions I had left.

Chris held my hand as the anesthesiologist injected me and as I counted down,

"Ten, nine, eight . . ." That was all it took.

And the infamous blue dye shot straight to the nipple? True to Dr. Good Karma's word, his skillful hands kept the pain away. Although he assured me that I felt it because I "tried to help" — which is to say I tried to knock it away. Also true to Dr. Karam's words, I urinated turquoise blue for several days.

There was, however, one promise Dr. Good Karma did not keep. He was not at my bedside with a Starbucks short, double, nonfat latte when I awoke from the surgery in my anesthesia fog. This is how I learned he had other patients. (The nerve!)

When Chris and I returned to the hotel that evening, I thought I was doing pretty well, but I was tired. I needed to lie down. I took off my light pink hoodie jacket and headed for the bed. Chris gasped.

"Baby, don't lie down yet."

"Why? I need to. I need to sleep," I said, leaning wistfully toward the mattress.

"Well, you're bleeding. A lot."

I looked down at my breast, fully expecting it to be squirting blood from the nipple. Thus, I was relieved to see that it was only a five-inch circle of dark red blood that had seeped through the gauze, the bandage, my shirt, and the formerly cute hoodie jacket at right breast ten o'clock, across to my under-arm.

Chris reached Dr. Karam on his cell phone while I grabbed a towel and lay down on the bed to sleep. That or I passed out. I really can't deal with blood.

When I awoke, it was after 8:00 p.m. and Dr. Karam was standing at my bedside.

I looked around the room. The lavender and gray furnishings and mid-century look told me I was still in the hotel room. "This brings a whole new meaning to house calls, doctor."

"It does! And this is a nice house you've got." He knelt down beside me. "I didn't want Chris to wake you, and I was finishing up my rounds anyway. I'm sorry I didn't get to see you after the surgery. I had another surgery, and it got more compli-cated. But for you, everything went very well. I'm very happy."

He changed my bandages while telling me that preliminary reports indicated no lymph node involvement and he believed he got the tumor. He was hopeful we'd have clean margins, "just like Seamus." He handed Chris a bag of supplies for future bandage changes and informed me that I bleed a lot. I would discover this again and again as I went through treatments, but at that point, snuggled warm in bed, bandages freshly changed, assurances that surgery went well, and the world's greatest boyfriend and Dr. Good Karma nearby discussing wine again (we'd now had the chance to give Dr. Karam the thank-you bottle of Pinot Noir), further treatment was far from my mind.

CHAPTER 17
THE GAMBLER

I'd like to tell you Seamus is the kind of dog who senses when his master is sick or tired or just not having a good day and cuddles, stays by my side, brings me my slippers, and licks my tears (if there were any) away. But you've read this far, so you know better. He isn't that dog.

He's Seamus. He is the master.

As I recovered from surgery, he spent time on the couch with me but usually stole the cashmere-blend throw blanket for himself and left me with the cotton one. He wanted cuddles only when he wanted them, whether I needed them or not or was awake or not. He continued to force the breakfast issue by bounding up into our bed at seven in the morning and shoving himself between Chris and me. Luckily, my surgery was on the right side and I sleep on the right side of the bed, which meant my left side generally bore the brunt of Seamus's morning demands. He kept me in good spirits and laughing, though, and he kept my mind off me. I liked being home with just Chris and Seamus and the occasional visitor. I liked the peace and quiet, and Chris seemed more than able to handle taking care of me. I couldn't lift my right arm, I needed regular medication, and I was tired, but other than that, I was functioning.

My mother had come out to California when she and my stepfather were on their vacation, before my surgery, and even then (when I looked and felt healthy) it was clear my diagnosis had caused her a great deal of stress. She was calling regularly and initially wanted to come out to help as I recovered. I told her to wait. It seemed more likely that if I needed more help than Chris could provide, it would be during chemotherapy. This turned out to be a wise decision. My mother broke out in stress-related shingles before I even recovered from the surgery.

Dr. Karam called, emailed, and texted to check on me the day after my surgery and again the next day. By the time he called on the third day with the pathology report, I had forgotten I was waiting for it. I'd finally been able to shower and vaguely blow-dry and style my hair with limited success since I couldn't raise my right arm above my shoulder, which happens to be where my head and hair are located. I felt good enough that my neighbors and friends Jane and Francis had come by to visit, bearing food. Between our conversation and Seamus's howling for the food, I almost didn't hear the phone ring.

"*Hola*, T. This is Amer. Your margins are all clear. I'm so happy. This is all good news."

"Oh. Hi, Dr. Karam. Right. Clear margins. Wait, I thought we knew that already?"

"This is from the pathology report, so it's all good. Now we know for certain. And your tumor was 1.7 centimeters so the mammogram was actually more accurate than the MRI."

"And that means?"

"Stage 1c, but smaller than we thought. Not as close to two centimeters. And you're all done with surgery."

"So you're breaking up with me?"

"Ha! No. I'm still your doctor and primary contact. You still need to see me."

"Am I still having chemo?"

"Likely, yes. We'll get you to Dr. Glaspy for that. Chemo is really going to be good for you — necessary for this. It's an aggressive cancer, and chemo is best. But today this is good news. Clean margins are very good news."

"Yes, I remember that. Clean margins. That was a big deal for Seamus, too."

"How is Seamus?"

"He's good. He's right here with me."

"Yes! I hear him."

One should always have an enthusiastic doctor. And one who listens. My surgeon not only could remember my name, my condition, and my medical history, but also could remember my dog's name. And he cared about all of the above.

I shared the news with Chris and Jane and Francis, who happen to be three of the smartest, most articulate people I know. But what vocabulary suffices as a response to "I'm now cancer free"? We were all reduced to simple exclamations of relief that weren't much more than a teenager's "ohmygawd!" Luckily, in addition to being charming, intellectual, and Irish in all the best ways, Francis Carney made a mean martini. I celebrated my clean margins with a dirty martini. The green olive played the role of the green dog biscuit perfectly.

After my follow-up appointment with Dr. Karam, he walked with Chris and me over to the oncology department in another building to meet Dr. Glaspy, the oncologist.

"You're going to like him. He's the best there is. He will tell you exactly what you need to do," Dr. Karam said.

"He's going to tell me I need chemotherapy. Chances are, based on that alone, I'm not going to like him." I was still hoping that somehow, some way, I'd be spared chemotherapy. Although Dr. Karam had been very good at leading me gently to the near certainty of it, I was too frightened of chemotherapy to have yet accepted the message.

"That may be, but what is that expression? Don't shoot the messenger."

After introductions, Dr. Karam left us with a parting, "You're in good hands." He gave me a hug and shook Chris's hand.

Dr. Glaspy was nothing like Dr. Karam. He was a large man and his demeanor was serious and somewhat reserved. I thought perhaps I'd been spoiled by having a funny, gregarious surgeon who was so kind and empathetic, so perhaps my judgment was skewed.

Dr. Glaspy began to explain his role in my care.

"My job is a little like a guy on a riverboat with the gamblers. You know those riverboats with tables of guys playing poker?"

My mind flashed to Mel Gibson and Jodi

Foster in *Maverick.* Was that a riverboat? And how does it end? The only other riverboat I could think of was the Mark Twain Riverboat at Disneyland, and surely there was no gambling going on there. Mickey would not have it. Wait. What does this have to do with my cancer?

"Um, sure. Right. Riverboat gambling," I answered Dr. Glaspy, but I was looking at Chris. Chris smiled and raised his eyebrows.

"My job is to walk up and down the boat looking at the cards each player is holding. I can tell you your odds based on the cards you're holding, but I could be wrong. You could be dealt a different hand completely. All I can do is look at your hand and tell you your odds and the best way to play that particular hand."

My worries increased. I started arbitrarily calculating my odds of survival. Fifty percent? "Okay. So, what are my odds? What have I been dealt?"

"Well, it's not a good hand."

Thirty percent chance of survival? Chris told me later he was thinking 20 percent. We both had our greatest moment of fear right there on the *Delta Queen.*

"How not good?"

"Without chemotherapy you have a 30 percent chance of recurrence. And if it recurs we're not talking about cure then, we're talking about treatment to extend your life."

So, wait, that's a 70 percent chance it won't be back? That's not bad. Not bad at all. I expressed my relief, much to Dr. Glaspy's horror.

"No," he said, "that's not good at all. Those are not acceptable odds. You are the poster child for chemotherapy. With chemotherapy we can cut those odds in half. With chemotherapy you will reduce your odds of recurrence to 15 percent — that's still higher than we like, but it's better than 30 percent."

"Oh, right. No, I get that. It's just that the way you were talking, I was expecting a lot worse. I thought I had no face cards and not even a pair of twos." I spent many a day playing poker with my grandfather and our next-door neighbor Art when I was a kid. I was an excellent poker player at seven years old. I knew a bad hand when I was dealt one.

"It is a bad hand. Triple-negative is a very aggressive form of cancer. When I say you're the poster child for chemotherapy, I mean that you could go to any oncologist anywhere and they would all recommend chemotherapy. It's all we've got for this. Oncologists love to debate and argue the most effective treatments for various cancers, but not with yours. Every oncologist would tell you the same thing. You need chemotherapy."

I realized then that my response had concerned him that I wouldn't agree to chemotherapy. But the good and great Dr. Karam had done a fine job of slowly but surely turning up the chemo heat, and Dr. Glaspy was now bringing things to the inevitable boil. It was clear what I needed to do, and I would do it. Right then, though, I was thinking about Seamus and the hand he'd been dealt — the terrible odds that he'd beaten anyway.

Dr. Glaspy continued his explanation. "If we took one hundred women with your cancer exactly and put them in a room together, we know that with no post-surgery treatment thirty of them will have a recurrence of the cancer and seventy of them won't. We just don't know which thirty."

I wasn't picturing women in a room. I pictured one hundred beagles. Thirty of them immediately ran howling to one side of the room. In Seamus's case, it was probably thirty that would not have a recurrence. The seventy beagles on the other side of the room would have a recurrence. I figured if the doctor could be on a riverboat, I could be in a beagle rescue. Now, if those beagles were at a card table, playing poker . . . Stop! Listen to the oncologist! He's talking about your cancer!

"So we give them all chemotherapy. The chemotherapy will cut that number to fifteen. That means fifteen of those women will still have a recurrence, but another fifteen will not. Again though, we don't know which fifteen."

Fifteen beagles ran across my mental room and joined the other thirty safe beagles. Which side of the room had Seamus been standing on after his surgery? Either way, there was, as I knew, as I had insisted to that sorority-bitch of a doctor, always the chance he would survive. There's always a chance. Seamus had shown everyone that much.

Later when I explained to a friend why I was undergoing chemotherapy even though there were no signs of cancer in my body after surgery, when I explained what these statistics meant, what the science could and couldn't tell us, and most particularly when I told her about the beagles racing across the room in my mind, she clearly thought I had lost my marbles in that beagle stampede.

"Teresa, the doctor is talking to you about your life, your diagnosis, and all you can think about was your dog? You're not taking this seriously," she said.

Not taking cancer seriously. As though that can be done. She was not the first nor the last to make this comment to me. I was taking cancer seriously. I was also taking those odds very seriously. Seamus's experience helped me understand my odds in a very positive way, whether my friend understood that or not.

I addressed Dr. Glaspy. "So, I could have the chemo but never have needed it — I could have been one of the original seventy?" Dr. Glaspy did not strike me as the kind of doctor one discussed her beagle's cancer diagnosis with, at least not then, so I stuck to questions geared toward understanding my own chances.

"Yes, but you could also be one of those fifteen women whose life was saved by chemotherapy."

Like Seamus. I understood now, far better than I had then, why Seamus had to undergo chemotherapy even though the surgeon had achieved the coveted "clean margins" around his excised tumor. Chemo gave him the best chance to be the beagle that crossed the room over to the safe side and walked out the doggie door to health. And he did it. Would I be that lucky?

There was only one way to know.

Once I agreed to the chemotherapy, Dr. Glaspy and his physician's assistant explained the protocol to me. I'd have Taxotere and Cytoxan four times each, spaced three weeks apart. I recognized Cytoxan — Seamus had been given Cytoxan. They really do give the same chemotherapy to dogs and humans. I made a mental note to check to see if Cytoxan was what caused Seamus's white blood cell crash.

Dr. Glaspy reviewed the possible side effects with me. "You may be fatigued, and you may be nauseous. We have ways of controlling that, and it's certainly better than it used to be, but some patients do get nauseous during or immediately after treatment. Your long drive may be an issue. Do you have someone who can drive you?"

"I'll be with her for each appointment. Do you think we'll be able to head home by 2:00 p.m. and miss the traffic?" Chris said.

"Hard to know. And probably not for the first treatment. You might want to consider staying in a hotel if that's an option for you. Or I can refer you to an oncologist closer to where you live."

I considered that option. I'd had such

good care at UCLA and trusted Dr. Karam's opinion of Dr. Glaspy so much that I did not want to go anywhere else. On the other hand, I knew I couldn't afford a hotel room each night of chemo, not with missing work on those days as well. The thought of being nauseous in a car for sixty miles and possibly as long as three hours was also not appealing. Things would be easier for Chris, too, if I had treatment closer to home. I decided to at least get the referral and meet the other oncologist.

Hi Everybody, Chris here.

As you probably know, Teresa has cancer. I know, big-time shocker! But her surgery was successful and now she's on to chemotherapy. Huzzah! Where, as the oncologist said, she's GUARANTEED to lose her hair. GUARANTEED. (His emphasis, not mine.)

Expecting this even before the surgery (apparently some of her pessimism is rubbing off on me), I did what any good boyfriend would do — I offered to shave off my hair. I mean, if you're going to have one bald person in the family, why not two, right? Three, though, wasn't going to be an option. Seamus is far too reluctant to go the shaving route with us. He gets freaked out at the sight of a Mach 3. Plus, apparently he's vain.

Teresa, though, was just as reluctant as Seamus to go through with my whole head-shaving scheme. She's always loved my thick, full head of hair ("Democrat hair," she calls it — think Kennedy, Kerry, Clinton. . . . yeah, you got it), and the last thing she wanted was for me to get rid of it when she lost hers. Why have two bald people in the family when you only need one, she said? And who am I to argue? I mean, she has CANCER, for crying out loud! (And don't think she ever lets you forget it.)

So, I decided to go another way with it instead: instead of shaving my head in solidarity, I would grow out my hair during her chemo and radiation sessions. I get to look like Clinton, she gets to look like Jimmy Carville.

Long story short, I had what may be my final haircut of 2009 (gulp! or at least until August — gulp!) Saturday.

But here's the thing: (1) My hair grows really, really fast. Like Usain Bolt speed-of-sound fast, (2) I think the longest I've ever gone without cutting my hair is three months — all told, this is going to be at least six months of growth, possibly seven or eight or even longer (if I keep it up post-treatment while Teresa is still, well, shiny. We'll see. That will be a game time and psoriasis-related decision). I've never grown my hair out that long. I have no idea what's going to happen, and (3) unlike most normal people whose hair grows down as it gets longer, mine doesn't. It grows up. And big. Like pompadour big. Like Del Shannon in 1957 big. Like Roman centurion helmet big. As my hair grows, it develops into a White Irish Afro (or Whi-fro).

Anyway, that's what I'm doing to support Teresa in her fight against cancer.

See you all later. Longer, shaggier, and substantially more democratier than before.

A week after our visit with Dr. Glaspy, Chris and I met with Dr. Blaine, the oncologist closer to home. I was immediately discouraged by the sight of her office. Valentine's Day was coming up, and thus there were pink and red streamers, Cupid cutouts, and hearts adorning every spare inch of wall and ceiling space. As though chemo wasn't going to be nauseating enough, I was going to have to put up with a cuteness overdose? I quickly calculated my three months of chemotherapy and realized I'd have to suffer through St. Patrick's Day and Easter décor as well. My hopes that the treatment rooms were not likewise vandalized were dashed when, thirty minutes after my scheduled appointment time, I was led back to the exam room, past plates of heart-shaped cookies on heart-shaped doilies, more streamers, and Mylar balloons shouting, "Happy Valentine's Day!!"

I waited in my paper dress uniform for another twenty minutes before the doctor made her appearance. Where Dr. Glaspy had seemed reserved and somewhat humorless compared to Dr. Karam, he seemed endearing, warm, and fuzzy compared to the icicle that was Dr. Blaine.

She quickly introduced herself and then commanded I lay down for an exam. I did.

Her cold hands poked and prodded.

"You can sit up now."

I did.

"So you're a lawyer," she said as she reached for a file. "What kind of law?"

"I do estate planning, mostly for family business owners."

"Estate planning? Don't a lot of lawyers do that? Isn't that just wills and trusts?"

Nice move. It's always endearing to add "just" in front of someone's occupation. Aren't you just a priest? Just a schoolteacher? Just an oncologist?

"No. It's not 'just' that at all."

"Oh. Well, I've had lots of lawyers as patients. Do you know John Allen? He's not a patient, but we've done lots of work together."

I knew of John Allen. He was a well-known, well-respected attorney who sued insurance companies for breach of good faith and abuses of their insureds. I wasn't sure how I felt about her working with him so much or how I felt about discussing legal matters. She had a motive for this discussion though.

"Well, my staff tells me you've declined to sign our waiver," she said.

"I did. For two reasons — first, I'm only here for a consultation so I shouldn't need to waive anything, and second, that waiver reads as though you could completely screw up everything and I'd have no redress whatsoever."

"John Allen drafted it." She smiled in a manner clearly meant to convey "Checkmate, bitch." And she continued, "If you don't sign it, I won't treat you."

I wanted to ask what had caused her to be so defensive about lawsuits, but I didn't. I was too floored by her response and demeanor.

With my surgical scar still healing, I was not able to discuss my choice of oncologists with Chris in the hot tub. Perhaps that is why our decision was not a good one. I wish I had more vividly recalled my encounter with Seamus's Dr. Sorority Chick and been able to recognize when I'd walked into yet another alpha-female battle that I could not win, especially not when dressed in a paper towel, stitches in my right breast, and the nightmare of chemotherapy on the horizon. If I had recognized what was happening with Dr. B, I would have spared myself much frustration and pain over the next several months. But once we learned that Dr. B was also the oncologist who had treated the mother of Chris's friend Ashley (who'd been at dinner with us the day we first met Dr. Karam), and Ashley gave her glowing reviews, it seemed she was an obvious choice. Dr. B came highly recommended by Dr. Glaspy as well.

I was there for health care, not to find a new friend, I told myself. Maybe she'd just had one bad day and I happened in on that day.

Maybe.

I've learned many surprising things, but way up on the list was this fact: by the time a breast cancer mass (fancy word for "lump"; unless you are trying to apply it to your spouse — it doesn't work the same) can actually be felt, those dastardly cancer cells have been hard at work in the breast for six to eight years. Years! I've had cancer for years! (I'm totally expecting phone calls, cards, and flowers from some of you. . . . the way you've treated me. . . . and I had cancer then!!!) Modern technology can't detect the cancer in the beginning years of growth (nope, not the mammogram, not an MRI, and you can't feel it either. . . . these are just little tiny bad-guy cells), so it's only after they've divided and multiplied and turned into a gang that they get discovered.

Basically, a fertile little cancer cell reproduces to be two cells in about one hundred days, then four cells at two hundred days, eight at three hundred, sixteen at four hundred, up until at about five years the cancer party is now about 1 mm in size. Millimeter. . . . not centimeter. Only at eight years have they divided in number to get to the 1 cm size, which is generally considered the smallest "palpable" tumor (meaning you can feel it — if you were trying; the machines might pick it up before this. . . . if you were getting regular mammograms). At ten years that could be 2 or 3 cm or larger, depending on the rate of growth.

Let's just think about my rude little invading tumor bastard (just a little pet name I have for it). I have had a mammogram every year since I turned forty. So that would be five mammograms that didn't pick up on the party going on. The last of these was July. Then in November I could actually feel something. By December it was clearly "a lump." And it turned out to be a 1.7 cm lump. It had maybe been growing there for eight years??

Quite a party of evil. Which explains the change from July to December. It also, in part, explains the chemotherapy as necessity. We don't know if there are other cells starting a party o'bad somewhere else in my body that just hasn't been picked up yet — some of the gangbanger party attendees could have flowed out into the street and down to a neighbor's where they are hiding out (cowards, really) until there's enough of them to make their presence known. We need to flush those out and banish them.

CHAPTER 18
A COVER-UP

I sat at my desk with the prescription in front of me and read "Cranium Prosthesis." I flattened out the blue slip of paper, picked it up, put it back down, read the fine print, and ultimately stared blankly.

I needed hair.

I had no idea how to go about getting a wig, yet I would be bald in a few weeks' time. Dr. Glaspy had guaranteed it.

"And you will lose your hair. Guaranteed. One hundred percent. No question. But it will grow back. It will take" — and here he looked at my hair, a few inches below my shoulder, blond, and relatively healthy — "a couple of years to get back to that, but you'll get it back."

Dr. B was equally direct, although she threw in a gratuitous eye roll when I asked if I really would lose all my hair and she answered, "Of course you will."

Chemotherapy is almost as frightening as

cancer. Every chemo patient must hang on to the idea that maybe they won't lose their hair; maybe they will be one of the lucky ones. These oncologists had obviously had the discussion too many times.

At UCLA, in my initial meeting with Dr. Glaspy, he gave me several prescriptions to begin preparing for chemotherapy (several very serious prescriptions, just to be clear) — antinausea, pain relief of varying degrees of strength, and a cranium prosthesis. The latter cannot be filled at your neighborhood pharmacy — which is why I was sitting in my office, twirling a blue piece of paper, and contemplating synthetic hair.

I'd been stumped for a few days. My "cancer to-do" list was long, and I was busy taking care of most of it with the help of my family and Chris. My mom sent me sweatsuits with zip jackets to wear during the infusions. My dad sent antioxidants, vitamins, and books. Chris stocked our pantry with the foods I liked most or that had been recommended (much as I had done for Seamus, I couldn't help but note). I read as much as I could on the Internet, and I made an appointment for Chris and me to attend chemo "boot camp" training at Dr. B's office.

But with only a week left until chemotherapy started, I still had not bought a wig. I was quite simply flummoxed by the whole idea of it. Once again, I could not get from here to there (or, forgive me, hair to . . . not hair). I felt foolish. I'd been able to handle everything else relatively easily. I'd maintained whatever control I could wherever I could, but the thought of buying a wig drew me up short.

How? Where? When? What? I had nothing.

Online I finally found a cancer center that offered free wigs and fittings for cancer patients. I didn't need a free wig; in fact, that struck me as odd and wrong. I wondered if I'd have to qualify as financially needy. I recalled my Irish grandfather's insistence on getting his share of the free government cheese handed out in the Reagan era, even though he didn't need it. I didn't need a free wig, but the fitting would be helpful. I had not the slightest idea how one selected, wore, or cared for a wig.

When I called the center to find out more, the woman who booked my appointment and explained the simple process to me was named Hope. This, I thought, was like Destiny calling to see if I was ready to adopt Seamus. I wondered if there was Faith and Charity in my future somewhere.

Once Chris and I knew all the appointments we'd be having and how many days we'd need to leave Seamus, we put out the APB for help. Anyone who offered assistance received a "how do you feel about dogs?" response. Luckily for us, and for our neighbors, many people love dogs and Seamus in particular.

My cranium prosthesis appointment was on the same day as our chemo boot camp appointment. The folks at the Mary S. Roberts Pet Adoption Center, Seamus's old home, offered to watch him for me for that day, which we all suspected might be a long one. Chris and I kissed Seamus good-bye, dropped him at the offices of the adoption center (with clear and comical instructions he was not to be adopted out, as though anyone else would be so nuts), and headed to the cancer center.

Throughout our UCLA experience, I continued to marvel at the youth of the professionals. But marvel as in "wow, what a young genius" and "wow, you got through Columbia, Harvard, and fellowships at Johns Hopkins and UCLA, and you're only, like, twenty-five?" That kind of marveling. On this day, we marveled at how young the girls we dealt with were in the "yesterday she was babysitting" and "I realize the bell just rang to let you out of class, but you are working, right?" way.

We were greeted at the Cancer Care Center by a teenage girl at the reception desk. I explained why I was there, and she stared blankly at me. Finally she said, "Today?"

"Yes. I made an appointment." I must have looked as abandoned as I felt, since another woman hurried out from behind her desk and offered to sit at the front desk so the teenager could attend to me.

Wig-teen is the "cosmetologist" I'd been told would work with me and find the "perfect wig"? I looked to Chris for his response, and he seemed as startled as me. Well, at least it was fake hair she'd be dealing with.

Wig-teen led us to what she referred to as a "wig room." "Wig closet" would have been more accurate.

"Usually when people come in for wigs they have less hair. So that's why I was confused," she said and pointed to a chair in front of a mirror.

Yes, well, hair can be confusing at a cancer center. I sat and explained that my chemo starts this week so of course I still have my hair.

She looked at me in the mirror. "Yeah,

but now I can't get the wigs on your head. I don't know how to fit them."

I was worried she was going to want to shave my head then and there just to make her job easier. But she had an idea. She opened a drawer and pulled out what looked to be a wide knee-high nylon. She stretched the nylon over my head, tucking all my hair up into it. Very pretty.

"Do you want to be blond? I mean stay blond?" she said.

"Yes. That seems safest. Let's stick with blond."

Wig-teen pulled out a bin of brown wigs. Short, curly, roadkill-looking wigs in styles last seen on *The Golden Girls.*

"Those are brunette," I said.

Wig-teen gazed into her box of roadkill and without looking up said, "No, these are blond. These are our blond ones."

"Those aren't blond. Those are brown."

She turned the box and looked at the label made from masking tape. It said "Blond," and clearly she was not capable of winning an argument with masking tape. "Yeah, these are blond," she said, holding up a small beaver pelt.

"Okay, how about some longer ones? At least to my shoulder, but preferably longer."

"We don't have any longer ones. Just

these." She held up a guinea pig corpse.

This would have been useful information to have before the half-hour drive, before the nylon was stretched over my head, and before I strangled her. I said, "Okay, well, what's the longest you have because I've never had short hair."

She selected a hoary marmot and squeezed it onto my head. Suddenly, I was Bea Arthur. Only older. And a lot crazier. Chris and I both laughed. I began chanting, "NO NO NO NO NO!!" and he began singing, "Thank you for being a friend . . ."

We tried three more rodent-wigs, each more ridiculous than the last. The wigs were stored in their plastic wrappers, flattened out, un-styled, and packed together in a bin on a closet shelf. Like craft supplies. When they were plunked onto my head, they were flat, and the wire-like hairs went in every which direction. There was no way to know what, exactly, or even remotely, the style was supposed to be. And clearly Wig-teen didn't know so she just randomly moved the wire brush around lightly on top of the wig, hoping something would eventually make sense. Because *Golden Girls* was off the air before she was born, so really, she had nothing to go on.

Chris broke the spell of despair. "I can't

believe you don't have any long-haired wigs."

"Everyone always likes the shorter ones. They look more natural."

He guffawed. There really wasn't any other response. "I disagree," he said, pointing to the thick perfectly straight crease with hair sprouting upward across my forehead.

She said, "No, everyone thinks so."

I wondered to what they were comparing these wigs. If you are only being offered short-haired squirrel pelts from a box of craft supplies, then what do they look more natural than? The Styrofoam head staring down at us from the upper shelf?

Chris asked the logical question, "Well, what's the age range of your customers?" This is what I had been wondering but couldn't find a way to ask, having been stunned into silence by my gerbil head. Even when we had pulled into the parking lot, with one look at the building, I had said, "Why do I feel like I'm going into a nursing home?"

Wig-teen assured us they had many young customers. We didn't believe her. She didn't care.

In the next thirty seconds, Wig-teen gave up on us and we gave up on her and her rodent collection. I'd rather be bald than wear one of those, free or not. She removed the knee-high from my head, leaving my real hair smashed down, messed up, and falling into my eyes. Naturally, she had no brush or anything available to help with that, because, as she'd already explained, her customers don't normally have hair. However, she did suggest we go next door to the boutique so I could see about "turbans" as an alternative.

The boutique was twice the size of the wig-fitting room, but alas they had only three turbans for adults. One. Two. Three. Not three models. Three of the same kind — one pink, one red, and one white all in size medium/large. If instead I were a child looking for a turban, I would have had a vast selection to choose from (vast being six). We spent about eight and one-half seconds in the "store" — long enough to get the explanation that they were low on inventory and I should come back in about a week. Right. That reminder did not make its way into my Blackberry.

We barely got out before Chris burst out laughing — because the closet of a store had two "shoplifters will be prosecuted" signs. He still wants to ask exactly how many times the store had been hit by renegade shoplifters desperate for pink turbans before they had to install the signs (which, of course, would scare the hair off any shoplifter).

I had no wig, and only fifteen minutes had passed.

We drove to the lab to get my pre-chemo blood work done. I was taken into the back, and after a short wait a nice, older woman who was about four feet tall came and quickly drew my blood samples. She put the square of gauze and the bandage on and sent me on my way. I was only ten steps down the hall when I felt a little squirt and then warm liquid running down my arm.

Back inside the lab we went. Only now both nurses were occupied with a screaming child and neither could see or hear me over the squirming, terrorized child and her two parents. I put pressure on my blood-soaked bandage, held my arm up, and waited. I hoped I wouldn't pass out or lose another jacket, and only then did I remember Dr. Karam telling me I bleed a lot. A third nurse finally came by and took me into another room, cleaned me up, stopped the bleeding, and bandaged me.

"Remember to tell nurses drawing your blood that you bleed a lot. They need to bandage you more tightly," she said.

So I've heard.

When I rejoined Chris, I mentioned this to him. "Since I'm busy concentrating on not passing out while they draw blood, maybe you can be the one to remember to tell them I bleed a lot."

"Good to know. I'll add it to my list," he said.

Our next stop was Dr. B's office for chemo boot camp.

Chris was seated on a stool next to the hospital bed where I was seated in a small room adjacent to what we had surmised was the chemotherapy infusion room.

"Do you think they give us a tour? Have you sample the chemo?" he said.

"I don't know. I assumed this would be a group thing. I thought several patients would be getting chemo training together. Though as I think about that, there are all sorts of privacy issues that would create."

"I don't know what I pictured, but I know it didn't involve a hospital bed. Though I'm getting quite accustomed to these wheelie-stools as my regular seat."

Chris was much too large of a man to be resigned to these tiny stools, but he was. It's what he'd been given as a seat in every exam room we'd been in.

The door opened, and we were joined by

a petite young woman with pale skin and long, stringy, mousy-brown hair (her real hair, I should note, lest the rodent reference throw you off). She shyly introduced herself, opened a large, overstuffed file, and started to read things to me. Slowly. Very. Slowly. And. Quietly. And she. Kept. Getting. Confused. No, lost. Wait. Confused. She was confused. No. Lost. She was. Lost.

Luckily, Chris and I had already read the same brochures, and we could redirect her.

"Okay, so I'm supposed to drink a lot of fluids during chemo. My dad gave me these antioxidants and immune boosters — mega greens and mega reds — they're powder form and you mix in water or fruit juice. Is there any reason I shouldn't be taking that?" I said.

She looked at me with a blank expression, highly reminiscent of Wig-teen.

"It's got vitamins and things also. Like a holistic health, natural thing," I said.

"You mean like Crystal Light?"

"No, not at all like Crystal Light."

Nothing.

"Are there vitamins, herbs, anything like that that she shouldn't be taking?" Chris tried.

"It depends on what it is."

"Well, do you have a list of the things I

376

should avoid?"

"We'd have to see the ingredient list. You'd have to bring it in."

I flipped through the materials she'd handed me — including two booklets from the American Cancer Society. I came across a page that lists the foods to avoid. To wit:

greasy, fatty, or fried foods
raw vegetables and unpeeled fruits
high-fiber vegetables
very hot or very cold foods
foods and drinks that contain caffeine, such as coffee
beer, wine, and alcohol
be careful with dairy products

Ummmm. . . . what the hell can I eat?? If I'm supposed to give up even one of the four to five cups of coffee a day I drink, it would have been nice to know that ahead of time to ease on out of the withdrawal symptoms. And what happened to the doctors telling me that if I felt like having a glass of wine, I could?

The nurse slowly backtracked away from most of what was in the booklet (and later that night at home I noticed the book was written in 1997 — and they've learned a lot about chemotherapy treatment since then).

Eventually we gave up asking questions because, as we discussed later, we could have said, "What about grass? Am I allowed to go near grass? Is air a problem? Should I avoid air?" and she would have smiled slowly and said, "What? I'll have to check. Ummm, it's different with everyone."

She, like her soul mate Wig-teen, gave up on us. She left to go get the billing person to discuss the "financial arrangements" with me. And that's when I noticed the song playing over the speakers was Sarah Mc-Lachlan's "I Will Remember You." I pointed to the speaker and looked at Chris. We both burst out laughing. He had already noticed they had also played "You Had a Bad Day" and James Ingram's "Just Once." All we needed was "Seasons in the Sun" and we had ourselves a chemo mix tape for all time. Chris even went into the chemo room to find out if we could expect this sort of serenade when I was hooked up in the chair. Thankfully, the sound system did not play in that room.

Where the chemo no-training nurse was quiet and soft and confused, the financial person was loud (really, really loud) and quite detailed (down to the penny) and full of information (down to the penny). So I learned that I was $2,114 into my $3,000 deductible and I needed to bring a check for $800 toward my deductible plus the $20 office visit co-pay on Thursday — then $96 the next time, and then $20 each time after. This part they were very, very clear about. Whether I could drink coffee or add mega greens and antioxidants to my fruit juice, which of the possible side effects I should phone in about, and what we should bring with us to the chemo session (food? water? blankets?) they were less sure of.

For that day's useless training and the opportunity to have Dr. B whoosh by me in a frost, I handed over the same credit card I'd used when Seamus was in treatment. I'd be getting airline miles for this, too.

As the receptionist handed me back my card, I thought clearly, "Seamus's card." Suddenly I realized why I'd been so baffled by the concept of a wig. Everything else had followed a familiar pattern. With the diagnosis, the search for a doctor, the surgery, the pathology report, the chemotherapy training, and now even the method of payment, I'd had experience and knowledge. I'd had a frame of reference. Because of Seamus.

But Seamus didn't lose his hair. Seamus hadn't needed a wig. I had to figure out hair loss and a wig on my own. There was no beagle-guide for that part of my journey.

Suddenly, I missed my diabolically cute guru.

I turned back to Chris. "Let's go get Seamus and go home. I'd like to forget about this day."

"I couldn't agree more," he said.

I slept as we drove home, waking as Chris pulled into the Pet Adoption Center. I hurried in to get Seamus.

But Seamus wasn't there.

"Destiny took him home," the young woman at the counter told us.

"Took him home?"

"Yeah. Wasn't she supposed to?"

Chris and I looked at each other, bewildered and hoping the other had an explanation.

"Uhhhhhh . . ." I looked around the lobby. "Is Denise here?" Denise was the same Denise who had run Ruff House Pet Resort and helped spoil Seamus with me. She was now the executive director of the adoption center. I had confidence she'd know why Seamus had been sent home with Destiny. Unfortunately, I was right.

Denise explained to us that he had howled so loud and so often all day that Destiny took him home with her after her shift ended, hoping to soothe his nerves. Seamus must have had a premonition of how badly our day was going.

"He howled too much for a facility with fifty other dogs?" I said, wincing.

"That's our Seamus," Denise managed to still be smiling. Seamus was lucky his charm was as far reaching as his howls. "He probably just senses the stress in the house. You guys have a lot going on."

We drove to Destiny's home, only a few miles from our own, wondering the whole way how we'd ever get me through all the upcoming medical appointments if Seamus's howling was even too much for a pet adoption center.

Destiny handed me Seamus's leash with him jumping and howling on the other end, while Chris loaded the crate in the back of my car.

"If you need help," Destiny said, "I'm happy to watch him for whatever appointments you have. We love Seamus. And he doesn't howl when he's here."

I looked down at the happy, twirling dervish on a leash. Destiny had interceded again. Seamus was a handful, but he was a lovable handful. His charm worked magic. All he really wanted was to be loved. And never left alone. Well, and fed a lot.

"That is really nice of you, Destiny. I may have to take you up on that. I have a lot of appointments coming up. A lot."

The next day, with a new determination born of necessity, I began a search for a wig shop. I emailed a few breast cancer survivors I knew, and I went online until I found what I needed. One name kept popping up.

When I telephoned Splendor Wigs, I heard a dog barking in the background. And, though I'm not big on "signs," I knew then that this was the place to get my wig. Much like understanding my survival statistics through poker-playing dogs, I found comfort in the bark of this dog. I'll follow a sign from the canine universe.

When I arrived at the little house of wigs on a busy commercial street, I asked about the dog. The owner, Diedre, hesitated only a moment before saying she didn't have a dog. I looked around the room for any sign of a dog while also assuring her that I wouldn't mind in the least if she did have a dog hanging out. My dog comes to my office all the time, I said. But no, she did not have a dog. She seemed quite sure of this.

Did I imagine the dog? Was it a neighbor dog? It didn't matter much, except, perhaps, for the sake of my sanity; this was the place I needed to be to get a wig that would fit properly, look natural, and come with instructions from someone who actually knew what they were doing. The dog barking in the distance, real or not, was enough to get me to the shop with a large selection of wigs and to a woman who knew how to select, fit, and style a wig.

Chris and Laureen, my friend and paralegal, met me at the wig shop. Though I was still overwhelmed, their enthusiasm and excitement over the options eased my worries. Diedre sat me in a chair and carefully placed on my head each perfectly combed, styled, and cared-for wig that Laureen and Chris selected. Some choices were good, others were ridiculous, but the three of them cheered me on, and Chris and Laureen even tried on a few wigs themselves while making comments and suggestions — some were even helpful.

"I don't know if I want to stay blond," I said, surprising even myself.

"Really?" Chris said.

"Well, yeah. It's not like I'm trying to hide that I'm in chemo or wearing a wig, so maybe I'll just have a little fun with it."

"I like it. It's like I get a different girlfriend for a while," Chris said.

"Go brunette. You can see how the rest of us live," Laureen said.

"You can always get two," Diedre said, smiling.

I went from having no answers to my wig dilemma to too many options.

But I had an idea.

I immediately went home and posted photos of me wearing several of the wigs on my blog. Then I set up a poll and let my friends and family (and, as it turned out, quite a few strangers) decide what look I should choose. Seamus might not have been able to help me with this part of my cancer odyssey, but my friends could.

CHAPTER 19
COCKTAILS FOR ONE

Seamus wore a "Beagles for Boobies" shirt to my birthday party. His shirt and my matching sweatshirt were gifts from my mother.

Since my birthday fell between surgery and the start of chemotherapy, Chris and some friends decided a "Post-Operation/ Pre-Chemo" birthday bash was in order. The party was quickly dubbed the "POP-C Party" and, alternatively, the "Boobie Bash."

Destiny came as a special guest to corral Seamus and make sure at least some of the food remained available for the human guests. (Seamus still snuck more than his fair share.) As for the refreshments, I don't think I've ever seen so many variations of pink food and drink. It wasn't even October, Breast Cancer Awareness month, and yet my friends were able to find pink vodka, pink ribbon wines, pink cakes and cookies, pink ribbon tablecloths, plates, and cups, and even pink martini glasses. What they couldn't buy, they made. One friend even made what she called "boobie pops" — small cake balls on a stick with pink frosting and a darker pink jellybean "nipple."

My mom and stepdad sent flowers, and Chris's parents sent a basket of very useful items including a gorgeous periwinkle soft cotton wrap that Trudi assured me would be perfect to use during the chemo infusions. A group of friends surprised me with a lithograph from an artist I loved and whose show I had to miss because of the surgery (and the obvious fact that I needed to spend money on health care, not artwork). The colorful lithograph was of a hound dog, standing on a lush green lawn, empty liquor bottles surrounding him. The title was "Booze Hound." It made me laugh for so many reasons. I was thrilled to see that the artist, Robert Deyber, had signed a program from the show wishing me well in my treatments.

I was able to forget, for just that one night, what lay ahead.

Soon after, though, I began to count down the days before I'd have to start chemotherapy. I was not sleeping well. I fell into a habit of waking at two each morning. I'd get out of bed, grab a book off my nightstand, and head to the recliner in our library. When Seamus started waking with me and following me to the other room, I thought it was cute. When he crawled onto my lap and slept there with me, I knew my nervousness was palpable.

I thought I'd gotten used to the idea that I would lose my hair, but I kept trying to picture how it might happen — would I wake up one morning and my hair would all be on my pillow? Would I wash it all down the drain in the shower some morning? Or would I be sitting in a client meeting when suddenly my hair would begin to fall into clumps on the conference table? What if it was a new client? They'd be too frightened to come back!

The doctors and nurses seemed confident nausea wouldn't be an issue, but I'd always had a weak stomach, so I wasn't convinced. And the list of other possible side effects was horrific. My fingernails and toenails might come loose and fall off? Skin rashes? Thrush? Swelling of the hands and feet? Severe bone pain? Fluid retention? Mouth sores? Anemia? Nerve pain? Life-threatening infections? Seizures? Neuropathy? Debili-freaking-tating fatigue? My memories of Seamus's white blood cell crash were fresh and frightening.

I had to remind myself that these were just possibilities and that they would not all occur. Surely they couldn't all occur. And yet, the only way to know how I would respond to the chemotherapy — the only way to know which, if any, of these side effects I would experience — was to undergo round one.

So, I'm all set for chemo this Thursday at 10:00 a.m. Tomorrow I go pick up my prescriptions and my wig (I'm pretty sure I'm going to have to name "her"), and tomorrow night I start the antinausea medication. Chris has done the preparatory grocery shopping based on what we've surmised — because goodness knows we had to figure it out ourselves. Between the materials UCLA had given us, the book the good and great Dr. Karam gave me, and our many prior conversations with doctors, it does seem that it comes down to this: there isn't really a chemo diet/nutrition plan. It's just about controlling the side effects. So really, until we know how I react, we won't know what diet restrictions I have or what foods/liquids might help. I can drink coffee. I can have a glass of wine now and then. I have to avoid some obvious problem foods like sushi, mushrooms, raspberries (hard to wash), etc. Basically, that's to avoid getting an infection of any kind since my immune system will be shot. Common sense will suffice.

People keep asking me if I'm afraid. I really don't feel afraid. A little anxious, but mostly, I'd just like to get to Friday night. There's a lot riding on Friday — the day after the treatment is usually the "worst" day and will give me an idea what I'm in for. I'd like to be at the point where I know that. I feel prepared, and that's really all I can do.

Thanks again for all your thoughts and support. I'm bringing my laptop to chemo and will blog from there if I can. I'm wondering if they'll let me take pictures. If they do, you can count on it!

Two days before my first infusion appointment, I sat at my desk at home staring at the medication chart the nurse had given me. The chart was similar to the one Seamus had, only where his had been carefully designed and printed from a computer, mine was a poorly copied calendar with handwritten notes squeezed into the boxes for each day. The chart was a pill regimen meant to reduce or eliminate nausea and pain. These were "good" pills.

There were pills to take the night before, the morning of, the evening of, and the next two days following the chemo infusion, and there were optional pain medications, one for mild pain and one for severe pain. I had filled all of the prescriptions as well as purchasing all of the over-the-counter drugs that had been suggested — Benadryl, anti-diarrheal, stool softener, Tylenol — and two thermometers so I could constantly monitor my temperature at work and at home. I wondered if pumpkin pie filling worked for relieving side effects in humans like it did in dogs.

"Maybe you should put the chart somewhere we can both find it," Chris said, entering the office.

"I can't imagine forgetting it, given the dire consequences," I said.

"You never know. Plus, you might not feel like getting up and getting the list, so I should know where it is."

"I was thinking I'd leave it by the coffee pot. Then I'm sure I'll see it."

"What if you aren't drinking coffee then? Remember they said your sense of taste might change."

While it was difficult to picture drinking my usual gallons of coffee while nauseous, or worse, vomiting, it was equally hard to imagine getting through this stressful time without coffee. I can't imagine getting through a morning without coffee.

We decided instead to leave the chart by my computer in the home office, and I lined the pills up next to the chart once again, going over each one with Chris. "I guess you need to know the instructions, too. In case, you know, I'm a vomiting, shaking, unconscious mess."

"You'll be fine. You'll be like Seamus was — all appetite and energy."

"I'm not that lucky. Plus, really, the silver lining to chemo had better be weight loss."

I awoke at five on the morning of my appointment. Seamus stretched, yawned, and then followed me, waiting for me to get down the stairs before racing ahead of me. The one good habit I'd managed to teach Seamus would turn out to be a very useful thing.

When I first brought him into my home, Seamus regularly raced ahead of me, cut me off, and thought nothing of running between or under my feet. Before Chris moved in, I had fears of Seamus tripping me on the stairs in his mad dash to the food bowl. I envisioned myself sprawled on the floor, back or neck broken, days passing before anyone came to look for me. And then it would only be because Seamus, having missed breakfast, was howling at the gate. So I trained him not to run down the stairs ahead of me. He had to sit (not so) patiently until I reached the bottom of the stairs and gave him the signal that he could descend. He challenged me regularly, rushing ahead of me when I was three or four steps from the bottom. I'd stop and make him go back upstairs and wait before I'd continue down, and even then, occasionally he'd bolt down after I took just one more step. I'd stop and make him go back upstairs and we'd do it again. Finally, he'd wait, sitting at the very edge of the top step, dancing back and forth on his back end, shifting the weight on his front paws — left, right, left, right — and groaning with anxiety, until I stepped down from the last step and turned back to him to say, "Okay." Then he'd let out a victory howl and launch himself, screaming, *AAAAAARR-ROOOOOOOOO! Hurry the fook up! Get my breakfast, woman! I don't have time for these fookin' games! AAAAAARRROOOOOOOOO!!!* as he bolted for the laundry room where his bowls were. It was a game to Seamus. I knew that. The only way the training worked was because Seamus knew if I never got to the bottom of the stairs, he'd never get breakfast.

Now, if I was going to be ill and weak and perhaps have numb or painfully swollen feet, it was a very good thing I'd managed to teach Seamus this particular game.

Seamus followed me to the laundry room and I scooped kibble into his bowl, giving him a little extra. Chemo morning seemed to call for leniency and empathy for all creatures. I poured myself a large cup of coffee and drank it downstairs, letting Chris sleep. After breakfast, Seamus cuddled in next to me on the couch.

"What do you think, buddy? Shall we have toast?" I was supposed to eat something.

Seamus thumped his tail at the word *toast*. He also thumped his tail at *what, buddy,* and *shall* — since he'd just had his own breakfast and knew he'd be getting mine next.

Dr. Dutelle had told me Seamus could have carbohydrates now and in fact would need some. Since I kept him on the high-protein, low-carb kibble, I gradually returned to our codependent toast-sharing routine. I made two slices of wheat toast and slathered them with peanut butter.

Chris came into the den as I handed Seamus the last bit of crust.

"Did you pop your pills yet?" he said.

"I'm headed upstairs now to take them. I figured food in my stomach was a good idea. And coffee in my brain . . . so I can read the pill labels. No OD'ing on Vicodin the first day."

"Good plan. I'm going to pack us a lunch while you get ready."

Seamus's tail thumped again. *Lunch? Yes, please!*

But I had less enthusiasm. I had to go "get ready." And how does one get ready to have their body flushed with poison? Should one wear black?

I showered and dressed, choosing comfortable black pants, a short-sleeved periwinkle blue cotton top, and the huge, soft cotton wrap Trudi had given me. She told me the infusion room was usually cold, but you can get hot flashes from the drugs, so the wrap would easily come on and off without disrupting the tubes coming from my arm. Practical advice. And fashionable — the wrap was gorgeously soft and in my favorite color. I blew-dry and styled my hair, trying unsuccessfully to not think about how many more times I'd do that before there was no hair.

I went back downstairs, where Chris waited, showered, shaved, and dressed, snuggled up with Seamus on the couch.

"Okay, pills are popped. I'm ready for the chair."

"And lunches are packed. It's only 7:30. We're even early."

"Obviously cancer has changed us. And not for the better."

"Surprisingly."

"Let's just get going. It's not like I'm going to sit down and rest."

Seamus followed us out to the courtyard, and we stopped for photos of me, new cancer warrior, and Seamus, the veteran. I petted Seamus for good luck, kissed the top of his forehead, and then put him in his crate in the backseat of our car.

We dropped Seamus at Destiny's home. True to her offer, she was watching Seamus for the morning. Or however long my appointment took.

I was relieved to see that the oncology office had removed the Valentine's Day décor. The office seemed more professional without pink and red streamers and hearts. And this time, I was in my paper dress and being addressed by the nurse practitioner by 9:15. She deemed my surgery scar healed sufficiently and the blood work I'd had done earlier in the week came back fine.

"Go ahead and get dressed and we'll find a chair for you," she said.

Although I'd been calling it "the chair" myself, the expression got more ominous the closer I came to having to sit in it hooked up to a bag dripping poison. Chris followed me to the infusion room. We both stood in the doorway and looked around the room, waiting for instructions.

After a few minutes a nurse showed me to my chair, on the left side of the room, next to an elderly woman reading a book. I sat in the chair, and Chris took a seat on a small chair next to me.

"We're mixing up your chemo cocktail now. I'll be right back," the nurse said as she departed.

I looked at Chris. "I've never been so disappointed to hear the word *cocktail.*"

"No kidding. It's like an abuse of a perfectly wonderful word."

The infusion room was small. The chairs (large and reminiscent of the massage lounge chairs usually found in places named "Happy Nails") were positioned up against each wall of the room. Which meant, like it or not, the patients, ten of us (nine women and one man), were all staring at one another in silence.

I wondered, what is the etiquette? What do you say? "I'm new here"? Or, "Come here often?" Or, "What are you in for?" It was hard to know. I think the etiquette should have been covered in my chemo training. The dogs with Seamus didn't seem to have this problem. In that oncology waiting center, the patients sniffed butts indiscriminately as a greeting. Such knowledge was not going to help me here, although having the nonchalance of a dog would certainly have.

Most patients merely glanced at us and returned to their magazines. A few were sleeping. All had IV drips on poles next to their chairs.

Chris began to unpack all that we'd brought with us — some books, my journal, my laptop, Chris's laptop, the large bag of foods Chris had prepared, two liters of Gatorade, several magazines. Because the chemo drip is done slowly so as to observe any negative reactions, we were told, the first day of chemo was going to be a long one. We had prepared for that. Maybe we'd over-prepared. We looked like we'd come to stay.

In addition to taking the steroids and other medication the night before and morning of my appointment, I'd also packed up enough work and other items to keep me busy for the day. One would not want to be bored while poison is pumped through one's veins. As I understood it, I likely wouldn't be sick until the next day. That meant I could still work during the infusion. The comfy recliner even had a little table at the side for my computer. The nurse approached the side of my chair and asked to see my left arm. The chemo is delivered in the arm opposite from the side the surgery was done. Right breast, left arm.

I extended my arm, moving back the soft cotton wrap.

"Oh, you're lucky. Great veins. You didn't need a port?" the nurse said.

"No. They didn't even ask me about it. But yes, I've been told I have great veins. At my age, I guess that's a compliment."

Chris perked up. "Those veins bleed a lot. I've been told to let you know that."

"That's good to know, but it won't be a problem here," she said, rubbing alcohol on the back of my hand.

The needle easily, quickly slipped into a large vein. I winced. Not because it hurt, but because it had begun. I watched as she taped down the catheter on the backside of my hand. She hung the chemo cocktail — clear liquid in an opaque, sturdy plastic bag — from a hook at the top of the IV pole and bent down to push some buttons on the monitor attached to the pole. Chris held my right hand tightly, and I rested my left on the arm of the chair. We watched as the liquid began to seep through the tubing and made its way to my hand and into my vein.

After sitting with me for a few minutes and asking if I felt okay, if I was warm, if I was itchy or felt anything at all, the nurse left to tend to other patients.

I turned to Chris. "So here we go." There was no turning back now.

"Well, this has got to help," he said, pointing to the top of my IV pole.

I looked up. Attached to the pole, hanging from its neck was a Beanie Baby panda. A little lower down, but also hung from its neck, was a brown bear. Both bears were slumped and depressed. I turned back to Chris. "What the hell?"

"Look — they're everywhere. As though this experience isn't bad enough, they've attached suicidal Beanie Babies to each and every IV pole."

I glanced around the room — there were unicorns, angels, blue bears, a dog, a lamb, and what may have once been a kitten or perhaps a raccoon before it gave up on life, all dangling from their broken necks from the tops of the IV poles.

"The person who decorates for the holidays obviously got her hands on this room, too. Is this supposed to cheer me up?"

"Look on the wall," Chris said, pointing behind me to the cheaply framed prints of angels, dolphins, rainbows, and bears dressed as angels, wearing rainbow dresses. "I like that one in particular." He pointed at a quilt square framed under glass. "What? In case of temperature drop, break glass?"

I laughed. Which caused most of the people in the otherwise quiet room to look my way. Several of them smiled, but only one laughed with me. She was a beautiful, dark-haired young woman, seated in one of the "normal" visitors' chairs in front of us. She had a textbook open on her lap.

"I'm sorry," she said. "I don't mean to be eavesdropping; it's kind of hard not to listen. And you guys have been cracking me up."

"I'm sorry. We didn't mean to interrupt your studying," I said.

"No, it's fine. It's nice someone is talking."

We learned that her name was Elizabeth and she was there supporting her mother, who was two chairs down from me on her fifth visit. Her mother didn't like to talk during the sessions, preferring to read. Elizabeth shared a plate of chocolate, walnut, and cranberry cookies that she'd brought for the nurses and other patients.

The woman in the chair next to me declined any cookies and minutes later was vomiting into the trash can between us, a frightful reminder of what was happening in this room. To my disappointment and surprise, the oncology center had no wireless Internet connection, so there would be very little work I could get done. Instead, I read until Chris set out our lunch spread — cheese and crackers, peanut butter and jelly sandwiches, a pudding cup, and grape Gatorade.

"It's like a picnic," I said.

"Close. I figured comfort food was good, plus we needed stuff that could just sit in the bag all morning. Just pretend the Gatorade is wine and this is a park. With, you know . . . suicidal unicorns."

Later, when I needed to use the restroom, the nurse pointed me in the right direction and explained that I'd need to wheel the IV pole (panda and bear, too) along with me. I made my way, pulling the pole and struggling to get the wheels headed in the same direction, my luck with IV poles no better than it usually is with grocery carts. I closed the door behind me and was immediately confronted with a sign over the toilet: "Chemotherapy Patients: Please Flush Twice." Yeah, that about summed up what was happening to me.

By one in the afternoon most of the other

patients had left, including Elizabeth and her mom, and I was just being switched to the second chemotherapy drug, Cytoxan. This was not the drug Seamus had a problem with, so I figured, however insanely, that this one would be easy.

After fifteen minutes, I was cold. I gathered the wrap around myself and asked Chris if he was cold. He wasn't.

I sneezed. Then I sneezed again. When I sneezed a third time, two nurses were instantly at my side.

"Are you hot? Itchy? Nauseous?"

"No, I'm cold."

"We have to watch for allergic reactions."

"No, I think I'm just cold."

She gave me a warmed blanket.

I wrapped myself in the blanket and slept until nearly three. Seamus hadn't had a problem and neither would I. When I woke, it was over. The nurse was removing the needle from the back of my hand.

"So that's it?"

"That's it. You did great. Most side effects, if you have any, don't start for twenty-four to forty-eight hours. Be sure to take your medications and call us if anything comes up. When you stand up, stand up slowly."

I stood slowly, but I was steady. Chris had

already packed up our things. We were the last ones to leave the infusion room. All that was left to do was pick up Seamus and wait to see how I'd react.

Chapter 20
Beaglefest

I awoke at three in the morning, bursting with energy. I wrote a blog post on the chemo experience, cleaned out my desk, and then read for a couple of hours. Seamus followed me into the library and stayed with me, sleeping on a pillow and blanket on the floor, until I went back to bed. We both woke again at eight, hungry. Chris made scrambled eggs and bacon, with toast (for me and Seamus), and I had two cups of coffee. The steroids were doing their job.

That wasn't all good. When I went to the bathroom, I had the worst bout of constipation I'd ever had or even heard of. That was on the list of possible steroid side effects; I had the medication for it, but I just hadn't taken it, because chances were just as good that the opposite problem would occur from the chemo. How was one supposed to know?

As arranged previously, Stacey came by to sit with me on side-effect watch so that

Chris could spend the day interviewing Princeton hopefuls as he'd volunteered to do for the Alumni Association many months before. He was going to cancel it, but I encouraged him to go. I had finally had the discussion with him about how unfair I felt it was that he had to be going through something like this at his age. He dismissed it with a response that it was even more unfair that I was going through it. Still though, I wanted to minimize, in any little way I could, the effect of all of this on him. In that way, I was like his mother had been when she had cancer.

I was awake when Stacey arrived, and although I hadn't bothered to do my hair and makeup, I didn't look sick. By the relieved look on Stacey's face when I answered the door, I knew she was expecting much worse.

"This must be confusing for you," I said.

"How so?"

"Well, if I looked really well put together, you would have thought I was doing awful, based on your theory. But if I looked really awful . . . under these circumstances wouldn't you have also thought I was doing terribly and you'd have your hands full for the day?"

"Ah. Yes. So I'm thankful you just look

somewhere in between. You feel okay?"

"I feel surprisingly well."

We spent a few hours sitting on my bed watching old television shows and getting caught up with each other. The day reminded me of being a teenager again when one had time to while away the day with television and a good friend. Except for the part where we were anticipating the effects of poison on my innards.

The doorbell rang, and Seamus ran, howling violently, slipped out his doggie door, and flung himself at the gate.

"Poor FedEx guy. He looks scared to death," Stacey said as she brought the package upstairs to me.

"Yeah, I get that Seamus is loud and looks a bit crazed, but I never get 'fear of a beagle,' especially on the other side of an iron gate. He's only hoping for another cookie delivery."

"The love of a mother blinds you." She handed me the package.

Inside were the wigs Chris and I had picked out together and ordered online. Not the one I'd bought from Diedre, but a few cheaper versions. We'd had so much fun trying on different styles and colors that I ordered extras.

I pulled out a long, layered, jet-black style.

"Oooh, very Natasha-esque," Stacey said.

"True. And obviously this one will henceforth be called Natasha." I set Natasha down and pulled out a blond bob. I put it on and turned to Stacey.

"Sienna."

"As in Miller?"

"As in Miller. Let me have that one." She took it off my head and plopped it onto her own.

I laughed. "I'm sorry, but you don't look a thing like Sienna Miller."

"No?" Stacey got off the bed and walked to my bathroom mirror. I heard her howling laughter echo off the tiles. "I look like a crack whore! Or a washed-up stripper!"

"Then this one we shall call 'Sienna Chablis' — she's quite versatile."

I tried on the next wig, a thick, strawberry-blond, shoulder-length style. I'd always wanted thick hair.

"Kind of '70s housewife," Stacey said.

"Yeah? Okay. I don't know why, but I'm calling her 'Connie.' "

"I don't know why either, but that works. And now, I want to be a blond." She pulled the last of the wigs out. It was a long, blond, stick-straight style — exactly like my hair had been in high school. She put it on, over her short, dark hair. "I expect to instantly have more fun."

Stacey was not meant to be a blond. I laughed again.

"Fine," she said, removing the wig and handing it to me. I tried it on, and she immediately dubbed it "Britney-Bitch." I thought that worked nicely. When Chris came home, he joined in our fun. When he put on Sienna Chablis and looked so much like some English band member from the '80s we considered renaming the wig "Nigel," I laughed so hard my stomach hurt.

I figured that was a pretty good first day of chemo. The only pain I had came from laughter. I can handle this.

I held that thought for the next several days, encouraged by my steroid energy boost and a huge appetite.

Soon, though, my energy waned.

By midafternoon in my office on Tuesday I needed a nap. I closed my office door, unfolded the futon I'd brought, and napped for a half hour. The short nap allowed me to work straight through until six that evening. On Wednesday, I did the same but only made it until five. Still, I felt better than I'd expected.

Emboldened, I talked to Chris about a weekend trip to Phoenix. Seamus and I wanted to go to Beaglefest. Chris questioned the sensibility of this.

I called my oncologist. I was once again passed over to the nurse practitioner, but I minded less when she gave me approval to go. I was thrilled.

"Are you sure?" Chris said.

"Yes. It will be so much better than sitting around the house. If I get tired, we can just go back to the hotel."

"She said it's okay for you to be around all of those dogs?"

"Yes. Especially since it's outside. But she said I should stay away from anybody who is visibly sick or coughing or anything like that."

"I don't know. It seems a little crazy to drive for five hours with a dog in the car to spend a day with hundreds of other dogs, only to turn around and drive back the next day, all while you're all chemo'd up."

It did sound a little crazy, but that's exactly what we did.

The drive from our home to Phoenix is almost entirely desert and thus peaceful. We stopped every hour or so for food or water and to let Seamus stretch and walk and sniff. In six hours we arrived at the one hotel near Beaglefest that allowed dogs.

The hotel clerk gave us a room on the first floor with "easy access to the grass area" —

which turned out to be a six-foot by three-foot strip of grass next to the stairwell, which was also in front of our room.

I napped before we went to dinner, and by then the temperatures had cooled significantly and the wind was strong.

Because we had Seamus with us, our only option was eating outside on the restaurant patio. The servers and bussers took turns coming by and petting Seamus, bringing him first a bowl of water, then some bread, and finally a large bone from the kitchen. Other diners coming and going from the warmth of indoors also stopped and petted Seamus, who sat quietly, looking adorable. Chris and I sat shivering at the table, while Seamus collected his due.

Back at the hotel, things did not improve. Seamus barked each time headlights flashed into our room and again when two teenagers chose to hang out in the stairwell talking. Just as we'd drift off to sleep, lights would flash and the beagle would howl. We only got uninterrupted sleep after three in the morning. When we awoke, I walked across the parking lot to get a large cup of French roast coffee and bagels for all three of us. We were an hour and a half late to the event.

Beaglefest is, as it sounds, a celebration of beagles. There are hundreds of hounds there, baying, jumping, howling, and being beagle-y. We missed the howling contest but did see the very unsuccessful "best trick" contest, which made us feel much better that we weren't the only ones who couldn't train a beagle. At least we were smart enough not to enter Seamus in the contest. The "best kiss" contest also seemed to be a bust, since it would seem that most beagles, like Seamus, are not face-lickers. (Someone should have thought to put bacon grease on their face.) I noticed the organizers weren't silly enough to stage an eating contest for the beagles.

The day was windy, and my eyes watered, and I tired earlier than I normally would have, but I was blissful. The entire day had nothing to do with cancer. I was just a girl on a date with her boyfriend and her beagle. Just like hundreds of others that day. Seamus and I both slept for most of the drive home, so it's possible Chris was not as thrilled with the trip, but he didn't complain.

The next day I woke when my alarm clock went off at 6:30. Seamus and I both went downstairs. I gave him his breakfast and made my toast and coffee. We returned upstairs, and I sipped my coffee while checking emails, just like any other morning.

By 7:15 I began to feel fatigued and unusually warm. I took my temperature. 99.5. Chris was in the shower then, so I didn't say anything to him. I took Tylenol and lay down. After twenty minutes, I felt better.

I went back to my computer to email work that I'd be late. My hands shook on the keyboard. I felt a rush of heat. And then I was cold. And then it wasn't just my hands shaking.

I walked slowly back to the bedroom and again took my temperature. 102.

We'd been given instructions repeatedly that if my temperature passed 101.5, we were to immediately phone the doctor. I got in bed, holding the covers as tightly around me as I could, while calling my oncologist. Only she wasn't there. I received assurances someone would get back to me.

Fifteen minutes later my temperature was at 103. I was too weak and shaky to make another phone call. Chris called and received the same assurances that someone would return the call, along with instructions to have me rest and take Tylenol to reduce my fever.

The Tylenol worked to reduce my fever

enough so that I could sleep, but I slept fitfully, wrapped in several blankets and still shaking. I didn't have the energy to sit up, to eat, or to drink water. Chris brought me a damp cloth and placed it on my forehead. I can't remember the last time that was done for me. He sat on the bed with me, watching me and checking my temperature every so often. He called my office to let them know I wouldn't be in.

In the early afternoon, my temperature hit 104 and still the doctor's office had not called back. Despite my temperature, I was unable to get warm. The only movement I could manage was the uncontrollable shaking.

My temperature hit 105, and I slipped in and out of consciousness. I was vaguely aware of Chris screaming on the phone to my oncologist's office just as I was vaguely aware that I was likely experiencing the same white blood cell crash that Seamus had endured. But like Seamus, who couldn't follow me downstairs for toast that fateful morning, I couldn't follow the thread of Chris's conversation. I just wanted to sleep. I was beyond fatigue. My body was shutting down.

Chris grabbed me, pulled me out of bed, wrapped me in a heavy blanket, and rushed me to the car. Seamus was left behind, howling at the gate. We had no choice. I didn't even have the capacity to make a choice. I curled up in the front seat of the car with the blanket wrapped tightly around me.

I can recall getting in the car, but I cannot recall the drive. Likewise, I remember getting out of the car, dragging my blanket, Linus-like, with me and entering the waiting room. Chris had to fill me in on the rest later.

"You know how at the emergency room or urgent care or even a doctor's office waiting room there is always that one really sick person, coughing, hacking, pale, shaking, or vomiting? And everyone moves away from that person? You were that person. Only there was nowhere for people to move. Every single chair was taken. I actually had to ask someone to let you sit down."

"You'd think they'd triage better," I said.

"Believe me, I tried. I was up in the receptionist's face every few minutes reminding her you had cancer and were in chemotherapy. She continued to insist it was first come, first served and if I needed more, we'd have to go to urgent care."

"I still can't believe they sent us to a lab to get my blood drawn instead of the emergency room."

"Twice. We had to have two different blood tests, and the second one couldn't be done until twenty minutes after the first."

"I don't remember that."

"Do you remember sitting in the car in the parking lot?"

"Kind of." I remembered wanting to sleep. I remembered being cold and extremely exhausted, in an unable-to-keep-my-head-up way.

"That was between blood tests. You kept saying you were freezing, and the waiting room was cold, so I took you out to the car and turned the heater on."

"Weird to be so cold with a 105 fever."

"Yes, well, that apparently happens when you get down to your last six white blood cells."

"Like Seamus."

"What?"

"That's what happened to Seamus. He wasn't shaking, but he was pretty out of it. Shaking would have freaked me out even more."

"Believe me, I was freaked out. I wasn't there when it happened to Seamus, but if it was even half as frightening as this was, it was horrible."

"It was. It definitely was. Thank you for

taking care of me."

"You and this dog — I can't believe you had the same white blood cell crash. I really could have done without that part." He was petting Seamus in bed next to me when he said this.

"I know, baby. I know." I petted Seamus, too. Seamus and I both received Cytoxan chemotherapy, but that wasn't what had caused his white blood cell crash. I had foolishly assumed it wouldn't cause mine.

We didn't notice the flashing red light on our answering machine until the next morning. The neighbors on each side of us had called, complaining of Seamus's howling at the gate. I told Chris I would at least handle that much. I'd email the neighbors, explain what happened, and ask for their patience and understanding. I wasn't convinced I'd get it, but I didn't want Chris to have to deal with angry neighbors, too.

I sent the email and told my neighbors, for the first time, about my cancer. Judy called immediately. She let me know that she too was a breast cancer survivor.

"Please don't worry about the dog. You have enough to worry about. I'm so sorry we called. We didn't know," Judy said.

"Oh, I know. And I'm so sorry he bothered you. We usually don't leave him alone."

"You had no choice. Please let us know if there is anything we can do to help. Anything at all. And don't worry at all about Seamus. You do what you need to do."

Our neighbor on the other side responded shortly after and, much to my surprised pleasure, offered to watch Seamus for us if we ever needed it. I wouldn't have been more surprised if she had offered to assume my cancer for me.

So it occurred to me in an odd, rambling way (which is how things tend to occur to me) that cancer treatments are in many ways all about keeping the wolf at the gate away or at least on the other side of the gate. But this week, as I think we're all clear on now, has been all about dealing with the side effects of the chemotherapy, which is all about keeping the cancer-wolf on the other side of the gate. There was the white blood cell count crash. That's mostly under control. I have some energy back, my temperature has returned to normal but still tends to creep up slightly right around the fourth hour after I've taken Tylenol, and I've still got to avoid being around crowds or sick people. I have three more days of antibiotics. And I'm just not a good sick person. Unless it's completely obvious I'm sick (see Monday), I tend to forget. So today I

forgot the antibiotics and the wolf started licking its chops. I took them with dinner. The
antibiotics, not the wolf.

Then there's the mouth problems. I have no
taste buds anymore. Well, I do, but they are
mostly programmed to "under the car hood"
and "dirt." Of course, this doesn't stop me from
eating. It just means I eat a little of everything
trying to find something that tastes good. Then
I try to remind myself that I'm supposed to eat
for nutrition, not taste. Then I laugh at myself.
Then I berate myself. Also, now my gums and
mouth in general are so tender the electric
toothbrush is a no-go and I have to use an
extra-soft bristle brush. I was already using
special toothpaste and mouthwash designed
for dry mouth and to increase bacteria fighting. It was recommended by my dental hygien-
ist when I went in for my final cleaning until
after chemo (right, that's another thing you
can't do during chemo). The mouthwash in
particular is very soothing. So now I am
completely a special needs dental care person. I brush my teeth completely differently
than you do. I also take a lot more Tylenol.
(And chemo.)

When I woke Thursday morning, exactly
two weeks from the chemo infusion, I
hesitated to lift my head from the pillow,

suspecting my hair would not come up with me. I'd been told this was when the hair loss would start. In the shower, I washed my hair gently, fearing it would drop out all at once. I combed it out slowly and let it air dry, carefully pulling it back in a low ponytail. So little hair came out that day that I began to think maybe I'd be lucky. Maybe Wednesday's hair loss was it. But then Dr. Glaspy's words came back to me: "One hundred percent guaranteed your hair will fall out."

I called Kelly, my hairstylist, to arrange for her to shave my head on Friday evening. I got my wig ready — I'd be a redhead soon. All dog owners begin to look like their dogs eventually, right? It was not the wig that won in my blog polling, but it was a respectable second place, and the process helped me determine what I really wanted to do. And what I wanted to do was have a little fun with the situation.

I was tired of the stress of constantly worrying when and if my hair would fall out. I wanted to get it over with. Somehow I felt the sooner I got the hair loss out of the way, the closer I'd be to finishing all of the treatments. I could move on to the recovery stage.

Kelly arrived at 5:15, and Chris made us

all margaritas. But Kelly was not anxious to get the shaving over with. She kept asking me if I was sure I was ready.

"Kelly, I have to be ready. Let's just do it." I sat down on the chair Chris had brought into our living room on the wood floor. I could see Kelly was fighting back tears. "No crying! This is not supposed to be harder for you than it is for me."

"I know, I know. I'm sorry. You're really brave."

I'd heard "brave" from a lot of people since my diagnosis, but really, what's the other choice?

While Seamus watched, seated in front of me, staring up, and Chris took photos, Kelly wrapped a cape around me and began cutting. At first she cut six inches of length, and for a brief time I had a bob. Then she cut the sides much shorter, and we laughed at my mullet. The hair in the back went next. I did not look down at the floor; it was easier to look ahead — sometimes at Seamus, sometimes at Chris. It's only hair. It grows back. It's a small price to pay for living.

Kelly pulled out men's hair clippers. "Are you sure you're ready?"

"It's a little late to stop now," I said. There was only about an inch of roughly chopped hair left on my head. "Go ahead."

"I'm not going to shave it all the way down. It's too risky that you'd be cut. If I leave a quarter to a half inch, you'll have less scalp irritation." She turned on the clippers.

I heard the humming noise of the clippers and felt the tickle of hair falling down my neck, and in only a few moments it was over.

She handed me a mirror.

I was not shocked by my appearance. I had the same face, wore the same clothes, was the same person. I just had a lot less hair. No one would refer to me as "blondie" now. I wondered though, without makeup and colorful clothing, and when all of the hair was gone, how bad would I look?

"You look cute," Chris said.

"Cute is an overstatement, but thank you."

"You have a great face. You can totally pull this off."

"I was thinking the same thing," Kelly said.

"Thanks, you guys. I'm okay. Thanks."

For the next several days, small hairs dropped everywhere I went. I shed worse than Seamus ever did. Within a week I had only a few wispy baby-like hairs on the top of my head and around my ears. I did not ever get the shiny bald look that many get, but I was certainly bald. After a few more days, the baldness was almost a relief. I was too tired to have to mess with styling hair anyway.

CHAPTER 21
SIDE EFFECTS

After my day of medical bills and taxes yesterday and then missing out on such a fun event today [Chris and friends in San Diego at a Wine and Food Festival] staying home and working instead (you know, to pay those medical bills), it was hard not to launch into a full-blown pity party. I came close. More than once.

But luckily I had Seamus and he abhors pity parties. If you suffer from depression, get a beagle. Then get some food. You'll be endlessly amused and laughing in no time. Seamus even convinced me to take him for a walk. (This is when I was explaining to him that I am fat and ugly and now broke; he was sure a walk would cure all of that.)

That's two days in a row of walking! For me, that's like a full-blown exercise routine. I'm sure I even worked off the potato chips I ate at some point during the pity party (because come on, what's a pity party without potato chips?). I'm thinking keeping busy is somewhat key to this positive attitude thing. Just maybe not busy with a bag of chips.

I did not wake as early for my second chemo session, but without hair or the ability to enjoy the taste of coffee anymore, I was able to get ready quickly. I wore the Sienna Chablis blond wig, but I put a soft cotton newspaper-boy cap on over it, which I felt made it look less wig-like. I looked and felt fine, I thought. Once again I hugged Seamus for luck and took a picture with him, and then Chris and I loaded up the car with our "picnic" lunch, books, and Seamus, along with all of his required paraphernalia for the day.

We dropped Seamus off at Destiny's house.

As we parked at the oncology center, I said to Chris, "I think I'll be okay if you don't want to stay with me the whole time. I have a feeling I'll sleep. Now I understand why all the other patients seemed to be sleeping last time."

"Okay, if that's the case I might run out and do some errands."

"You should."

For the first half hour of my infusion, Chris stayed and chatted with me and with

Elizabeth, back again for what we learned was her mother's last treatment.

"I think I'm going to read, so you can go now if you want," I said.

"You sure?" Chris said.

"Yeah. This is boring, and you have things to do. If you're back for us to have lunch that will be fine."

Once Chris was gone, I leaned back in my chair and opened my book.

Fifteen minutes later Elizabeth said to me, "Do you feel okay?"

"Yes. Why?"

"You're kind of red."

"I am?"

The woman in the chair next to me turned and looked. "Yes, you are. You're very red."

Just then my face began to sting. Then my hands tingled and quickly numbed. And then I was hot — very hot. A bolt of pain shot through my lower back just as I was ready to ask for help. Instead all that came out of my mouth was a gasp. The nurse across the room raced over.

She flipped the switch on my IV pole and stopped the infusion. "How do you feel?"

"Hot. And my back is killing me. I should have taken the sedative you offered."

"I'm giving you Benadryl and Decadron intravenously; you should feel better quickly." She changed out the bags of fluid on my IV pole and turned the pump on again.

In minutes the pain in my back subsided. And, the ladies around me were quick to comment, I'd gone back to normal coloring. The nurse then hooked up a saline solution to flush out my system. Once that finished, the chemo was started again, with a slower drip. I lasted fifteen minutes before the tingling hot flush returned. The nurse had to repeat the intravenous flushing process one more time.

By the time Chris returned for lunch, I was no further along in getting the actual chemo than I had been when he'd left.

"You missed all the excitement."

"I did? What happened?"

I told him, while Elizabeth added color commentary (mostly red).

"Geez. I shouldn't have left," he said.

"It's okay. You couldn't have known. And I'm fine now."

"Have I mentioned how much I hate chemo? I'm not leaving again."

"Okay, well, settle in then. The nurse says that now they'll do the infusion much more slowly to avoid any reaction. And next time, they'll keep my steroid dosage up. So that should be fun."

Chris dropped heavily into the chair beside me. "I thought it was going to be another white blood cell crash."

I reached over and held his hand with my free right hand. I had thought the same thing.

Once again, we watched as each of the other patients that day finished treatment and headed home. We said good-bye and good luck to Elizabeth and her mother, who received her "diploma" for completing treatment. The doctors and nurses and we fellow (envious) patients all applauded her as the staff gave her a "graduation" ceremony.

Chris and I were the last to leave, along with our nurse, at nearly six that evening.

"The steroids are working," I said as soon as Chris and I were in the car. "You know how I know?"

"You have a sudden urge to bat? Or you're angry and wanting to fight?"

"Pizza. I want pizza."

"We can do that. I certainly don't feel like cooking. We'll get a pizza, get our dog, and get home."

"Sounds good."

The next day we'd have to return to the oncology center for a shot that would prevent the white blood cell crash from happening again. The shot itself had a long list of possible side effects, including "severe bone pain" in 30 percent of patients, but that evening we had a quiet time at home before us.

Seamus, however, had other plans. He must have had steroid sympathy the way he howled for the pizza.

AAAAAARRROOOOOOOOO!! Pizza! I Love Pizza!! Pizza is my most favorite. AAAAAAR-RROOOOOOOOO!!! Pizza! It's like toast with sausage!! Pizza!!! Give me fookin' pizzaaaaaaaaaaaaaaa roooooooooooooohhh!!

I handed Seamus my pizza crust. Chris shook his head.

"You can't imagine how much sympathy I have for this dog right now," I said.

We only lasted twenty minutes after devouring the pizza before all three of us fell asleep on the couch.

Turns out this breast cancer club is kind of a woman thing. Yeah, that's a problem. I have never been good at women's club things. Never. I may not be a "group" person in general. For example, the thought of a cancer support group, to me, is worse than the disease. And not surprisingly, no one (not even my health care providers) has suggested that I attend one. Okay, well, the oncologist's office did hand me a calendar of "events"

(which has an awful lot of support groups —
but none for generally grumpy, sarcastic souls
such as me), but the calendar was for January and February and she handed it to me on
February 26.

So here I am — breast cancer person, thrust
into a world of pink ribbons, cute T-shirts,
inspirational talks/signs/poems/books, woman
power, and. . . . cliques. Yeah, cliques. Now
don't get me wrong, I love the shirts. But I'm
not that big of a fan of pink (fuchsia, sure, but
not baby pink). I also tend to find myself
uninspired by things that I'm just sure are supposed to inspire me. I want nothing more than
to get through this and return to being me, not
a better me, just me.

This feeling that I'm a member of a club has
been around since early after my diagnosis.
And hey, like Trudi said, it's not a club anyone
wants to belong to so that's no surprise. The
feeling that I might be a loser member of the
club and not living up to expectations is new-
ish. But the fact that there are "cliques" within
this club and a sort of "rule book" is only starting to sneak up on me. I'm not sure I'm finding my clique. Maybe because my people
don't go to pink events?

I might now be the equivalent of the goth
kids in high school.

■ ■ ■ ■

The shot to prevent the white blood cell crash required its own round of side-effect-fighting pill-popping. I was given another cocktail recipe of sorts. It was a "cocktail" of Claritin, Benadryl, and Tylenol, with a Gatorade chaser. Seamus had been given Tagamet and Zantac. Until then, I had no idea there were so many over-the-counter drugs used in combating cancer.

As a result of these new drugs, I didn't have nearly as much energy as I had on day three of the first round, and I was disappointed with that. I kept searching for the slightest silver lining. (I had gained, not lost, weight.) I napped, I watched TV with Chris for a bit, and then I zonked out. Since I was taking the steroid medication and drinking a lot of fluids, I had to get up and head to the restroom a couple of times a night. When I got out of bed in the middle of the night, my limbs were heavy. I felt like somebody was pushing me back down. It wasn't painful as much as awkward and frightening, as though cement was hardening in my veins. How was I going to lug all four limbs to the restroom?

I rocked my limbs into something resembling momentum and flung myself down the hallway to the restroom. I took a Tylenol while I was at it and then fell back into bed, thankful I didn't cause the bed to crash down to the bottom floor. I stayed in bed most of the morning, without energy and weighing six hundred pounds.

For the first time in seventeen years, I didn't make it to the Walk with the Animals, benefiting the Mary S. Roberts Pet Adoption Center. I asked Chris to go and to take Seamus. I felt like I would at least be represented. Chris emailed me photos from his cell phone, each one showing a familiar person waving or giving me a thumbs-up sign. He made me feel a part of the event even if I couldn't make it physically. And Seamus received treats and petting from just about everyone there.

The cement in my veins feeling lasted for nearly a week. I recovered from that just in time to deal with my eyelashes and eyebrows falling out. I had assumed that since they did not fall out with my hair, they would be staying. They had other plans. I could make up for my loss of eyelashes with eyeliner or, perhaps, fake eyelashes. But the loss of eyebrows changes a face. I looked sad. I looked sick.

Then I woke up with a rash on my hands,

which throughout the day spread over my body. I drenched my skin in calamine lotion and popped the maximum dosage of Benadryl, but nothing seemed to help. I scratched. I bled.

When I woke the next morning, the rash had worsened and my body was covered in deep-red welts from where I'd torn at my skin in my sleep. Chris phoned the doctor's office and after several calls back and forth was told by the nurse that I should take Benadryl and Tylenol and to keep checking my temperature. Here we go again, we both thought. And again the doctor was not available. We'd never heard from her during the white blood cell crash, and it did not appear she would be available for this.

The Benadryl kept me sleeping most of the day. But when I slept, I had nightmares usually involving a car spinning or sliding out of control or with me in the backseat and no driver up front. Analysis of the dream was not difficult — everything was spinning out of my control. At night there were no dreams because there was no sleep. Instead, I played what I called Misery Slots. I had three things going wrong intermittently all through the night, any one of which was enough to keep me wide awake. First there was the hives — which periodically would flare up and keep me tearing at my skin. Then there was the hot flashes — chemo had sent me into early menopause, so hot flashes, night sweats, all those lovely lady things, occurred. And then there was the indigestion — the common name for the elephant stepping on the middle of my chest. Every so often I felt as though a tennis ball had lodged in my esophagus and all I needed to do was swallow it. My father had told me about drinking a mixture of baking soda and water and usually that relieved the indigestion better than the over-the-counter drugs. But not always.

Hives. Hot flashes. Indigestion. These were the reels at my Misery Slots. Sometimes one of these things would occur, sometimes two, and if I hit the misery jackpot, all three were up together and the bells would ring, the siren would go off, and . . . there was no jackpot payoff. Except total misery.

I could not sleep. One particularly terrible night, I gave up and swung my tree trunk limbs out of bed, careful not to wake Chris.

In the guest bathroom at the end of the hall, I ran an oatmeal bath to try to reduce the red, bumpy welts covering my body. I undressed and climbed into the lukewarm water, letting it surround me as I tried to find a comfortable position. Oh, how I missed the spacious hot tub with seats shaped for comfort and water surrounding me up to my neck. But the hot tub, like raspberries, spicy foods, and pedicures, was off-limits during chemo. The tremendous, deep, long bathtub in my old rented condo would have been a beautiful respite, but that was in the past. I made do with the shallow, short tub available and the lukewarm water I was allowed. I waited for relief. Any relief.

I closed my eyes and tried not to look at what had become of my body — what had become of me. I was a bloated, hairless little girl suffering from early menopause and hives. I was tired. And I was sick. I could no longer pretend otherwise. Too soon the water cooled.

I rose slowly, using the wall to balance myself and my heavy limbs, and stepped out of the tub. In two steps I came face-to-face with a monster in the mirror. There she was: bald, no eyelashes, no eyebrows over her eyes but heavy gray bags under them, red welts all over her body (made much more vibrant by the warm water), darker red scratches ravaging her skin, a two-inch scar across her right breast, and a full-body steroid bloat.

I was hideous. Hideous.

I was Chemo-stein.

In preparing for chemo I'd thought about the hair loss, of course, and concentrated on the fact that it would grow back. I thought about losing my eyelashes and decided eye shadow and liner would work miracles. I knew of the bloating weight gain the steroids could cause but told myself that was better than nausea and again it was temporary; after all, Seamus had gained 20 percent of his body weight and just as quickly was back in fighting shape. Menopause would come, sure, but it was going to do that sooner or later anyway, and before it happened I was no more aware than anyone else of the true meaning of hot flashes and how you burn from the inside out, so that hadn't bothered me either. Somehow I had overlooked skin rashes as a side effect and never, never had I given thought to what these side effects would all be like together. Not until that moment, face to mirrored face.

How does one recover from this? Impossible. There was no way my body would ever be the same. And I still had two more chemo sessions to go. I sank down to the floor, away from the mirror, and dropped my head into my palms. I closed my eyes tight. I'd never be the same. I'd been kidding myself that this was all temporary. One cannot possibly come back from this. My head pounded. My chest hurt and I gulped for breath. I can't do this. I can't.

And then a familiar noise.

AAAAAARRROOOOOOOOO!!

I jumped up, banging my forearm into the edge of the sink.

AAAAAARRROOOOOOOOO!!

"Seamus, no," I hissed at the door. He'd wake Chris, and I did not want Chris to see me like that. I grabbed my robe and threw it on quickly, flinging the door open simultaneously.

Seamus blocked the doorway.

He was at my feet, sitting in that cute stance I loved, butt on the ground, back legs splayed in what seemed to be six different directions, front legs locked and straight in front, head tilted, one ear flipped back, and big kohl-lined brown eyes staring up at me, tail wagging. He looked at me as though nothing was wrong.

But something was wrong. Something was horribly wrong.

I bent down to pet Seamus. Instead of curling into me as he usually did when he wanted love, he barked and spun around, heading toward the staircase. He did it again and again, his head jerking from me to the staircase and back to me with each bark.

Downstairs. He wanted me to go downstairs.

Seamus had a lot of issues, but an inability to express himself was not one of them. I hurried after him, still hoping we wouldn't wake Chris. As I passed the bedroom, I glanced in and realized that Chris was no longer in bed.

I followed Seamus to the cause of his excitement.

Chris was in the kitchen, wide awake with the lights on.

"Aw, you look cute," he said.

Cute? "I look horrible. I can't believe how awful I look." I sat down at the kitchen counter. "I don't know if I can keep doing this."

Chris slid a tray of hot, fresh cookies out of the oven. "You're all pink from the bath, and with your white, fluffy robe and the hood pulled up around your little face, you look cute. Not awful at all." Unperturbed, he began to scoop the cookies onto a plate. "You can do this."

"I don't feel good. I feel really, really shitty."

"I know, baby. I know. But you're halfway there. Remember our mantra: the dog lived and so will you."

"I may live, but I may also forever more look like a monster."

"No, you won't. Look at da Moose." Chris pointed to Seamus, who was balancing on his hind legs, head and neck stretched out, snout in the air, sniffing at the plate of cookies on the counter. "You'd never know he'd been sick."

Chris poured two glasses of milk.

"I'm not a dog. I'm not that lucky."

"No, you're not a dog. But you are just as stubborn as this one." He came out from the kitchen, carrying the plate of cookies and the glasses of milk. Seamus trotted behind him. "This will help. I'll stay up with you. And as long as there are cookies, I think Seamus is in, too. Maybe we can find a movie on."

He made cookies. He'll stay up with me. And it's four in the morning.

He hadn't even flinched at my appearance. The tension in my face relaxed. My shoulders dropped, and I moved over to join Chris on the couch.

I looked like a monster, he'd given up so much to stay by my side every step of the way through this, he'd been scared and tired and had to take on so much more responsibility in our home and our life, and he'd never complained once. No, instead he quietly slipped downstairs and made me cookies and milk, and he was ready to stay up with me all night if need be. What more proof did I need that I have finally, finally chosen right? I've gotten this "relationship" thing right. What more proof did anyone need?

My Misery Slots were shutting down. I was winning an entirely different jackpot now.

There on the couch, snuggling with Chris, chewing on soft, gooey, homemade cookies, I realized I'd just been saved. What happened in the bathroom could have gone in an entirely different direction. That moment could have broken me. But it did not. Seamus, whatever his reasons, had managed to pull me out of it. He'd taught me this before. I needed to remember the very important lesson: sometimes, you just need to focus on the cookies. And if I focused on the cookies, I couldn't help but see the love from the dog and, more importantly, from Chris. And that's what really mattered, then in the middle of the night and always. Focus on the cookies.

I rested my head on Chris's shoulder and breathed deeply. The feeling was similar to when I'd had the rollover car accident — the moment when I'd walked away and realized I was unharmed but then turned to see the wreck of a car and what could have been. The moment I realized how much I could have lost.

Cancer has a way of focusing one on what is being lost, I realized. It was time for me to focus on what I had. I smiled. Any urge I had to burst into tears dissipated. All I wanted to do was pet my soft, cute, cancer ass-kickin' beagle and snuggle in next to Chris.

Yep. The dog lived. And so would I.

CHAPTER 22
A BASKET CASE

I made Chris breakfast. It was simple —
bagels with cream cheese and some fruit —
but I brought it to him in bed.

"Nice. Did I forget my birthday?" he said.

"No. I just figured it was my turn to do
something for you."

"Thanks, but you didn't have to."

"I did." I sat on the bed next to him. "You
know I almost lost it completely last night,
right?"

"I figured it was bad."

"So I didn't really look cute? You were
talking me off the ledge?"

"You always look cute to me. But, yes, I
like you a little farther back from the ledge."

I was not fond of staring over that cliff
either. "I don't think I'll be there again. I've
been thinking."

"That can't be bad."

"You've been telling me this for a while
now, but I don't think I really got it until

last night. I need to handle this as I did for Seamus." We both looked down at Seamus, who was, naturally, at Chris's bedside doing his toast dance.

Having our attention, Seamus howled.

"I assume you don't mean you're going to eat your way through chemo?" Chris said.

"No, but I am going to talk to the doctor, and if we can't get her attention, I'm going to switch back to Dr. Glaspy. She hasn't been there at all. She never talked to either of us through the entire white blood cell crash and after. She never responded to you about the hives. She's never called to check on me. I don't think she has a clue what's going on with my case."

"I can't argue with that. Best I can tell, she's not even in the office."

"Exactly. So what's the point of being referred to her if she never sees me?"

"We know now the drive home from chemo isn't when the problems happen. So if you want to switch back to UCLA, I'm with you."

I tossed Seamus a piece of my bagel. "And there's another thing I've been thinking about."

"Apparently you've been up thinking for a while."

"I have. And this is about your parents."

"Uh oh." He sat up straighter and adjusted his pillow behind his back.

"No, it's okay. It's fine. I'm fine. With them I mean. I think it's time I cut them some slack. Your mom has been really kind through this whole thing. She's given me great advice on handling the chemo and sent those gorgeous wraps. She calls. They've sent cards and flowers constantly. And I know your mom reads the blog. So, yeah. I think it's time for me to let go of all that past crap."

"Okay." He dragged out the word, still nervous about what was next.

"You said they offered to come out here and take us to Easter brunch, right?"

"Yep."

"Tell them yes. We'll go."

"Brunch? With my parents? Again? Are you sure this isn't another chemo-fever?"

"Nope. We're going. Doctor first. Then the parents."

"Well, all righty then, the Teresa I know and love is back."

When we entered the oncology office, our senses were attacked with pastel hues and garish paper cutouts of eggs, bunnies, and chicks. Easter was blooming all over the reception area in such a purposefully cheery manner it seemed to be mocking the very patients it was presumably meant to help. I hadn't been nauseous, but I had a consistent metallic taste in my mouth, and not even eggs sounded good, let alone chocolate bunnies. And they were so condescending. We were really going to be cheered by bunnies in straw hats and dresses?

"This might be the worst one yet," I said, waving my hand around the waiting room as I took my seat with the clipboard and chart of questions they handed me each visit.

"Easy, tiger," Chris said.

I pointed to my questionnaire. "They want to know if I consider myself to be healthy. I'm bald. I've barely recovered from a full-body rash, and, most importantly, I'm seated in a freakin' oncologist's office. I wonder if this is a trick question?"

Chris laughed. "I see you are in rare form this morning. This should be good."

When I returned my clipboard, I let the nurse at the desk know that I would not be going forward with my treatment unless and until I was able to speak with the doctor.

"The nurse practitioner will meet with you in your exam."

"And she's great, but no. I want to see the doctor."

"The nurse practitioner is doing the pre-treatment exams today."

"Is the doctor in?"

"Yes, but she has appointments."

"And now she has another one." I sat down without waiting for a response.

Shortly thereafter Chris and I were both in the exam room alone, me in my customary paper vest seated on the exam table and him in his customary small stool next to me.

The doctor entered the room and greeted me without making eye contact. She stared at her clipboard. "I understand you need to talk to me."

"Yes. It seems unusual that I haven't been talking to you. That there's been no communication and I've had a few things go wrong."

"These side effects are very common, and the nurses know how to deal with them. We deal with this stuff all the time." She moved toward me with her stethoscope aimed at my chest.

I leaned back, dodging her weapon. "It's not common to me. I don't deal with it all the time. And your nurse sounded like she was guessing on what to do about my hives."

"We like to have you come in so we can see what we're dealing with." She moved toward me again, stethoscope at the ready.

I again leaned back, putting my hand in front of the stethoscope. "I offered to drive in. It's not like I was going to work looking like that, so my calendar had been cleared. But your nurse said the nurse practitioner was in Pasadena. And you were in Switzerland. It was obvious there was no other doctor in this facility because the nurse was waiting for return phone calls from Pasadena. Obviously there wasn't anyone for me to come see."

"Well, there's always the emergency room, but that's not a good choice." This time she merely raised the stethoscope hopefully, but without moving toward me.

"No, it's a terrible choice. I'd just like some assurance that somebody is overseeing my case and knows what to do about it. I feel like it's all the nurses and they're overwhelmed. I was referred here because of you, but it doesn't seem like you are the one taking care of me."

"I know everything going on in your case. They call and they email me with all updates and changes. I know what's going on. Now, we need to proceed with your exam."

"Can I reach you by email?"

"Absolutely not. I see way too many patients for that."

"My surgeon didn't seem to have an issue with that. It really helped to be able to contact him with questions."

"Oh well, sure, he only sees you five times."

I held her gaze. "That's three more times than you've seen me."

She stepped back, leaned back against the counter, and crossed her arms over her chest. "What do you want from me?"

"I want to know what's happening. I want to know if that was an allergic reaction I had and, if so, what's being done about it. I want to feel confident in the care I'm receiving. I don't think that's so much to ask." My voice was shaky. I was trying to be firm without showing my anger. I was also trying not to scream at her.

Grudgingly and quickly, she reviewed my case with me. My reaction to the last chemo was not acceptable, and she had decided not to give me that chemo again. She was switching me to another related chemotherapy that would give me the same benefit but was far less likely to cause an allergic reaction.

"What happens if I have another allergic reaction?"

"You won't."

She was infuriating. "What if I do?"

She let out an exasperated sigh. "If you have another allergic reaction, we will likely stop the chemo. You will have had three sessions and we likely will not do the fourth. We'll just continue with the hormone therapy."

I looked at Chris. His face registered the same alarm I was feeling.

"Doctor, my cancer is triple-negative. It's not hormone receptive. My protocol does not call for hormone therapy."

She turned back to my chart for a brief moment. It should have said "TRIPLE NEGATIVE" and "ALLERGIC" in brightly colored letters, but it did not.

"Of course," she said, much more quietly than she'd been speaking to me.

"You see why I'm concerned you're not involved in my care?"

After that, she spent twenty minutes examining me and listening to my concerns. I went forward with the chemo that day, and by the time we left, she had come in to see me to suggest I take the antinausea and sedative medication prescription she'd given me to help with my insomnia and given me an herbal remedy to help with the night sweats. She also agreed with my father about the baking soda for the indigestion. I got the impression she'd finally not only listened, but also had gone back and read my entire file. She addressed concerns I'd only mentioned to the nurses previously.

I slept through most of the infusion. It turns out it's exhausting to sit in a paper vest dodging a stethoscope while cross-examining a fast-talking doctor.

So this new chemo. . . . it's Taxol instead of Taxotere. And I was switched to it on Thursday with, oh, about thirty minutes' warning, during the stethoscope tango I was doing with the good doc. I was surprised to start feeling queasy Friday night and all day yesterday. Of all the side effects chemo brings, that just hadn't been one of them. I sort of feel like I've had my share, so I wasn't really expecting that one.

But then I went online last night and looked up Taxol. Hmmm. . . . seems that's a really common side effect of Taxol. More than the others. Gee. . . . wouldn't that have been nice to know? Perhaps I would have taken the extra antinausea medicine earlier. Oh, and it causes. . . . I'm just going to go with "the opposite digestive problem from the one I'm used to." Also would have been good to know ahead of time. Like, say, twelve hours ahead of time so I know which of the medications to take to combat the side effects. But you know, chemo is just one of those things you drop by the doctor's office for on a whim and then head on out. It's not like you need to prepare or, you know, plan for anything. I'm clearly just a big wimp. In a head scarf. And just about when I learn how to anticipate all these things, I'm going to be through with chemo.

Dressing to meet Chris's parents for brunch was easier this time. No one could really judge a chemo patient, and of course my hair would look perfect. All I had to do was decide if I wanted to be a brunette, a blond, or a redhead. I chose blond. While Britney-Bitch might not seem like an appropriate choice for Easter, it had one advantage: Britney was only a headband of hair — nothing covered the top of my head, which meant I could tie — over my head, pirate-style — the beautiful aqua scarf my friend Gary had just sent me. I liked the look; it seemed both cool and stylish. The look was certainly better than me sweating it out underneath the redheaded, more conservative wig I usually wore to work.

Wigs are hot and scratchy, and by Easter, Riverside was already heating up to be over eighty degrees. I wanted to stay cool, to go with my new calm, forgiving outlook. The scarf also matched perfectly with a new blouse I'd bought. I chose off-white linen pants and flat shoes; for weeks my feet had been too swollen and sore for high heels.

Chris's family arrived at our home, bearing large Easter baskets. Trudi handed one to me.

"For me?"

"You're part of the family now, you get an Easter basket."

Chris did not even try to contain his smile, so I knew he too was remembering that it was a missed Easter brunch that had caused his mother to "out" our relationship. And that I had mocked giving Easter baskets to adults. As I opened the gifts in my Easter basket, though, I became an immediate convert. My basket held two designer scarves and gift cards from Nordstrom, Starbucks, and Barnes & Noble. (Later I told Chris that he must have really loved me to have given up, that fateful Easter, the kind of stash his mother put in an Easter basket.) The only candy in my basket was jelly beans and a white chocolate bunny.

"I remembered that you don't like chocolate, but I hope white chocolate is okay," she said.

I was impressed and touched. "It's perfect. My own parents have trouble remembering I don't like chocolate. That's amazing you remembered."

"I have a niece who doesn't eat chocolate either."

"Really? I don't think I've ever met anyone else who didn't like chocolate."

"See, you fit right into our family!"

"Well, thank you. Very much. It's a perfect basket filled with all of my favorite things." I gave her a hug. And I am not one who hugs.

We went to brunch at a friend's restaurant, and the servers were all wearing black aprons adorned with pink ribbons. The warmth and support I was feeling was almost enough to make me forget the queasy feeling in my stomach.

I scanned the menu, looking for something my stomach could tolerate that also stood a chance of overcoming the iron dirt taste in my mouth.

"You should order the ginger ale, Teresa," Trudi said.

"Ginger ale?"

"The menu says they make it with fresh grated ginger. That'll settle your stomach."

"It will?"

"Absolutely. Ginger is great for an upset stomach."

Throughout brunch, I gulped down three large glasses of ginger ale, which not only helped my stomach, but also tasted fantastic. I wanted to order gallons of it to go. By the end of brunch I was able to eat nearly my entire omelet along with fresh orange slices and melon.

"The girls want to see the Mission Inn. Do you think you're up to walking over there?" Trudi asked.

Chris turned to me. "I can take them over there if you want to rest."

"It's no problem. It's right across the street, and I'm feeling pretty good. The ginger ale really helps."

The six of us walked through the vine-covered pergolas to the gorgeous tiled courtyards of the Mission Inn, enjoying the bougainvillea-drenched arches and balconies, the parrots in the large wrought-iron cage at the entrance, and the smell of eucalyptus wafting over from the adjacent spa. I pointed out the custom carpet with the portraits of each of the California missions, and Kati, Courtney, Chris, and I each found the mission we'd made models of in our grade school days, a rite of passage for California schoolchildren. The weather was Southern California perfect — bright blue sky with cotton clouds and exuberant sunshine. We stopped for photos on one of the balconies outside the chapel, with a view of the Spanish courtyard below. Trudi insisted I be in the photo, so Chris took the picture. I didn't even worry that I'd be "accidentally" pushed over — surely a sign of mental progress on my part. But so was the fact, plain and simple, that I had enjoyed my time with his family.

I felt fine today. I even worked until after 6:00 p.m. The feet were a little better. Perhaps because I wore sensible flat shoes (still cute; adorable Coach ballet flats) and then followed Doctor Dad's orders and soaked my feet in cold water and then elevated them for a bit when I got home. Seems to have helped.

That and I'm distracted from my own health issues by the fact that Seamus clearly isn't feeling well. He was waiting for me at the gate when I got home. . . . all sad and moving slowly (which almost never happens with a beagle). He took a nap with me but was slow to get off the bed and then yelped when he jumped up on the couch with me later. I think he injured something (back possibly), so we're letting him rest and see what it looks like in the morning. I've tried to feel around, and he let me without any more yelping or wincing, so I can't really figure out what's hurting him. He's awfully cuddly/needy though. Currently, he is sleeping soundly in his own bed, snoring up a marching band's worth of noise, and I'm hoping that's a good thing. Poor Chris. Too many patients in the house.

Chapter 23
Hairy Times

We were looking forward to a weekend of debauchery.

My fourth and final chemo infusion went smoothly with only one exception. I forgot my antinausea medication in the morning.

Chris turned the car around. "We're like parents of a fourth child. With the first one, we did everything perfectly and by the book. Now we're down to the fourth, and the only rule is 'no heroin on the good couch.' "

My forgetfulness made us an hour late and hence, in keeping with our tradition, we were once again the last to leave the oncology office. No diploma or "graduation" ceremony for me. And naturally, no sad good-byes with my doctor.

I didn't care. It was over.

Bring on the partying.

I had three more weeks of possible side effects, and of course there were thirty-three radiation sessions ahead of me, but I would never again be infused with poison. And Chris and I were looking at a long Memorial Day weekend when I'd finally be off restrictions from the hot tub, strawberries, sushi, crowds, and other dangerous things. I was hopeful my taste buds would return to normal by then as well.

Over the next two weeks, in addition to my usual side effects, my feet swelled to where I only had two pairs of shoes I could wear, the bone pain increased and infiltrated my skull, my throat was sore, and the night sweats were ferocious. But I focused on the cookie, which in this case would be a weekend spent in La Jolla, courtesy of a friend who'd offered up her beach house.

One morning, I woke up craving coffee. When I stepped out of bed, gingerly as usual, I put my foot down. There was no searing pain shooting through! I did not stumble! I could go down the stairs without needing to put both feet on each step. And, the most wonderful sign that the side effects were receding, my Starbucks French Roast tasted like . . . coffee! Heaven!

Immediately, of course, I scanned my head to see if there were signs of hair sprouting, as though it made perfect sense that all the negative effects would clear up simultaneously. I made Chris look, too.

"It's fuzz, right? There is visible fuzz!"

"More like touchable fuzz, but yes, fuzz. Congratulations, baby. Your bald days are over."

Seamus's x-rays show a little hip dysplasia, but they think he probably injured it and needs to rest. No stairs. No jumping. This is nearly impossible to accomplish because (1) he's a beagle and (2) our house is multileveled and has stairs pretty much everywhere. He now has anti-inflammatory medicine as well, and judging by the effects of the first one, it makes him feel like he can run up and down stairs. . . . until he can't. And Seamus hates to be picked up (he hates not being in control actually), so this carrying him up and down the stairs is going to be interesting.

In other news, I officially have "skull stubble"!!! The hair has definitely started its comeback. Not that you could tell, but I can definitely tell. As can Chris. We asked Seamus for his opinion, but he honestly doesn't care. That's part of what's so great about dogs.

I tied a pink scarf around my fuzzy head. A wig seemed ridiculous at the beach.

The weather was warm, with clear, sunny skies, which I figured was why so many people smiled at us as Chris and I walked the La Jolla beach, holding hands.

Then I noticed the head tilt and the slight squint of their eyes as they looked at me.

"Ah. The sympathy smile. Everyone is thinking I have cancer."

Chris slid his arm around my waist. "I don't know about everyone, but yes, it's fairly obvious you've been battling breast cancer. If not the T-shirt or sweatshirt, the scarf would be a clear indicator."

I looked down at my attire. He had a point; I was wearing a "Cancer Vixen" T-shirt and the sweatshirt emblazoned with "Beagles for Boobies." And then, yes, there was the scarf — the waving chemo symbol. "It's ironic. This is the best I've felt since surgery, and now I look sick to everyone."

"Not to me you don't."

In the weeks ahead I chose mostly to wear only scarves, and I'd be frequently surprised by doors being held open, chairs offered up in waiting areas, a free drink, and once, a free banana cream pie, which I shared at my radiation appointment. I began to think of my scarf as having superpowers, and it all began there on Windansea Beach in La Jolla as I celebrated getting my life back.

The regular blog postings have been interrupted due to the following circumstances:

a. the end of chemo restrictions;
b. the presence of a fresh, clean, refilled hot tub;
c. Chris, and
d. a nicely chilled Four Graces Pinot Blanc.

Enough said.

My secretary Michelle returned from maternity leave. She brought her infant son, Jayden, with her. We'd agreed she could bring him to work with her for as long as we could make it work. She was efficient and hardworking enough that I knew she'd be able to get as much done in a day with a baby as most people take two days to accomplish. Plus, Jayden was an adorable and content baby. He was very popular with our clients and a nice, happy offset from my "cancer patient" look. He didn't fuss or cry and judiciously chose to nap for most of the day. He brought another benefit as well.

"He makes me feel better about my hair," I said.

"I know. He's just got fuzz. I'm wondering when he'll start growing real hair," Michelle said.

"I'm wondering the same thing about me.

Is it mean if I challenge him to a hair-growing duel?"

"Not if you let me take pictures."

She handed Jayden to me and I removed my scarf. Holding babies terrifies me (I mentioned my lack of maternal instinct, didn't I?). I was thus distracted from the fact that I was now bald in public. A small public of two (one of whom was only an infant), but a public nonetheless. I was too worried about dropping the baby to worry about what a freak I may have looked like.

Michelle took pictures of Jayden and me from the front and the back, with our bald, slightly fuzzy heads together.

"Hey, you both have that red rash thing at the base of your skulls in the back," she said.

"We do?"

"It's called a stork bite on babies."

"Well, I suppose it's a chemo bite on me. Does it go away? Or does everybody have it and eventually the hair covers it?"

"I guess we'll find out."

(For the record, I won the hair-growing competition, but Jayden ran away with the "cuteness" category. And the stork bite does go away — on babies and chemo patients.)

Chris here with another Growin' It Out for Cancer report, currently entering month four.

We're inching closer (inching. . . . get it?) to the mythical three-inch mark, clearly the longest I have ever worn my hair. Honestly, some days I feel like Richard Marx when I'm brushing back my long, flowing locks after a shower. Other days, I feel like that homeless guy who lives under the overpass. It's the hair on the back of my neck that's really getting to me. That and the hair falling down over my ears. Teresa says if I give it another half an inch, I'll be able to push my hair back behind my ears and slick it back, but I don't know. I don't think I'm swarthy or exotic enough to pull off that kind of look. I feel like if I slicked my hair back like that I have to start growing a goatee or a full beard, and to be quite honest, I just can't do that (not that I don't want to. . . . I think I'm physically incapable of growing a thick, full beard or goatee. Honest, all the hair on my face is on my neck, and let's face it, neck beard looks good on no man).

One more leg of my cancer odyssey remained. Radiation was to start four weeks after chemotherapy ended. Since these treatments were more frequent than even chemo had been — I'd go every weekday for thirty-three visits — returning to UCLA was not an option. But I was very concerned, given how chemo away from UCLA had gone.

Dr. Karam remained Dr. Good Karma by personally researching and finding an oncology radiation center close to my office. He also researched and interviewed the radiation oncologist herself over the phone. "I think you will like her. She seems very good. Very good credentials," he said.

"I'm glad you found someone so close. Her office is about two miles from mine."

"Really? That is perfect then."

"Yes, it is. Especially since there is a Starbucks nearby."

"Oh, I know that. I searched for a clinic near a Starbucks."

"You did?"

"Ha! No, T. I searched for a good physician to continue the excellent care you deserve."

"Awww. Well, I deserve Starbucks, too."

"And wine! When are you and Chris coming back to LA? When you finish your treatment, we will celebrate with wine."

"That sounds wonderful."

"And how is Seamus?"

"He's doing well. He had his own issues with a little hip dysplasia and inflammation, but he's healing fine now. Running crazy as always."

"He was jealous you were getting all the

medical attention."

Dr. Good Karma hadn't met Seamus yet, but he had him figured out. "Sounds about right." It was Seamus's ego that was inflamed.

With Dr. Karam's help, my radiation treatment plan fell into place quickly and easily. Chris went with me to the initial consultation. When Dr. Hocko entered the exam room smiling and cheerful, she made eye contact with us both and had clearly read the information sent to her by UCLA (who now also had my chemotherapy files). She also commented that she liked Dr. Karam and enjoyed talking with him. I took that as a very good sign of her character.

In the days before I began the radiation, I again prepared myself. I bought sports bras with no wires, the natural deodorant that was the one kind allowed, and plenty of aloe vera. I also spent a little time reading outdoors, soaking up some sun while I could. I was instructed to stay out of direct sunlight during radiation.

I also decided that radiation was like the California bar exam had been. The bar exam itself, I thought, was not that difficult. After all, I'd spent the prior three years of my life studying for that very exam. What was difficult was the physical and mental aspect of being tested for eight hours a day, three straight days in a row. If you allowed yourself to think about that too much, you'd have a much harder time in the exam. Back then, I hadn't figured out the "Seamusness" of concentrating on the cookie, but I wasn't far off. Then I had focused on the test in increments — one essay at a time or one three-hour test segment at a time, never more than that. Now I'd be counting down thirty-three radiation zaps, one at a time, with a latte after each.

Radiation patients have the same appointment time every day. I chose the 9:15 appointment slot. Even though I had no hair to wash or blow-dry, no eyelashes to lengthen with mascara, and my legs and underarms did not need shaving, I still didn't move quickly in the morning, and I knew I'd be grumpy the rest of the day if I had to be anywhere before nine in the morning.

On the morning of my first appointment though, I again woke early. Moments later, Chris followed me downstairs. "Are you sure you don't want me to go with you?"

"Thanks, but no. It seems like a waste of your time. Besides, there's Seamus."

Hearing his name, Seamus wagged his tail and picked his head up.

"Well, the doctor said it's only like fifteen minutes. I'm sure we can leave him for that long," Chris said.

"I'm not at all sure of that. But it's okay. I'll be fine. If there's a problem, it won't be until much later on."

I managed to maintain that bravery right up until I was on the radiation table, breasts exposed, arms up over my head and lasers pointed at my chest.

"Okay, stay still. We're going to leave the room now, but we can see you and there's an intercom so we can hear you and you'll be able to hear us. This won't take long." The radiation techs were cheerful and efficient, but that only made me feel more alone when they left the room. The metal door they closed behind them was huge, over eight feet tall and at least a foot thick. The room fell silent.

Alone on the table, I thought of Seamus. Each time he was taken from me and led back to the hospital quarters for his chemo infusions, I worried that he'd be frightened and feel alone or abandoned — like I felt then. But each time he'd come trotting out, happy and full of energy, just searching for his new cookie.

I hoped the same for me.

The machine started up with its space age

noises, humming and dinging as the arm moved over me and the laser beams flashed across my chest. I could hear each time a radiation shot was fired. Ping, zip. The machine rotated clockwise. Ping, zip. The machine moved again. Ping, zip. More rotation. Ping, zip.

"You did great. Now just stay where you are and we'll come in to release you," came the voice over the intercom.

"That's it?"

"Yep. That's it. You did fine."

I would have wagged my tail if I had one. Good patient! Good, good patient!

Within the week, I devised a routine. A routine I began to look forward to . . . well, at least as much as anyone could look forward to a routine that involved radiation of one's breast. I woke, had my coffee while reading, showered, dressed, and drove to the radiation center. I greeted and chatted with my fellow radiation patients — Ms. 9:00 a.m. was an ovarian cancer patient, Ms. 9:30 was also a breast cancer patient, and Mr. 9:45 was, in addition to early to most of his appointments, a throat cancer patient who on some days could talk and on others could not. Usually I was in and out in under twenty minutes, longer if the machine was moody or if any one of my fellow patients or I were particularly chatty. Then I drove through Starbucks and picked up coffee and oatmeal on my way to my office. I was at my desk finishing breakfast by ten. For a cancer patient, I told myself, this was not bad at all. One day down, twenty-five, -four, -three more to go.

Folks keep asking what the radiation dosage is, how long it takes, and whether it's "low dosage." And, um, I don't know. I'm sure they told me, but I'm also sure I decided it wasn't information I needed to keep in my over-crowded brain right now. As long as the doctor knows, I'm good. I tried to count (one Mississippi two Mississippi three. . . .) how long each zapping was, but they seemed inconsistent to me, so I finally asked. And the radiation nurse told me it isn't about the time, it's about the dose. So I'm zapped for as long as it takes to get 180. . . . um. . . . I think she said centigrams. (Dad . . . I know you'll let me know the correct measurement and then demand repayment of some of that tuition money you wasted on me.) She said to think of it like pouring a cup of sugar. It's not how long it takes; it's just done when you get to a cup.

By week two, I'd come to know my fellow

radiation patients. After my Wednesday zapping, when I returned to the waiting room, Ms. 9:30 and Mr. 9:45 and his friend, a heavyset African American man whose e-reader I'd begun to openly covet, were seated, each quietly reading.

"I'll get changed and wait for you," I said to 9:30.

"Great, I brought a scarf. I can't wait to have options besides all these hats," she said.

"But you look cute," I said.

"I'm sixty years old! Cute is not what I want. I want sophisticated. I want to look like you."

"Well, we have the same hairstyle, so you are off to a great start," I said. Everyone in the room laughed. We all had the same hairstyle.

The day before, Ms. 9:30 had asked me how I tied the head scarves I wore. Just as I'd given up the wigs in favor of scarves for the summer, she had given up wigs in favor of a variety of cute, sporty caps.

I'd now amassed an impressive selection of scarves, including the several expensive, large, luxurious silk scarves Trudi had given me and the many my mother had sewn especially for this purpose. My mother was still battling shingles and could not come out for another visit, so she'd busied herself sewing. And quilting. (I now also owned a pink ribbon quilt.)

I received daily compliments on my head-gear from the staff and other patients. I promised Ms. 9:30 I'd teach her how to tie the scarves. My verbal instructions failed, as did my demonstration on my own head, so today we were moving on to full demonstration with class participation. I took off my scarf to demonstrate the tying.

"You have hair," Ms. 9:30 said.

"No, I have stubble. And it's weirdly dark."

"You have more than I do. If I had that much, I wouldn't be putting anything on my head."

I thought about that for a moment. At home, I'd begun to go without any head covering. But I wasn't quite ready for a full public viewing. Still though, it was nice to hear.

After a few tries, she mastered the art of pirate-scarf tying.

"I need hoop earrings," she said.

"And heavy, dark eyeliner, a la Johnny Depp."

"Very cool!"

I liked this group of people I was getting to know. All of us were fighting the battles of our lives, but everyone had time to be kind to one another. The nurses told me how the dynamic of a waiting room changed with the groups that came through, and ours was a particularly kind group. They'd had nervous groups who increased the anxiety in one another, groups who flashed their scars at one another, and groups who competed over who'd suffered the most. I was happy for my group.

But then one day, about halfway through my treatments, when I exited the dressing room, dressed for work, I walked into a discussion among the other patients. A new patient had joined our ranks and was demanding to know everyone's numbers.

"So what's your number?" she said to me.

"My number?"

"Was yours breast cancer?"

Cancer patients are possessive of their cancers, I'd noted. There is much talk of "my cancer" or "your cancer."

"Oh, um, yes. Breast cancer. Triple-negative." I looked at my fellow patients — the regulars. Ms. 9:30 looked like she was trying not to laugh and others were just shaking their heads slowly. I was aware that "triple-negative" was not a number, but I wasn't sure what she was getting at. At least "triple" was number-y.

"So like 5 percent?"

"I'm sorry. Five percent what?"

"Five percent chance of recurrence. You know. These doctors all give us our numbers. So we know. We know if it's coming back. What's your number?"

Wow. This total stranger wants to know the odds of me dying? Why? So she could decide if she'd be wasting her time getting to know me? "Ah. That number. Well, I have an 85 percent chance my cancer is not coming back."

"So you have a 15 percent chance of recurrence."

"No. I have an 85 percent chance it's not coming back."

"That's a 15 percent chance of recurrence!" She stepped closer to me, her brow furrowed, as though I was failing to understand and it was her job to set me straight.

"There's nothing wrong with my math. That's just not how I'm going to look at it. I prefer to think I have an 85 percent chance it's not coming back. But thank you for asking." I looked past her to the patients seated in the room. Ms. 9:30 gave me a thumbs-up, and I could see that several of the other patients were now smiling. As I left, I heard the newcomer explaining to the others that I was in denial.

That evening Chris and I took a fully

recovered Seamus for a long walk, and I told Chris what had happened. We'd been banned from our hot tub for months. Walks with Seamus had become our new talk time.

"That's shocking," he said.

"I know. Right? Like I need reminding I might die from this. From a total stranger!"

"Well, that's not all that surprising. People are rude. No, I'm more surprised at you."

"At me?"

"Giving scarf tying lessons, cheerful talk . . . when did you become little Miss Pollyanna Optimistic? Focusing on the positive? Are you sure your brain wasn't zapped in that lightning storm during radiation? Maybe they swapped your personality with some poor cheerleader somewhere who's now yelling 'just do your fucking job and let us go home' on the sidelines of a football field somewhere."

I laughed. He had a point. Not about the poor cheerleader, of course, but about me. My first response had been a positive one. An optimistic thought. No doom. No gloom. Me!

The dog lived and so did I.

And it seemed I really believed that now. It wasn't just a hope or a mantra. I gave Chris a quick kiss and finished the walk still smiling. On the last day of radiation, Chris came with me. I finally got my diploma and a cheerful graduation ceremony from Dr. Hocko and her wonderful staff. I thought, briefly, that I'd even miss the radiation oncology center. I'd come to know my fellow patients and the staff well, and in many ways my recovery had started there. When we left, Chris took a picture of me in front of the center, clutching my diploma and throwing my hat into the air, proudly displaying my half inch of hair and grinning ridiculously.

Be warned — if you are looking for some sad, crazy, or even funny cancer treatment story you've got the wrong blog today. Yeah, sure, this is a blog about my cancer "odyssey," but I took the day off from cancer. Instead, it's a happy little post about Chris and me celebrating our anniversary. June 12 was our first date — at an Angels game. So, this June 12 found us back in the Diamond Club at an Angels game. Because it was a special occasion I went in drag (fake hair and eyelashes! This was big!).

Our first date was a lot of fun (yeah, um, that's why we kept dating), and it also marks the anniversary of me learning the term *cougar*. (I've now perfected my knowledge. Ahem.) There was a pair of cougars in the seats in front of us at that first game. This time, there was a family of four. Both times, however, there were obnoxious drunk guys behind us. Ah, public sporting events. I like these times when I get to return to normal, however briefly. And nothing says normal like drunk guys and fireworks at a baseball game. I may have been a little more tired than normal, and "in drag," but it was a great night out with a fantastic man who doesn't care if I'm in drag or bald or fighting cancer or cranky or any of those things I've been in the last several months.

Chris didn't even mind that for the second time in five days a stranger came up to him and commented that he looked like Jay Leno. He didn't even mind when drunk Angels fan asked him to do a Jay Leno impression (yes, he did it and yes, it's very good). When his hair is long, people think he looks like Jay Leno. When it's short, Vince Gill. To me, he's all Chris. And all mine.

CHAPTER 24
ALOHA, CANCER

As we headed into summer, daylight was lasting longer and so was my energy. I came home from work one evening to find a group of friends with Chris on our back patio, sipping French rosé wine and watching the sun go down.

"We were just telling Chris how wonderful he's been through this whole awful experience," Jane said.

I pulled up a chair, and Chris poured me a glass of wine. "Yeah, I know. I tell him that, too. I also told him how popular he'd be with the ladies if I didn't make it. He'd have his choice of women."

"It's true. Oh my god," Becky joined in. "A guy who not only stuck by his woman and went to every single doctor's appointment, but also did this crazy thing with his hair just to show support? They'd be lining up. Wait, where do I get on the waiting list?"

"Seriously. I'm in," Laureen said.

"You can't be; you're already married," Becky said.

"Okay, well then I'll just be his pimp. I'll handle the scheduling for Mr. Popular Young Widower. This will call for great organization skills."

We were all laughing, and the riff went on for some time. Chris added a few names to the waiting list himself.

"Hey, people, I'm still here! I'm not actually dying. A little respect for Cancer Girl, please!" I said.

"You started it," Becky said. "And seriously, I've never been around someone with cancer, and I never thought I'd be able to joke about cancer things. So I guess I have to thank you for that — for showing me how to handle this and making it easier."

"Well, I'm a little concerned I may have made you all a bit too comfortable. I'm worried about the next woman you all know with breast cancer. She may not laugh at you pimping out her man."

"No worries. We won't," Laureen said. "We'll be too busy pimping out Chris."

I was happy to hear the laughter, but even happier to hear the toast that Jane made next.

"I mean it, Chris. You were outstanding through all of this. So I'd like to make a toast to Chris." She raised her glass, and we all held our glasses up. "I've never been so happy to have been so wrong about someone."

I caught Chris's glance across the glasses, and I could see he was happy to hear this. After all we'd been through, finally everyone could see what Chris and I knew all along. (Well, Chris knew all along; I was a little slower to the realization of what we had.)

"That means a lot, Jane. Thank you," Chris said, touching his glass to hers.

It meant a lot to me, too, and I drank in the moment as the sun dipped below the hill and our friends continued talking and sipping wine on a gorgeous June night.

Chris here, subbing in for Teresa tonight. And since it's been about a month since my last Growin' It Out for Cancer posting, we're dropping Month 5 on you tonight. And what a month it's been in hair growth. We're sneaking up on four inches and we're definitely racing headlong into hair helmet territory.

In fact, we may have already sprinted through helmet territory and are moving right into a full-on lion's mane. My hair suddenly began to take on the same shape and form of Miss Havisham's garden. The hair around my ears (around, people, around!) can now be

stretched all the way down over my ears if I
so choose (I don't), and I'm starting to get
worried that soon, there won't be enough
room behind my ears to keep the massive
amounts of hair I have on the wings properly
tucked and stylish. I fear that soon the only
look I'll be capable of is Donny Osmond circa
1972, and even he didn't have to deal with
that, that, that THING undulating and breach-
ing and pluming across my forehead. Seriously, the natural waves forming in the front
and back of my hair would make Jacques
Cousteau gasp in awe and would send thousands of Indonesian coastal dwellers screaming for higher ground. I mean, check out
whatever that is going on in the back, those
little Fancy Dan girls starting to U-turn back
toward my neck. That's not natural. Hair's not
supposed to move that way, right? I'm not getting a mullet, right? RIGHT?

Chris and the friends at our house that
evening had begun plans for a *Survivor*-
themed celebration of the end of my treatment. They made invitations and T-shirts
with a parody of the *Survivor* reality television logo. The logo was pink and said,
"Out-Chemo, Out-Radiate, Out-Live." The
party would be held in our friend Michelle's
backyard, recently landscaped and looking

just like Provence. She had the added bonus of two large dogs, Will and Nellie, who were Seamus's best friends. Seamus viewed her yard as a sort of Doggie Disneyland, so much so that it was difficult to get him back in the car after we visited.

Over one hundred friends and clients came throughout the day to celebrate with me, despite the temperature hitting 118 degrees, one of the hottest days on record in Riverside. Folks came from as far away as the Bay Area, Oregon, and Colorado. Dr. Karam came in from Los Angeles, spreading his good karma and causing quite a ruckus among my female friends when he changed his shirt into one of our *Survivor* T-shirts, revealing a full back tattoo as well as one around his bicep.

He also finally got to meet Seamus.

"He's so cute," Dr. Karam said, kneeling to pet Seamus.

"Diabolically cute, that's the problem."

"But he survived cancer and he helped you, so he gets away with it."

"Exactly."

Dr. Karam stood up and Seamus ran off in the direction of the barbecue, howling for hamburgers.

"So, I have a question for you, Amer."

"Anything. Ask away."

"I know you were new to UCLA when we came there. Was I your first patient?"

He smiled sheepishly. "Pretty close."

"It's okay. Obviously it worked out fine, and I wouldn't have cared even if I knew then. Seamus was only the third patient of Dr. Dutelle's, and we loved her. So what number was I?"

"Third is probably about right."

"Ha! So, that's why you went to all my appointments with me."

"Yes, I was learning my way around the campus, too." He grinned. "And I got to meet some other doctors."

"Glad I could help. But I guess I can't tell everybody else to expect that sort of treatment."

"No, maybe not. But I will try."

I knew he would.

Chris's parents and both sisters, along with his aunt Susan, all came to the party as well. I tried to exercise my new powers of optimism to not stress over the fact that their attendance meant that members of my family — my dad and stepmother and my younger sister and her husband and kids — would meet members of Chris's family for the first time. But I was nervous. By the time we saw our fathers shake hands, Chris and I had been dating for just over five years and living together for three, but we still held our breath. I nearly hyperventilated when my dad met Chris's mother, but they smiled and complimented each other on their respective children and how well we'd handled our cancer odyssey together. In other words, they behaved like the civilized adults they were. The universe did not, in fact, implode. I could finally exhale.

Chris walked across the lawn and handed me a frozen margarita from the machine my friends insisted on renting. "So they've met."

"They have. And no punches were thrown." I raised my plastic glass to his.

"Not even verbally. Seems all is good."

I drank in the moment, standing next to Chris, watching my family and friends. I could feel myself healing in the warmth of the full sunlight.

Seamus ran howling by, Will and Nellie in full pursuit. "All is good," I said, leaning in to Chris's embrace. I was deeply happy. "Very, very good."

My own "any other dog" experience happened last night. I go for my first three-month checkup in three days. I've heard that this can be, much like the first post-treatment mammogram, a stressful time, as it brings back memories of the disease and the treatment just about the time one has started to get back to normal. Plus, there is that constant "it might recur" feeling until one hits the magic five-year mark (and, I imagine, even after that). I wasn't really thinking about it or concerned at all. Until Sunday night.

I wasn't feeling good. I was really, really thirsty and having to um, well, uh. . . . pee all the time. Then I got a killer backache. By yesterday, I also had the chills — which were highly reminiscent of my white blood cell crash experience. When I took my temperature, it was 102. Not good. I got online to look up my symptoms on WebMD. And I should add here, I've never done that before in my life. I either tough it out or call my dad. But I was a little nervous because I felt a lot like I did the morning of the crash. WebMD was pretty good — I either had bladder or kidney cancer or a bladder or urinary tract infection. Fook!! Then it also had a warning about getting medical attention immediately if the person was *X, Y, Z* or had a compromised immune system such as a person in chemotherapy. Um, okay, I'm going to start with the lesser of these choices. I'm going to pretend I am any other dog and rule out the easier one first. I had a compromised immune system (during chemo), but I don't any longer. Do I?

I drank lots of cranberry juice, slept like there was no tomorrow, stayed home from work today, and got antibiotics. I'm feeling a lot better. I am, I think, just any other dog. With a bladder infection.

I wasn't sure if I should be excited or not. Chris, though, was ecstatic.

We were getting haircuts.

As I'd promised my mom when she couldn't travel to me, Chris and I went to Missouri in August to visit (and, as it turned out, have another *Survivor* party). Chris, with his by then massive Whi-fro, had endured a humid Midwestern summer visit. I, on the other hand, had the perfect summer cut for such a trip, the same buzz cut my ten-year-old nephew sported in my honor. But Chris stayed true to his promise. He wouldn't cut his hair until I needed to cut mine.

By December, I had nearly two inches of wavy brown hair. It didn't need to be cut so much as shaped. But that was good enough. We were heading to Hawaii, and I did not want Chris to have to vacation with that hair again. At the rate his hair grew, we'd have to buy another airline ticket for it if he didn't cut it.

"Do you want to go first?" I said.

Chris sat one chair away from my stylist Kelly's chair and extended his hand from me to her chair. "After you. I can't cut mine until you've cut yours. A deal is a deal."

"I can't believe you did that," Kelly said. "It's almost crazier than shaving your own head. And, in your case, definitely more difficult."

"Eh, it was fun," Chris said. "And I've single-handedly revitalized the hair product industry."

Kelly trimmed my hair, mostly in the spots where some original hair had hung on — never leaping from my head through all four rounds of chemo. (Chris called them "little hairs — big attitude.") She then used a shaping product to give my hair some texture and hold. She ran her hands through my hair and pulled some pieces in different directions.

Then she spun my chair around so I could see my new look.

"Wow. I actually have a hairstyle."

"It's really cute," Kelly said.

"You can pull off short hair. I told you that," Chris said.

I liked the look. Kelly had given me a funky, sporty style and done away with my chemo-victim look. I'd just have to get used to being a brunette now. "And at last, it's your turn." I rose from the chair and offered it up to Chris.

"I cannot wait!" Chris excitedly moved into position.

Kelly ran her hands through his tsunami of hair. "I'm going to have to chop at this with scissors before I can use the clippers!"

"Hack away. You'll probably need new scissors when you're done."

Massive chunks of salt and pepper hair fell and instantly overpowered and covered my wispy little brown chemo curls on the floor.

When Kelly finished, a half hour later, Chris looked in the mirror. "And I'm back!"

"You look great. More Vince Gill, less Jay Leno."

When we decided to go to Hawaii to celebrate the defeat of cancer and ignore that holiday that shall not be named, friends offered us the use of their condo in Maui.

"Just let me know the dates you want to use it and we'll reserve the place," my friend Ted had said. He was aware of my history with December and his wife, Sandy, a nurse, had followed my treatment progress on the blog.

"That's incredibly kind of you. As for the dates, I only have two requests: I want to be there on the twenty-fifth and I don't want to be flying on December 23."

Ted barely skipped a beat. "No, that really wouldn't be fair to everyone else on the plane."

Chris's parents then offered to pay for five nights at a hotel on the big island as well. I wasn't even suspicious that there'd be separate rooms reserved or that Chris would be kidnapped and flown home without me. I was simply grateful and thrilled.

Now I'd have to see if I could give December another chance at being kind.

On December 23, one year from when the doctor called to tell me the results of my mammogram were "highly suspicious of malignancy," Chris and I walked Keawakapu Beach in Wailea sipping mai tais and watching the sunset for the third night in a row, with no hurricane in sight. I wore no makeup and left my hair tousled in the salt air. My right breast still had remnants of the "reverse tan" from radiation (the breast was darker than the surrounding skin), but my scar had faded greatly. I wore my pink *Survivor* T-shirt to commemorate the day and the year we'd been through.

It simply didn't matter what I looked like. I no longer needed armor. We'd won the battle. Seamus had brought me some Irish luck after all.

And of course, walking the beach, seeing other dogs playing and running in the surf, I missed Seamus. But I knew he was safe at Ruff House with his adoring fans and, most importantly, we were both healthy. I figured I'd given up enough for Seamus without giving up a trip to Hawaii, too. (I could almost hear him howling at this thought: *Foooooooookers! I love the beach! Come get me! Get me out of here! Noooooooooooooow!!! Also, bring toast! AAAAAARRROOOOOOOOO!!!*) I'd already bought him a green aloha print collar.

Chris and I sat on the beach with our arms around each other and toes sunk into the sand. We watched quietly as the sky turned yellow, orange, pink, and magenta. The sun lowered on the horizon and the palm trees were silhouetted black in the sky.

This time they didn't resemble cancer at all.

ACKNOWLEDGMENTS

One book alone can only begin to express the immense gratitude I feel for those who saved Seamus's life and mine. The knowledge and kindness of Nancy Mount of Details Dog Grooming and the compassion and consummate skill of Dr. Autumn Dutelle each saved Seamus's life (and quite possibly my mental health). Dr. Wayne Davis and the talented and devoted staff at Small Animal Hospital (particularly Angel Redfearn, Mardell Denney, and Dr. Laura Schrader), then and now, keep Seamus happy and healthy, as they have with all my dogs before. Thank you all. (And Seamus says, *AAAAAARRROOOOOOOOOO!*)

Everyone facing cancer should be lucky enough to be a patient of Dr. Amer Karam's, who single-handedly may well change the reputation of surgeons everywhere. His kindness, humor, and, most importantly, those skilled hands will never be forgotten. Dr. Good Karma — words could never express our gratitude (so we'll keep sending wine). Dr. John Glaspy and the entire UCLA Medical Center are so good we no longer mind the 120-mile round-trip drive (though it will be nice when it's no longer necessary). Thank you all for your compassionate care. Dr. Janet Hocko at Vantage Oncology and her entire talented staff made my radiation experience nearly enjoyable — and that's saying a lot. Thank you, always. And while I was, perhaps, hard on a doctor or two in this memoir, it bears mentioning that the nurses and techs Seamus and I both encountered along the way were, to a person (okay, except Lurch . . . but you knew that), friendly, caring, and professional. Those and all nurses and techs (particularly in oncology) deserve many, many thanks for the difficult work they do, and I give mine here. And to my radiation "class" (mornings, spring/summer 2009 at Vantage Oncology), thank you for your companionship — you each made those mornings more bearable, and though some of you are now gone, I remember you all fondly. A special thank you goes to my blue-gown buddy, Melanie Pope.

To my parents, Jim McElhannon and Vivian Terbeek, who gave me my first dog (the much-loved Tippy), my sense of humor, my first library card, and a quirky childhood that left me no choice but to be a writer, thank you. To my stepparents, Ted Terbeek and Nancy McElhannon, thank you always for your support; stepparenting is a tough job (perhaps more so in our family, but that's a whole other book), and you both do it well. To my brother Jay, thanks for letting me crash your trip to Ireland — who knew it would start all this? Many thanks also to my sister and brother-in-law Shawna and Eli Robertson — it's great to be able to get medical help and home repairs from the same household, and goodness knows I've needed both these past few years. To my stepsister Laura Ballantine and my step-brother Michael Wakefield (look, I've already explained the family is complicated!), thank you very much for your friendship and support when it really counted. And I must of course thank my cousins in Ireland — especially Seamus, the genius observer.

To Chris's family — Jim, Trudi, Kati, and Courtney — thank you for your support and acceptance . . . and for Chris. I'm happy to be a part of your family (though I really want to make an "interloper" joke here!). And in fond memory of Chris's aunt, Susan Michel Santos, who succumbed to breast cancer while I was writing this book but will always be remembered for her strength and ready smile and, of course, her "bling."

Enormous thanks to my friends, some mentioned in this book by name and some not, who kept me laughing, who hugged me even though I don't hug, who lined up to date Chris if I didn't make it (you're givers, you really are), who brought food and drink (both while I was in chemo and while I was writing this memoir), helped me figure out that tequila cuts through chemo better than wine, tried on my wigs, read the blog, watched Seamus, sent cards and flowers, and who worried about me (then and now, I'm sure), and then re-lived it all while I wrote this book: Corby Rhodes, Stacey Aldstadt, Valerie Zucker, Tom and Kris DeGrezia (and Mimi and Loren, too), Laureen Pittman, Michelle Pierce, Becky Whatley, Zee Beard, Sue Mitchell, Jane Carney, Amy Harrison, John Goodman, Gary Berg, Rich Gold, Barbara Ryan, Tera Harden, Brian Pearcy, Brein and Roryann Clements, Mitchell Edwards, Michelle Pepke, John and Carrie Schutz, and Bob and Helga Wolf. And to my hairstylist and friend Kelly Koerber, thank you for sticking with me through thick and thin (okay, right . . . that's not even funny). A special thanks to creative genius Mike Easley, of Vital Excess, who took the cover photo and brought to life many clever marketing ideas for this book and so many other things in my life. A world of thanks also to my therapist, Joanne Simmons — I shudder to think where I'd be without your guidance.

A special shout-out to my Maui girls — Jane Gideon and Lori Lacefield — who have traveled this writing road with me since we first met at the Maui Writers Conference more than a decade ago. It's good to have friends willing to join me putting in the hard work of writing in Maui, Paso Robles, La Jolla, Ocean Isle Beach, France, Breckenridge, and San Francisco. You constantly encourage and inspire me — and you're a lot of fun to vacation with, too. Cheers, ladies.

And speaking of writing, I'm lucky enough (see how I'm getting the hang of this optimist thing?) to have two writers groups who went through countless drafts of this manuscript (mostly the first chapter, 642 times, because that's how writers groups work). Many thanks and undying gratitude to my LA group: Trai Cartwright, David Del Bourgo, Julia Elrick, Eileen Austen, Lorna Freeman, and Chris Kern (yes, him!). And the same to my 951 Writers: Barbara Abel,

Barbara Shackelton, Michelle Ouellette, Kristin Tillquist, Dulce Pena, Patti Cotton McNeily, Susan Knock, and Chris Kern (again!). Special thanks to Nancy Hinchliff, who I met on She Writes online and gave me excellent critique notes the whole way through this manuscript — I hope to meet you in person one day. I also had the good fortune of meeting fellow dog lover and writer Sara J. Henry through our blogs (and then in person at the LA Times Festival of Books) and cannot thank her enough for her encouragement, advice, and sage notes on this manuscript. Every writer should have a mentor like Sara. I cannot thank my writer friends without also specially thanking my writing instructor, Tod Goldberg, who not only got me back to writing after a long, long hiatus (also known as my marriages), but also is responsible for Chris and me meeting (it's okay, Tod — that's a good thing).

And speaking of traveling (well, two paragraphs up; there's no editor for acknowledgments), a writer does not get to retreat to places like those mentioned above without having some pretty fantastic friends with awesome vacation homes. Many thanks to Susan Medel and Norm Martin for making my La Jolla retreats possible, and to Bill and Willy Richman and Ted and Sandy Williamson (Maui), fellow Maui alum Tim Smith (Breckenridge), and Rachel and Raphael Pommier (France). You're all welcome to stay in Riverside anytime.

And speaking of editing (only one paragraph up!), even I can clearly see the good fortune I had in landing Sarah Jane Freymann of the Sarah Jane Freymann Literary Agency as my agent. Her tireless work, gentle pressure, and good advice (without her, there'd be no love story in this book . . . and hence, probably no book) was invaluable. And it was Sarah Jane who got me to editor Shana Drehs at Sourcebooks. Shana has been such fun to work with that no part of the editing process has felt like work. (This is helped greatly by my having been in Maui sipping a mai tai when the edits started.) This has been a joy. Many thanks, Shana, for your deft and subtle hand in guiding this memoir and your enthusiasm in bringing this book to life. Thank you also to the Sourcebooks team — you are a fantastic group of devoted professionals (and dog lovers, which really helps).

Seamus would like to thank his best buds Will and Nellie Ouellette (Boxer/Great Dane/maybe pitbull mixes of great beauty . . . especially that bo-hunk Will . . .

and brains . . . especially that faux-nemesis Nellie). Can he come over and play again soon? And we both want to thank the many fine folks — staff, board, and volunteers — at the Mary S. Roberts Pet Adoption Center in Riverside, California. On behalf of all of the animals, thank you for all that you do. Seamus gives an extra tail wag and *AAAAAARRROOOOOOOOOO* to Denise Perry, the executive director and substitute mom, and Destiny Glass and Shawna Dowd, who've brilliantly cared for him in their homes and hearts.

And finally, Seamus and I both give our thanks and love in massive amounts to the pack leader (we're even going to let him think that, such is our love) and most important part of our family of "Chree" — Chris. Chris's zodiac sign is Cancer — he had no idea that meant he'd become the consummate caretaker of not just one but two cancer patients before his thirty-fourth birthday. But nobody has done it better. Thank you, baby. We love you.

ABOUT THE AUTHOR

Teresa J. Rhyne is an animal advocate and breast cancer survivor. Eleven months after opening her own law office, she was diagnosed with triple-negative breast cancer. On January 28, 2009, she underwent a lumpectomy, followed by four rounds of chemotherapy and thirty-six rounds of radiation. She is pleased to note she has been "NED" (no evidence of disease) ever since. She lives in the Los Angeles area with her boyfriend Chris in a home completely controlled by their super-beagle, Seamus (the Famous).